# GOD TALKS TO YOU

## SECOND EDITION

# ROBERT R. PERKINSON

BLACK ROSE
writing™

© 2016 by Robert R. Perkinson
All rights reserved. No part of this book may be reproduced, stored in a retrieval system or transmitted in any form or by any means without the prior written permission of the publishers, except by a reviewer who may quote brief passages in a review to be printed in a newspaper, magazine or journal.

The final approval for this literary material is granted by the author.

First printing

The author has tried to recreate events, locales and conversations from his/her memories. In order to maintain anonymity in some instances, the author may have changed the names of individuals and places. The author may have changed some identifying characteristics and details such as physical properties, occupations and places of residence.

ISBN: 978-1-61296-750-9
PUBLISHED BY BLACK ROSE WRITING
www.blackrosewriting.com

Printed in the United States of America
Suggested retail price $16.95

*God Talks to You* is printed in Adobe Garamond Pro

Dedicated to Angela, *my miraculous sign.*

# GOD TALKS
# TO YOU

# PART I:
# GOD TALKS TO ME

# CHAPTER 1

My father took me by the hand. At about three or four, it was my first memory. I was so small. *Had I done something wrong?* I didn't think he was mad. It was just his big hand and my small hand. Daddy was finally home. I was happy. It meant I might get something to eat. For days, mommy and daddy had been gone and I was hungry. He led me downstairs to the basement to the tiny coal bin that long ago fueled the furnace. Now, it was fueled by oil. I don't remember if it was a box or a part of the basement but it was small, just enough room for the leftover coal and me. He didn't say anything – not a word. He locked me in. It wasn't the first time, but sometimes he would forget and lock me in there for days. A small crack in the door told me when it was day or night. It was always dark, so very, very dark.

For freedom from this hole, I listened to every sound. Every footstep, each cracking hinge of the back porch door, or a muffled voice meant someone might be coming. The open in the bin had a light, my only link to the outside world, and it tracked along the pieces of coal like a secret line of white birds flying over black mountains. As the hours passed, the darkness became my friend.

He locked me in, the first time, during the day and came back late at night. I was asleep but awakened to his shuffling footsteps on the back porch, the hinge sounding the alarm on the screen door. I knew he was coming for me. Maybe he had water or food. I was used to the dark by now and even comfortable in the little black hole. He turned the white wooden latch, opened the door, and reached in and pulled me out. I learned never to cry, never to look at my parents, and never to make a sound. Anything that brought attention to me was sure to end in pain: yelling, yanking, and pushing. He put me down on the kitchen floor. Leaving me there, he staggered up the long white hallway and held onto the walls for support. I searched for food on the table and anywhere I could reach. I was too small to turn on the water faucets in the sink or the tub. But there was water in the toilet. I scooped and drank the water. It was cool and good. Walking into the living room, I lay on the rug and dared not move or cause any noise. There was a coffee table, a couch, two side tables and lamps that were lit. But I wanted it dark and quiet to be safe. I looked for a place and found it under one of the side tables. I balled up inside of the little box and went to sleep.

In 1950, an old southern town in Virginia harbored the fugitives of my childhood life – a mother and father whose abandonment and neglect were fueled by the angels and demons of their own darkness – all of it intensified by at least ten million times by the non-stop drinking.

The next day, with daddy gone, mommy walked into the living room where I was half asleep on the floor. Uncertain of what was to come, I lay still.

"You're filthy," she said. "How did you get so filthy?" She grabbed me, walked down the hall into the kitchen, and stuck me in the sink. A perfect fit it was. Thankfully checking the temperature this time, she turned on the water and washed me down. Sometimes the water burned so bad I wanted to scream, but I never did. I just stared at the water pooling around me. This was the water I needed in the coal bin.

"How could you get so black? Looks like you have been wallowing in a pig pen," she said as she washed me.

*Don't look at her, I thought. That makes it go bad.*

She dropped me down on the kitchen floor naked, and then she reached up high at the counter and got a bottle of the smelly stuff and took a long drink. Gagging as if she was going to throw up, she finally got it down. I meandered up the hall to the safety of the rug and started playing with a little tomato paste can I called a truck. The label was red, just right for a pretend truck. It was beautiful and round with a hole in one end. I could use it as a truck or it could be a person, a house, a tree, a dog or even a cup for drinking water out of the toilet. It was the best toy in the world because it could be anything you needed. It could even be a person who loved you and treated you good. This friend of mine even had lots of water and food. We ate together: the little can standing straight or lying down to relax. In case I wasn't around, I talked to the can and showed it how to moan for company. My daddy would never allow the can in the coal bin. So I had to leave my friend and look back and promise to return.

I was always hungry, but I never asked for food.

*That made him mad.*

I had an older brother, Gordon, but he was always gone. I don't blame him. He was good to me. But, he went through the toughest times, too. When he would come home, daddy would take him in the bathroom and I could hear the belt tearing at my brother's skin. Then the whipping got worse because he never cried out. Slap after slap after slap of the belt until I was sure daddy was going to kill him. How he survived those beatings I'll never know. I was too small to be beaten. Blaming Gordon and my mother for his troubles, my father beat them with his fists and his words, but I was too small to blame. My mommy blamed me for her pain but not daddy.

Because I was handicapped with a speech impediment, a stutter, my father was ashamed and he wanted me to disappear in the coal bin, never to reappear again. That was fine with me. I was safe there. Over the long days and nights, over the weeks, over the months and the years, my moan turned into a soft, silent song. I sang to the pieces of coal as if they were friends. I sang to the darkness and I sang to the line of light. I sang about my loneliness and I sang about my fears. In my child's heart, I believed all of these things could hear me and they were comforted.

If I was upstairs, the bathroom door sometimes opened to my father and brother. I always feared my brother might be dead. His bloody body scared me and I didn't want to see it. As fast as I could, I would run away. Where did I go when I was afraid? To my only friend: the coal bin.

To escape the feeling of doom, I would run down and climb in my box of darkness and dust. Then, I would close the door. It's where I belonged and daddy didn't have to do it if I did it myself. I moaned and sang to keep myself company but not too loud for anyone to hear: quiet, silent enough to make me feel I wasn't dead. I would fall asleep to my voice. Sleep is the most peaceful thing in the world. There is no pain when you are asleep. Most of the time I wanted to sleep, sleep, sleep my life away. To be alive and awake was a never ending nightmare, but in sleep there was rest and peace.

My house was peeling white and small, about eight hundred square feet, two stories, with a screened in back porch. The coal bin was under the porch with the furnace. Large spider webs covered the dark corners of the basement. There was a substantial lawn and a concrete sidewalk that lead down to South Main Street. The town was about 2,000 people about seventy percent black and the rest white. I felt closer to the black people because they treated me like I was a person. They were kindred spirits, downtrodden like me. The black people were always kind and the white people ignored me as if I was nothing. I saw myself as the weakest most inadequate person in town, so everyone was better than I was.

One night, I was upstairs when I heard a knock at the front door. My heart fell. I knew who was there. Men who wanted to see my mommy. They wanted to get naked with her and get on top of her in the bed. They got her so drunk with the smelly stuff that she would be asleep and I couldn't wake her up – sometimes for a whole day. When they came, some of the men or boys would pretend to be my friend. They would say, "You're my little buddy." This was a lie. They just said it to get me out of the way so they could do stuff with my mommy.

As early as I can remember I tried to be invisible. No one would yell at me, hurt me or shame me if they couldn't see me. I taught myself to be an invisible boy. I developed a severe stutter, so no one wanted me to hear me talk. The speech defect made people so miserable that once they heard it, they never wanted me to speak again. A child in such pain is unbearable to watch. It was a beautiful strategy and it worked perfectly every time.

I learned how to make myself so invisible that people couldn't see me at all. How does a boy do that? Easy, I created a smile on my face like nothing was wrong. I learned to never look at anybody. I dressed and walked like everybody else – same pace, same tempo. The final key was I never made one single sound. A time came when even my mommy and daddy didn't see me anymore: completely invisible. I was at peace in my bubble of invisibility. I grew up like a whisper of wind – you could sense it but when you looked to see what it was it was gone.

Later, everything changed when I grew too big for the coal bin. My six-year-old body was bigger and my daddy was too drunk and incapacitated to move the coal to yield more space. That thought was way above my daddy's ability to think and plan. One night he pushed and pushed. Then he rearranged my arms and legs and tried again. Exhausted, he finally gave up.

At age six, I could do everything myself. I could open the refrigerator, cook food, run water, wash my clothes, take a bath, dress myself and walk to school. The first day of school, mommy watched out of the window and when a kid walked by who was near my age she said, "Follow that boy." She made sure I understood that I had to go to school every day and on time. It took me awhile to figure out that there were two days, Saturday and Sunday. On those days, I didn't have to be there.

During this time, I learned I could walk up town and go behind the grocery store and eat the great food they threw away. This was perfect food: peaches, tomatoes, carrots, bread, and meat – anything anybody could ever want. But sometimes the market wouldn't throw food away for days and days. Then things would go bad. I had water but learned to endure the hunger.

Three and four o'clock in the morning was the best time to go uptown. This time was safe – no cars, no people, no distractions. Even an invisible boy didn't have to hide. Where ever I went, I was safest in the dark. Animals also come out at night, I found as I wandered around town. If I went to a quiet place in town and didn't move, at first I became invisible to birds, then to squirrels, cats, and finally the deer. I would watch the animals for hours in the starlight or, better, the light of the moon. The nighttime creatures came out during the last hour of the day and went home during the first hour of light. More and more of them come out as darkness fades the light and it gets completely dark. Finally, when its pitch black dark, they are all out looking for food, just like me.

How does an invisible boy stay invisible during the day? That's not hard, but you have to know what you are doing and abide by the rules. When you are with people, you have to dress, walk, and move exactly the way they do. Any difference in outward appearance or behavior and you draw attention. If I was too still on the playground, I would draw attention. A teacher would come over and say, "Are you all right?" Of course I never spoke and moved quickly away. My smile told them I was fine. If I moved too quickly then that drew attention, too. It's best to copy people's movements exactly. Then you fit in and nobody sees you – the perfect camouflage. I wanted to blend in so no one could see me at all. I became an expert. I got to be a great shrugger. This means you don't know the answer. The key is if you keep shrugging and smiling, people leave you alone. When you are called on in class, this works great. The teacher asks you a question, and you shrug, this means *I don't know*. If she asks you again, you just keep shrugging until she gives up and asks someone else. People can't take up all day with a smiling shrugger, it leaves them lost and confused. I know there are a lot of invisible people who know exactly what I'm talking about.

My parents split up when I was six and my dad moved to his mother's house: we called her Ma, my grandmother. Every once and awhile, my dad took me down to her house. Get this – once we were there, we would have a meal. That's when somebody cooks food: meat, gravy, vegetables, bread, and more. Once it was all ready, everyone sat at a long table. There were several plates and many kinds of forks, knives, and spoons. The food was brought in on large steaming platters. Everyone smiled when they passed the platters around. You could take as much as you wanted, but you had to be careful not to take too much or you would get a dirty look. A serving size was about as big as your hand. Take much more than that and people got upset or sometimes they smiled secretly to acknowledge their cooking was good.

Being invisible here was nearly impossible, but I managed to stay hidden even as the plates were passed. Then, as if on cue, we would all eat. I mean we would eat and eat and eat. The platters would be passed again and again, and no one complained about anything. My dad would be drunk and my mother and brother would never be there, but I didn't care. I would try to stuff enough food in to last for the next week. When we were done, my stomach was a tight ball and I felt as if I was going to pop. I lay down in a dreamy stupor for hours. Finally, after dark, my dad would drive me home and I would slip back into the house and upstairs to my room that was my sanctuary. I had a single bed with a night stand and a small light which I liked to leave on to make me feel safe. Mom never noticed I was gone.

One night, a new group of men came over to drink the smelly stuff, which I now knew was alcohol, and to get my mother naked and do what they wanted with her. This group was headed by a man named Bob. He was about thirty years old, thin and dressed in an open shirt and black pants. He was staggering when he came in so I knew it was going to be trouble. I knew that they seemed to particularly like it when she was unconscious because they could turn her any which way they wanted. She was really pretty so they had a ball getting drunk and playing with her like she was a toy. They didn't act like she was a person at all, but like she was a rubber doll. The other men sat on the couch while he did the talking with my mom. I did my invisible act so the men couldn't see me. Bob wanted to take my mom out for a drive. This time, for a reason I did not understand, she wouldn't leave without me.

"We can't take him with us," Bob said. "We're going to have some fun."

No matter what he said, she wouldn't take a drink or go out without me. *For once she could see she had a kid*, I thought. I was completely invisible, but I guess this time she could see she had a little boy. Bob got mad. He picked me up, carried me outside, and threw me in the backseat of the car. This was not good. Nothing good could come of this.

About five other men climbed in with my mom in the middle of the front seat. Bob sat on the passenger seat while another man drove. They were all drinking heavily and some were smoking. They drove forever down asphalt roads, then gravel roads and then the dirt roads. Finally, we stopped at a lake way out in the middle of the woods. The drinking continued and the partying was heightened by them encouraging my mom to drink more and more until she passed out. I stayed invisible in the back seat. Then they laid her down in the back seat.

Bob opened up the trunk and got out a frog gig, a long stick with pointed barbs on the end. He handed the stick and a flashlight to one of the men and said, "Take the kid frog gigging. I'll come down and help you after I'm done. The man reluctantly agreed, took me by the hand, and led me down to the lake. Except for my brother, whenever anyone took me by the hand it was going to get very bad. I never tried to pull away because it would get worse. All I could do was follow and try hard to become invisible. I really needed to be invisible now because it was the only way I was going to escape these men.

"Hear the bull frogs," he said.

I could hear them: "jug-o-rum, jug-o-rum, jug-o-rum." These were night creatures, my best friends. I looked at the spear and shivered, imagining it piercing a frog's innocent body.

"Be quiet," the guy said. "If you scare them, they jump in the water. You have to sneak up on them and then shine the light that blinds them – then stick them hard." He pulled me alongside of the water. The evening air was hot and humid and smelled like mud and rotting vegetation. Along the lake, there were clumps of cattails and tall thin three-foot-high grass. I didn't know if I should pull away or run. I had learned the best way to avoid conflict was to cooperate and wait for a time to escape. All I needed was a second for him to let go of my hand and I was gone, gone, gone.

With the man occasionally turning on the flashlight, we slowly and quietly walked along the water. Finally, he shined his light on a big bullfrog, sitting alone on the bank, half of his body sticking out of the water. He was beautiful, solid green with little bumps on his back, a white underbody that cried of purity, and large gentle eyes that were filled with love. The light didn't seem to scare him, almost as if he was savoring being in the spotlight for the first time in his life.

Suddenly the spear stuck him through the back. I could almost feel it. He opened his mouth to scream, but like me trying to talk he couldn't make a sound – only a painful silent cry. Why me? Why now? I didn't do anything wrong. I never hurt you. All of these painful sounds and words were never spoken, but telegraphed over the lake covering the earth with shame. Stunned, I knew to kill another creature was to kill a part of you. I believed this frog lived forever and his cry cursed the land and everyone on it. Then I realized the frog was trying to breathe but the spear must have gone right through his lungs. He kept his mouth open, his legs tried to jump: a silent unheard scream. I was sure the other frogs felt his pain and looked around at each other in hopeless despair.

Then, in my mind's eye, I began the conversation.

"What can we do?" The frogs must have asked.

"Nothing can be done," the older frogs must have said. "Humans don't understand that we are an equal part of the earth. We talk each night of love and peace but they don't have ears to hear or a heart to understand."

The man screeched, "Got him!" He pulled the frog up as a prize. Then, as if a spear were stabbing through my own heart, he took out his pocket knife and sawed off back legs of the still living frog – a frog who silently screamed. Then he stepped on the frog's head and yanked the gig out. I saw that the frog's eyes had glazed over and he was, mercifully, dead. I learned a valuable lesson that night. Life was beautiful but so was death. Death was release from pain. In death there were no more fear, frog gigs, and no need for precious food. No more drunken fathers and mothers that slept with strange men. Best of all there was no more coal bins. The frog lay at peace. His body left to feed the flies and to fertilize the earth by growing new things. The universe wastes nothing. It just transforms it. I imagined myself cuddled inside of my coal bin, invisible to the world. *If people couldn't see you, I thought, they couldn't stick you in the back with a frog gig.*

"I see you got one," said Bob walking down to us.

Bob put his large hand around my hand and squeezed hard. I could smell the unforgettable smell of my mother on his body. I knew what he had been doing and I knew what the other men were doing and there was nothing I could do to protect her from their hairy legs and scruffy beards and slimy hands. Strangely, as invisible as I was, I saw myself as my mother and father's protector, advisor, and comforter. When they were crying or upset, I learned to appear from my invisibility and comfort them with just a touch on their arm or leg. This touch brought tears – someone had appeared out of nowhere, an invisible boy to bring a feeling of not being alone. When the comforting was done, typically after they passed out, I disappeared again.

"Now it's your turn," said Bob handing me the gig.

I didn't move. I could never kill a frog.

"Don't you want to get a frog?"

I was as silent as the night.

"Say something. What are you, stupid?" The ripple of the water echoed in the night.

# CHAPTER 2

I tried to disappear but he had me by the hand, like a prisoner.

"I see," he said. "You're a no good little coward. No wonder your mother hates your guts. She does, you know. She talks about how ashamed she is to have a retard as a son." He let go of my hand. "You stay down here. I'll be back for you later. Don't come up to the car?" He grabbed my shoulder hard. "You hear me. Sit down and do not move until I come back to get you."

Bob and the other man walked back up to the car leaving me beside the dead frog. At least the frog was at peace, his eyes open, seeing nothing.

Later that night, I heard the engine start and the car drive away. No one came and no one was going to come, not ever. I sat there until morning beside my dead friend and the night. It was a long night but the frogs kept me company and sang songs of peace to me. The pine trees were whispering to each other in a way I didn't understand. When a moist breeze would blow, cooling me, the trees would tilt their arms and turn their leafy hands. I didn't know what they were saying but I knew they were comforting me and that I was not alone. I didn't know about God then, but if I had, I know I would have felt his presence. He was here in the miracle of his creation but I was unaware.

As I lay there, the stars were blinking in a rhythm, communicating with each other in star talk. So far away and safe in the night sky – it must be nice to be a star. I listened intensely for a message from the heavens but didn't hear one. I felt like something bigger than everything or someone alive and benevolent was listening but I didn't know who it was. "Hello," I said. But nothing talked back, just the croaking frogs and the whisper of trees.

Morning slowly arose revealing itself by a glowing light on the distant horizon. This was the time of day for the deer and, instinctively, I didn't move. As the light slowly grew, a doe stuck her head out of the edge of the forest. She was so still, almost impossible to see: a symbol of peace. *Maybe she was mourning the death of the frog,* I imagined. For many minutes, she stood perfectly still, then without a sound she stepped forward. With gray brown hair and white spots that melted with the surroundings, two fawns emerged from the brush behind her. When their mother moved, I observed, they knew they were safe and they walked behind her. They were even smaller than me. Looking carefully in all directions, the mother walked twenty feet in front of me. I was paralyzed with respect and admiration. She reached the water, leaned down and took a drink. Soon, her fawns drank beside her. The mother didn't keep her head down long but constantly scanned the landscape for any signs of danger. When they'd gotten their fill, they walked onward, browsing and grazing on bushes back into the dark woods. I watched what the deer ate. Perhaps I could eat the green leaves of bushes if needed.

For a six-year-old kid, I was in trouble, many miles from home and I had no idea which way to go. I walked up to where the car had been. The men had scattered a few beer cans and potato chip bags around where the car was parked. I ate the crumbs out of the bags and tried to get a visual bearing as to where I was. There was a car track that led away from the lake. I walked the track till I came to a gravel road. Checking the pathway out, I had no idea which direction to go in – no clue about which way was home. I knew if I walked and walked in one direction, I would ultimately find an asphalt road. If I followed that, no matter how long it took, I would find a town and finally home. I tried to memorize each turn so I could find my way back if I ever had to switch directions. At each turn, I left something: two rocks together, a stick pointing the way to show which way I turned.

My toes curled inward as I walked. My mother had not bought me shoes often enough. Wincing at the blistering pain in my feet, I walked all day. Walking at school was misery, but now I was walking for my life. I trudged along until darkness covered me and I could only see a few feet ahead. I was determined to keep walking through the night, but I came to a four-way gravel road intersection. On one side, was a torn down farm house and a tired old barn leaning over itself. The barn door was latched. My feet burned and the chips were forever ago. With no other entry, I finally managed to open the door and squeezed my body inside. There was hay, so I lay down to rest, just for a minute. If feet could kill, I was doomed.

Exhausted, I decided to stay the night. I glanced around for something to eat, like an old can of food, anything. In the back of the barn, there was a metal cattle trough that held water. I drank until I could drink no more. Then I went back outside and around the house and barn. Taking my cue from my dear friends that morning, I ate the grass and leaves. If it was food, then that was fine – if it was poison, then that was fine, too. I didn't mind dying. If I died I would go with the frog to where the dead go. A place where there was no more pain, no more beatings of my brother, no more drunken mother or father, no more hearing the thuds of my father's shoes against my mother's body and head, no more stuttering, no more pretending I was invisible, – just the silent pleasure of death.

Piling some hay on top of me for warmth, I rested my head in the golden straw. Instantly, I was asleep, deep, warm, comfortable, wonderful sleep. I dreamed of a white house with a stream in the back. Frogs and crickets sat along the stream, untainted, unharmed. The water was pure and anytime you wanted you could scoop it up in your hands and take a drink. Inside the house food was laid out on a table for everyone: bread, meat, vegetables, mashed potatoes, apple pie, pecan pie, and all the ice cream anyone could eat.

When I awoke, I didn't move. I kept my invisible shield rigid. I shifted my eyes and saw an orange and white cat peeking around one of the barn's rafters. Soon, six kittens appeared around her — all wide-eyed and beholding the exciting mystery of life. They were small enough to fit in my hand. The mother walked proudly out of the shadows and the kittens followed her, chasing her swishing tail as if it was a mouse. One of the kittens, a gray one, came right up to my face. I didn't move and tried not to blink. She observed me with beautiful, innocent, curious, gray eyes. Perhaps the kitten had never seen a person before. As she gazed into my eyes, the pupil of the cat's eyes widened from horizontal slits to large disks. Her tail was up as if to say, "Hello." Then she rubbed her nose against my nose marking me with her scent. It was her way of saying, "This is mine."

I was honored, but still afraid to move. Letting the kittens and the mother cat get used to my presence and my scent, I lay there for a few hours. Soon, they were feeding in a corner, and then asleep. The mother focused right on me as I slowly got up. I unlatched the door and wandered out into the day.

At the dusty four-way intersection, I stood for a long time wondering which way to go. If I went the wrong way, I might go deeper into the woods: certain death. If I went the right way, I might find a house or an asphalt road.

Guessing, I turned right. I walked all day in my too-short shoes, drinking out of an occasional ditch. I found an empty beer bottle to use it as a canteen and then, I found another, so I had two. Night was falling when I came to an asphalt road. About an hour later, an old model white car motored my way. A black man and his son about my age were in it.

"Do you want a ride?" The man asked.

I climbed in the car and didn't say a word.

The car shifted into gear and the man asked, "Where are you going? What are you doing way out here by yourself? Where's your mom?"

I pointed straight down the road.

He took note of me, sadly shook his head, and then drove. "Have it your own way," he stated. Amazingly, he drove me right to my home town. Once we were close to my street, I motioned him to stop. I waved "thanks" as I got out.

"I'm Sam," the man said, "and this here is Ben, my son." Ben leaned over and gave a slight wave.

I didn't say anything.

"You sure you're going to be okay?" Ben said. "We can drive you to your house."

I kindly shook my head waved and walked down the street, I did not look back. I did not want them to know who I was or which house was mine. Down the long sidewalk of South Main Street, I walked the mile to my house. Once inside, I dropped on the living room carpet and slept for two days.

Over and over again, these dark, desperate, and desolate times repeated themselves. The men, the smelly stuff, the nakedness and my unconscious mother unraveled their train of destruction at the intersection of my small life. Miraculously, I kept finding my way home. Sometimes it took hours and sometime it took days. If this kept up, I knew there would come a time when I wouldn't find my way back, and I would die in the forest.

Bob would kill me if I didn't stop him and I knew I had to do something. He came over anytime and my mother would insist on me coming with them. Then, he would leave me in another dark place. At his next visit, I panicked. I used the phone and called my brother over at my first cousin's house. "Come…home." I got the words out.

He could hear something was wrong. "I'm coming," he said.

Sure enough he was there in five minutes and I told him what was

18

happening.

He was shocked. "You're sure they were naked?" he asked.

"Yes."

"The men were naked and lying on mom and she was naked?"

"Yes."

"I've got to call dad." Dad was living with his mother in a large farm house much too big for my grandmother and my Dad.

"No." I shook my head, back and forth furiously. "He'll go crazy. We need to keep this a secret."

"No," my brother said. "He needs to know."

I thought this was a huge mistake, like throwing gas on a fire, but he called. Within an hour dad was standing before us wobbling, sloppy drunk.

I explained all the dreaded scenarios to my father: the many men and boys – the many times. I was afraid my dad would be mad that I didn't stop them. But these men were trapped by their own desires and nothing would keep them from getting what they wanted.

This opening up began a long ten-year struggle whereby my father, my brother and I would try to catch, beat or kill all of these men. Dad gave me a code word, "keeper." I was to call him and just say that word. It triggered him getting in contact with my brother and the battle would begin.

The first time the code word came into play, Bob was lying in his underpants and my mother was naked in the bed: both drunk and passed out. I made the call and quietly gave the "keeper" code then stood in terror for the half hour it took for my dad to get there. I heard him drive up the drive way and met him at the back door.

"Show me," he said. This was real bad because he was sober enough not to be totally incapacitated.

I walked with him to the bedroom and he spied inside. His face stiffened and turned white. I knew that look and was terrified by it. It came a split second before my dad swung his fists.

He leaned over and whispered, "Go get me something long and heavy." He stretched his hands out about two feet apart to show me how big.

I went down to the kitchen, looked under the sink and brought him a two-foot metal wrench. I was too afraid not to help him even though I knew this was going to be bad. Bob was going to kill me if I didn't do something and there was no one left to protect me except my crazy father. I didn't know who was going to kill me now, Bob or my dad.

Dad crept to the room and slowly raised the heavy wrench over his head. He paused for a second to take aim, and then he hit the man right in the balls as hard as he could. The man screamed a sound I had never heard, like a high pitched wounded bird. Then a swinging blow to the head sent blood splattering all over the walls.

"Who's that?" My mom yelled sitting up and covering her breasts with the sheet.

Dad hit him again and again and again. Blood splattered over the walls, the ceiling, and the floor. Like a homerun hitter smacking a fastball, he never missed. Bob tried to protect himself to no avail and then he stumbled and staggered down the hall. Dad followed behind him calling him names and hitting him over and over again. Finally, not dying like I thought anyone would, Bob got to his car and drove away. My dad chased him in his car until he was gone.

I went back inside the house where it looked like a pig had been butchered. The walls, floor, and the ceiling were dripping with bright red blood. I, too, was covered with blood. The red liquid was smeared across my arms, face and chest. I sat on the floor numbed by the events and the blood. I waited in the kitchen. I did not know what I was waiting for and I did not know what else to do. I couldn't think. There was too much blood, hurt, and betrayal, for my mind to handle. I thought about my kitten in the barn. I wondered what she was doing, if she was nursing from her mother, or sleeping in the purr pile of her family.

About an hour later, two policemen stormed into the house.

"Whose blood is that?" One of them said, walking up the hallway following the blood trail.

Thinking of my kitty, I just sat there on the floor.

The other policeman, a man with a kind face, kneeled down beside me. "It's going to be all right," he said. I had seen him around town and he had a son in my school. He was a good guy. But I knew he was wrong about dad – he didn't know my father. He didn't know my mother either. Nothing was going to be all right ever again. We were driving through hell and the deeper we got into the fire; the more my dad liked it. It was like he was born in hell and he was Satan's main go-to-guy, his trusted confident, and his mighty warrior. Once the blood started from this contract with the devil, he had moved his rage away from beating my brother to hitting, stabbing, shooting and killing everybody who was messing with my mom.

After the news got around, and in a small town that doesn't take long, everyone had to stop and think about what would happen to them if they were found at my house. There was a pause in the fall of the year, as if the men stopped to question whether it was worth it or not. But as sure as animals develop an uncontrollable call to mate, a deep restlessness descended over the town. Cars drove by slow and sometimes men would call on the phone and hang up. Going against their better judgment, they didn't seem to be able to stay away. Sex and lust, like a deep thirst, had a powerful draw

The lure of sure sex made them risk their lives over and over again. Even Bob came back bearing the scars of my dad's vicious attack. Once they were drunk, they could not stay away.

# CHAPTER 3

One day my mom came home and dropped a paper bag at my feet. "I got this for you."

I was so shocked and almost dared not to move. Then after a moment, I opened the plastic wrapper and found a pink, blowup plastic baby seal. My mom blew it up and actually smiled as she handed it to me. Inflated, it was about three feet long, almost exactly my height.

What did this mean? My mom, my dear mother, the holy saint who gave birth to me, was giving me a present? I couldn't believe it.

I took my seal upstairs where we would be alone. "You're going to be all right," I whispered. "I'll take care of you." Somehow, I knew this was a troubled seal who was frightened of everything. I looked into its pink eyes with the long black eyelashes and whiskers. I knew it was a boy seal. His face had a forlorn, downturned mouth – like he had lost his mother and had no friends. This baby seal had no one. But now he was mine and I was going to see to it that he was happy. I ran downstairs and got him a bowl of water and some bread, and I hugged its plastic skin all that day and fell asleep with it that night.

So, began my first friendship. I was going to be the best friend anyone could ever imagine. I named my seal, Baby, and we were inseparable. We went everywhere and did everything together. We talked all day and all night and I told Baby every detail of my life. Because he didn't know anything, I showed him everything I knew: how to drink, dress, eat and sing. He had been abandoned by his parents at birth and never had any friends. No matter what I did or how much fun we had, however, he never lost those sad eyes. It's hard to live without a family, but he and I had each other and that's all that mattered. I understood Baby and he understood me. He talked to me in a silent voice and just the look in his eyes and the gentle turn of his mouth told me he loved me. He spoke volumes that no one ever heard but me.

The best thing was going out with Baby at night. In the early morning darkness, we would walk the streets and I would tell Baby all about the night creatures. We wondered together about the stars, the moon, and what the crickets were chirping for and why. I pointed out my friends, the deer, and told Baby about the frogs. I was going to tell him about the frog that was killed but Baby got so terrified when I described the frog gig that I had to stop. Baby was too innocent to hear about such terrible things. Because he was afraid, I always held Baby extra close. I kept telling him that he was going to be all right because he had me, but it was hard for him. I knew, though, that even if he was afraid, he would protect me to the death if I got into trouble. I loved Baby and he loved me.

One night, Baby and I lay in the damp grass and gazed up at the millions of stars. I could clearly see the long dusty cluster of the Milky Way. I made myself a promise that night and I said it aloud to Baby to make it seem real. Nobody had ever been there for me but, if someone ever needed me, I was going to be there for them. I hugged Baby real tight and made that solemn promise, a pact between me, myself and Baby. I have tried to live by those words my whole life.

One day, I took Baby down to see the coal bin. Both of us were afraid of being caught, but we snuck down the stairs into the dirty darkness anyway. Upon opening the door, we found many spider webs and one spider, in particular, sat in the center waiting for a snack. When we peered inside for a closer look, Baby silently screamed. It scared me and I ran upstairs into the daylight. "I'm sorry," I said. "I didn't want to scare you." We decided never to go there again.

During the summer before my first grade year, Baby and I passed the summer walking and talking together about little things and big things. He told me about his mother and father. He said he had a brother and a sister. One day his father came home and told Baby he had to leave. He didn't give a reason and he wasn't mad, he just showed Baby the door. Baby looked at his family but they were too afraid to say anything. Baby walked out and never saw his family again. He lived on a dusty store shelf until my dear sweet mother took him down and brought him to me. She saved his life and I loved her for that one act of kindness.

One night, I was jerked out of my sleep by a man I didn't know. He had on a thick yellow coat, a long metal hat, and big black boots. He ran me over to the next door neighbor's house and put me down in front of a picture window. Awakening from a sleepy haze, I finally realized the fact my house was on fire. Flames roared out of the upstairs windows. Gawking at the two fire trucks that sprayed water on the fire, it passed through me that hope was gone.

Then I wailed.

"Baby is in there!" I cried and ran for the door, but the old lady who lived there held my arm and wouldn't let me go. I wailed again. "Please, Baby is upstairs in my room!" I begged and begged but she called her husband and they held me down and would not let me go. I cried and screamed and fought as hard as I could. I could not get away. My covenant I'd made under the stars to never let anyone down – broken. I knew Baby was terrified and he couldn't walk. He was going to die alone in the burning house.

I had promised I would protect him. I was letting him die a horrible death. I hated myself. I wanted to burn up with Baby so he wouldn't die alone. I wasn't brave at all. I couldn't protect Baby. I was a stupid, stupid, stupid child. All I could do was cry and surrender to the guilt and shame. I knew I was no good, a worthless piece of garbage, and I would never be good. If you let your first friend down, you don't deserve another one. You deserved to live alone. I wanted to kill myself for letting my friend down.

The next day, I found out that my drunken father, who still slept in the house from time to time, had set fire to the house with a cigarette in bed. The firemen had pulled us all out of the fire, everyone but Baby. The house was gutted but the soot and black that permeated the rooms remained. When I got to my smoky room, I hoped that Baby might still be alive, but he was dead. A small pile of melted plastic on the floor was his remains. It was my fault my beautiful friend was gone. That night, I took Baby outside and buried him under a big black walnut tree in our back yard. The night creatures wept with me. I felt them. I told Baby I was sorry, but he was dead and would never hear me. He died with no family and no friends. All of my promises of protecting him meant nothing. I knew I would die alone too but it didn't matter, nothing mattered anymore.

For the next five years of my life, I stopped talking. There was no reason to speak. I became an expert in survival. Alone and at night, I walked the streets. Baby was dead and inside I was dead, too.

The small years of my life drudged on like this in the battlefield of my home, like a war that never ends, a truce that's never called, or peace negotiations that are never held. Vigilant and on guard at all times, I stood ready to give up the code word. The men could come anytime and if I wasn't awake, mother would go missing. That was all right, even preferable, because I began to take care of myself. Dad was counting on me to give up the posse, and the battle was the only evidence that we were a family. The war, weirdly, held us together.

We were like soldiers and, at times, it was an exciting, bonding event. Soldiers found great comfort knowing their comrades were with them. The pact was strong and each was imprinted with the knowing that if the time came, no one was going to die without them.

During the battleground days, grade school passed by as a series of succulent school lunches. I lived for school lunch. Often, it was the reason I survived. It was savory warm food. The difference in this and a meal elsewhere was it came on a plastic tray subdivided into sections for each delectable dish. If we had hotdogs, the big section was for the bread and meat and the other sections held vegetables and a dessert like Jell-O. They even had little cartons of milk. I loved that school lunch. I waited patiently for my one meal of the day because what they had was better than I could make. On weekends, I had to get buy on eating dandelion greens and red clay. Both filled me up and the hunger pains went away. The clay was gritty so I didn't chew it. If it was moist, I could swish it around a few times and swallow. It wasn't bad at all and it even left a good taste in your mouth.

One day, in my dad's room he had another of his great ideas: math. He was going to teach me to do math. Drunk and standing in his filthy underwear, he undertook the quest as any great professor. He had made some flash cards of addition, subtraction, and multiplication tables. I was sure he did not know them either. He didn't wear his glasses, so he had to hold the cards out at arm's length. He was off balance and balance was always difficult for him. He called out the problems and I was supposed to answer. Suddenly, I couldn't be invisible. It was one of the first times in a long time. I was shamefully present. I had to speak but I could not. To make things worse, I had to come up with the right answers, but I could not. So, I was stuck. If I said anything, I stuttered so bad my dad got furious. If I got a word out and it was wrong, he got even more furious. For every mistake, he began to scream at me and everything I said was a terrible mistake. If I made a sound, it was wrong and if I tried to be quiet and not answer that was a disaster, too. He began to scream at me, "You are a stupid retard. You don't have a brain in your head. I never wanted you. I wish you had never been born. I wish you were dead. Get out of my sight before I kill you!"

Like lightening, I bolted.

Passed the town and deep into the woods, I ran and ran and ran. I got away from the house and as far as I could. Exhausted, I fell into a pile of dried oak leaves. I wanted to be dead and save my dad from the shame of having me as his son. I surveyed the landscape for a way to die, but I couldn't find one. There was no rope or belt for a noose, no gun, and no knife. There was no way, no way, no way but to keep living. I clenched the earth in my hands and peered up into the sky. No hope but the life I was living.

As I sat there hoping for death, I noticed the squirrels scampering about looking for nuts and hiding them under the brush. The robins were skipping along – stopping and tilting their heads looking for worms. Now and then, they found one and pulled and pulled until the whole worm came out for a feast. The sky was still there. The white puffy clouds drifted along with not a care in the world. The trees still reached up for the sun and twisted in the breeze. Everything seemed fine except for me.

I wanted to be free of the pain of being me.

# CHAPTER 4

When my brother got to high school and I was in the sixth grade he got a white 1959 Chevrolet. I don't know how he paid for it but he loved that car. It had wings on the back like it could fly, four on the floor, and red carpet. It was fast and he sat in it like a king. He was always laughing and riding around with a bunch of girls.

One night I came home, and caught Bob walking out of the house with my mom. With four other men, they all clambered into an old car and motored off. I was grateful that I wasn't home earlier or I might be taken hostage with them, only to be lost again in the woods – certain death. I called dad and soon my brother in his beautiful car and my dad and I were staked out across the street waiting for the men to bring my mom home. My dad drank beer and with every can he became filled with more hate.

In the early morning, Bob came slowly up the road and turned in to the back of our house.

Dad had three guns a double-barreled 12-gauge shotgun, a 410 single shot shotgun, and a small automatic pistol. My job was to sit in the back seat and load. My dad's job was to lean out the passenger side window and shoot, and my brother's job was to drive his car like a bat out of hell. Mom emerged from Bob's car and staggered her way into the back porch nearly falling as she opened the screen door. Bob backed out of the driveway. As soon as he made his left turn to South Main Street, my brother gunned his car and was right on his tail.

It didn't take Bob long to realize he was in a hornet's nest again. When he saw my brother inches away from his bumper, he took off as fast as he could go. He sailed south out of town onto a winding asphalt road. The guy was going back to the lake where he had left me to die. Now it was his turn. We would kill him and throw him in the lake to be eaten by the frogs. For once, life seemed to slow down and have a certain justice. For the first time, the saying, "what goes around comes around" made perfect sense.

Bob drove as fast as he could, barely keeping his car on the road. Smoke and dust flared up, and his tires squealed like a pig as he made each turn. My brother's soldier's eyes were glazed and fixed on the enemy. The next time Bob made a right turn, my dad leaned out of the car and shot both barrels of the 12 gauge at his back tire. Amazingly, the tire didn't blow, and Bob kept driving. He had seen the fire coming out of my dad's gun because he drove even faster.

*Dad is so drunk he can't shoot*, I thought. Maybe Bob was going to live after all. I slid across the back seat every time my brother made a turn. It was hard to hold onto the guns and stick in new shells but I managed as well as I could. When dad leaned back for another weapon, one was always ready. We must have raced for twenty miles before we came out on the highway north of town. This was a better road, straight with no bad turns. My brother sped up beside Bob's car. Hurriedly, my dad leaned out of his window and emptied his pistol.

Dad missed him from ten feet. I could have hit the guy blindfolded shooting backward. We were with a great driver and we had a great loader, and we had a totally incompetent marksman. My father couldn't shoot his way out of a paper bag.

Bob drove to the outskirts of town and pulled over next to a policeman who was waiting for speeders. He jumped out and pointed to the bullet holes in his car then stood behind the policeman for protection. At least dad had hit the car in the twenty or thirty shots he had taken with the guns.

My brother pulled up alongside the policeman and my dad jumped out and walked up to Bob and shook his fists as if he was going to beat him up. Bob was clinging onto the police officer begging for protection.

"Go on home," the policeman said bluntly to my father. And, that's what we did.

Soon after this night mission, when I was ten years old, my dad brought me my own gun. It was a black .22 six shot revolver with a six-inch barrel. I took this to mean my dad knew he couldn't shoot and maybe I could. He left me with fifty cartridges, but I knew I could get all the ammo I needed at the hardware store.

I put the pistol under my bed and waited. I knew it wouldn't take long. I began to practice in the woods, shooting at tin cans and knots in trees. I got pretty good at distances of about ten feet. I found this gun might be helpful in selecting the men I would let in the house and the ones I wanted to keep out. A kid with a gun doesn't scare anyone until he points a steady hand at you and looks at you with the eyes of a killer.

Of course, the only man I had to run out was Bob. A few months after the car chase, he knocked on the backdoor drunk. "Hey, little partner. Want to go for a ride?" he asked me.

I stuck the gun in his face and said, "Don't come here anymore." Then I shot the gun at his feet making him dance. I didn't want to hurt anybody but I would kill him if I had to. It was either him or me. I had spent enough time lost in the back roads. With my gun, I knew I would never have to do that again: be lost. I never saw him again.

The other men and boys were fine as long as they behaved. I let them come and do their business. This was a major lesson for me. If you wanted something done, do it yourself. From then on, I didn't have to depend on anyone but me.

Over the years of family war and combat, or any combat for that matter, I watched my father closely. He never fought someone face-to-face, even if they were in the wrong and he was in the right. He always took people from behind. He would hit them with a stick, ax, knife, or gun, whatever was handy, but not with his fists. Never eye to eye. My dad was afraid of a fair fight and that's why he always won. If someone hits you from a blind spot like with a wrench, then it takes the fight right out of you. If you were helpless, my dad could take you.

Once, my dad told me about someone who blind-sided him. He was caught with another man's wife. "I peed in my pants," he said. So my dad wasn't a tough guy like he said. He was a coward, hiding behind the false front of being a big man. Of course, he was man enough to beat me and my brother. However, once my brother got to be a teenager, dad left him alone. I think this is because my brother had so much pent up rage. If they ever got in a fight, my brother would kill him. As long as dad didn't attack you from behind, he would be easy to kill. Dad was always drunk.

One hot summer day, my dad came home trembling from being sober. He was irritable as usual when he said, "Come on, I'm going to take you fishing."

This could only end in a disaster, but I couldn't say no. It was certain – I knew we were going to get killed either in a car accident or by drowning. My dad was sober but he wasn't going to stay sober and once he got drunk he became totally incapacitated.

We got in a white Thunderbird he got from somewhere and he started driving. One after the other, he smoked Cool cigarettes. His hands trembled badly as he lit each one. Until the marriage of flame to tobacco, his hands did an undulating dance as if he'd forgotten the simple task. "I'm going to become a fishing boat captain," he said, as if he already knew everything about the water and fishing. "It's easy. You just take people fishing and mix drinks."

I thought it was going to be more complicated than that, but as the summer air from the window cooled me, I began to get excited. I wanted to go fishing. I just didn't want to go with my father.

"The striped bass are running up the Chesapeake Bay," he said lighting another cigarette while he held the filter with his teeth. "You'll see. It's easy."

When we stopped at a stop sign a pint of whiskey slid out from under the front seat.

There it was – the kiss of death. Once he started in on the whiskey, we were doomed. I hoped we never reached the water. But, amazingly, he stayed sober for over a hundred miles. Further on, we somehow found a dirt road marked by a rusty sign: *Fishing Boats for Rent.* Dad left me in the hot car and ambled into a gray, rundown shed. Moments later, he walked out with a hefty teenage boy who donned a tattered baseball cap and who also held two fishing rods and a white bucket. They walked down to the boats and the hefty boy unhooked one. He taught my dad how to run the twenty-five horse power motor then started it. My dad looked back at me. Catching his glance, the boy scratched the side of his cap and looked my way, too.

The time to escape was getting short. I tried to come up with an excuse that was rational but the problem was I wanted to run, to flee, and to get out of this situation.

My dad walked back to the car and told me to go and get in the front of the boat. I looked back at him as he was chugging the pint of whiskey and how he gagged when he got it all down. So my fate was sealed. This was a good day to die. I got in the rickety twelve-foot aluminum boat and peered in the bucket. It was crawling with a dozen small crabs.

"Soft shell," the boy said. "The bass loves them."

After finishing the pint, my dad walked with determination down toward the boat and stepped in the back of the boat. Blue smoke billowed from the idling engine. The boy pushed us off and my dad picked up speed. As if he was a charter boat captain already, he actually knew how to run an outboard motor. I was amazed to see his competent look in the wind. With the intake of booze, the tremor had subsided. *Maybe we were going to live after all*, I thought.

The little bay was surrounded with tall grass and the channel we rode in had red and green buoys a fool could follow. But instead, my dad went right through them, away from the marked route. Somewhere down in a truthful part of myself I knew that this wasn't possible, because my father was a total screw up. We rounded the corner and the bay got wider and wider. Soon, we were so far out I didn't think we could swim back. This was dangerous. As I spied over at my father, I saw fear widen his eyes as if he knew he was in over his head.

My dad got loud as the booze plodded through his body. "The fish are over there," he said, pointing to rocky shoal about a mile away. "We have to cut over." He turned the boat too sharply out of the channel toward the rocks. I thought of my dead body where water would lap against it till the police found my body. As a poor little drowned kid, maybe I would get some sympathy.

I knew it wasn't a good idea to leave the channel, but my dad's eyes had been fixed and steady, his gray hair blowing in the wind. He really did look like he knew what he was doing, but he was also becoming drunk. The booze hit his brain and deprived him of sensation.

Going at full speed, we suddenly hit a sand bar hard and it threw both of us into the belly of the boat where the bucket of crabs spilled over. The spider-like creatures skittered wildly. They were trying to keep away from me and I was trying to keep away from them. Dad's nose was bleeding and he was cussing a blue streak. "Must have hit something," he said mystified. There was a confused look on his face like he needed another drink.

We were sitting on a long flat sandbar. The water was clear enough. The channel buoys were a hundred yards behind us toward the boat house. This was why we were here. If we hadn't gone through them, then a hundred crabs wouldn't be scuttling about and our boat would be riding fine.

Dad reached down and got one of the two long paddles. With his captain dreams fading, he was a little panicky. "Got to get off of here," he said, pushing the paddle in the water and trying to push us off. He strained with all of his might but the boat was stuck hard. "Get out and push us off," he said.

I stared scared at him with begging eyes. I had never been in the ocean before but had read about crabs, sharks, and killer whales. The water was nearly three feet deep, which was over my chest. This gave sharks plenty of room to attack. I was certain with all my heart that these killers would appear as soon as my skinny legs hit the water—fresh meat. I imagined them attacking all at once as soon as I turned my back to push the boat. I looked at dad hoping he would understand. *Why didn't he get in the water?*

Just then a twenty-five-foot white fishing boat sputtered toward us. It was huge and dwarfed our little craft. This was a real fishing boat with a real captain. He was definitely coming right to us. He could see we were in trouble. As he got closer, I could see twin diesels bubbling in the water. He pulled just off of the sand bar and skillfully turned his boat around the twin propellers churning up

31

mud but he never touched the bottom. I was so relieved I almost started crying, shouting or singing. We were in good hands.

"I'll throw you a line," he hollered, coiling up a long one-inch white rope and throwing it. My dad caught it like he knew what he was doing again.

The man went back to his seat at the wheel and turned in amazement to see my dad sitting down holding tightly to the rope.

"Go ahead," my father yelled.

"Tie it off," the man yelled.

"Go ahead!" my father screamed, getting angry now at the man's knowledge about boats, lines, and tying things off.

The man walked back to the back of his boat, his cringed look was apparent because now he knew he was dealing with a man who knew nothing about boats. He tried once more. "Tie the rope to that cleat right there," he said, and pointed to the piece of metal the boy had used to tie the boat to the dock. In boat language, a rope was a line and a cleat was the tie off point. It was easy.

But my dad would have nothing to do with it. He had made his decision, and to go back on that was a sign he didn't know what he was doing. My dad told the man to run his boat and stick the excess information up his rear end.

The man's face went white, his lips squeezed and pursed into a thin line. He turned around, sat down, put his hands on each throttle and pushed them all the way forward. My father braced his feet just before the rope got tight. He was going to hold on and show this man what a real charter boat captain could do. I saw him grit his teeth, the jaw muscles bulged. The big boat almost jumped out of the water. When the line got tight, it burned and seared into his flesh – little pieces of skin went flying and he let go.

The big boat turned slowly in the water and backed up to us again. The man walked back, with more sympathy than I would have expected from someone who had been cussed out. "Better tie the line off," he said.

My father meekly obeyed the commands and wrapped the rope around a cleat and tied a knot. Even with his mind misty and unclear, now he knew something about boats and power.

The big boat easily pulled us off of the bar and drove away. My dad peered around at his new enemy: the water. What would he do now? Fear was in his eyes and he licked his lips. I knew that hardened look. He needed a drink. "It's late, we better get back," he said.

At this point, he was able to get the boat started and we drove slowly toward the dock. Once in the channel, a fishing boat with nets began gaining on us from behind. Dad hated to be passed in a car so I assumed he felt the same way about boats. This big gray boat gained on us fast, but dad never picked up speed. He was on the wrong side of the channel but he didn't know it and the fishing boat had to pass close to us. The skipper in the gray boat left a four-foot wake behind him and never slowed down. He passed within a few feet of us and looked at my father like he was crazy. The wake that followed bolted us up in the air like we were a surfboard and when we came down over the wave, the force made us go faster than ever before. My dad screamed in terror as the little fishing boat tipped its nose down into the wave. We were going to get crushed when we reached the foamy bottom. The boat had enough bounce that we popped up, the fisherman never looking back to see what happened.

My dad was totally defeated. We pulled up to the dock and the boat boy came down to assist us. I was relieved we were alive. We had faced boats, sandbars, crabs, sharks, killer whales, and other fishing boats. The look on my father's face told it all. He would never be a charter boat captain. He would stay the failure he had always been. On the way home my dad got drunk and he never took me fishing again.

# CHAPTER 5

At the age of thirteen, I began to have a problem with girls. It was not a conscious decision. Try as I might to always look the other way from them, I was invariably attracted to their beauty, and their soft ways. It was to the point that it physically hurt. It was weird and unlike me and it put me at great risk – risk of losing my invisible shield, mainly. The physical pain wasn't bad. Pain was my old friend. No way would I ever ask a girl out, but, amazingly, several of the real pretty ones came after me. A girl would make up her mind I was going to be hers and she would hone in on me. They were relentless, clammy, red-faced, wearing lacy white socks and patent leather shoes. My best cloak of invisibility did not work. These girls could see me plain as day. No matter how hard I tried with my cloak, one of them would come over and want to dance, or talk, or go for a walk, or just look at me with love in their eyes. By the way these girls observed me; I knew they wanted something more than to just be friends. But sexual activity meant you might be killed. I wanted to do it, and I thought about doing it, but I would never put my life at risk for such a silly thing as rolling around naked.

This attraction to girls and their attraction to me, all seemed to happen overnight. One day I was with children and the next day I was with grown, women. I was still a child so it was both horrifying and thrilling and confusing. My mind and my body were at odds.

To make sure I stayed humble and full of shame, my extended family began trying to take care of me. I hated this but I couldn't stop them. I was fine where I was. But, one of my aunts saw some of the problems with the alcohol and the posse of men and took me home with her for a few months. Sometimes my mother would come with me and we would have weeks or months of being almost normal. Like a pack of wild dogs, however, the men would always find out where my mother was. Then once they sniffed her out, they began calling and coming around and the whole mess started up all over again.

On one of my first visits to relatives, I found out something new: toilet paper. This is a long roll of soft paper used for wiping yourself after going to the bathroom. It was fascinating. I was introduced to this amazing invention by my aunt. When I asked her what it was, she carefully explained and even gave a little demonstration. Then, every time I went in the bathroom, I looked at the paper as if it were waiting for me. The first morning when I had to go, I sat myself down and did my business and gazed at the pure white roll. It was a shame to mess it up, but I did what I was told, using it exactly like my aunt showed me. Afterward, when I opened the door to the bathroom, my aunt was standing and narrowed her eyes at me sternly. "You only use one square at a time," she said drawing a little square in the air with her finger.

This was a clear but profound symbol of my worth—I was worth one square of toilet paper, not two or three—just one. Because most people judge themselves based on how others see them that taught me a lot. When I wiped myself with one square of toilet paper, the square was immediately torn and everything smeared. It's worse than if you used water like I had used before at all. Only once did I use her toilet paper. Soon, she stopped listening at the door. But, I knew she was probably counting the squares, so I better not use any of her precious paper. I eagerly agreed with her judgment. I knew what I was worth. No problem. I got it loud and clear. This was no surprise and only confirmed of my own judgment of myself.

For a year, I lived with my mother's father, Big Daddy. This was the first good man I had ever known except my brother. He taught me how to hunt and fish and never went anywhere without me. He acted as if I was important and it seemed like he even liked me, although I knew this was impossible. His body smelled of old, musty wax and his fingernails were yellow with age. Long white hairs curled out of the black holes of his big nose and he had long ears. He moved slowly and I watched him for hours. His movements were exact when he would shave or eat. Every little thing he did was fascinating, like when he would sit in a rocker on the front porch and cut up an apple. With a little pocket knife, no larger than his little finger, he would slowly open the knife and then meticulously peel a Red Delicious Apple. He tried to peel the apple and never break the spiral core as it unraveled precisely with the blade. When the apple turned in his hand, I transcended and felt the earth turning under my feet, then the sun flew through space, and then the galaxies wound their way through time. A long white and red circular rind was his gift to me. I took it and was happy. He tried to make me a part of everything and this was very strange and sad. I knew this momentary joy. It was too good to be true. Three meals were placed in front of me every day for a whole year and it was way too much to ask for. I knew where I belonged, in a coal bin hidden in shame from the world as if I were a caged dangerous tormented animal.

When I entered high school in the ninth grade I had to ride the bus, a big yellow bus full of teenagers. Twice a day, I got on and off the bus with the same people. It felt dangerous to me, because I wanted to be by myself. However, when I got off every day, there was a whole group of kids. This was trouble because I had to walk home from school with a group of kids from my neighborhood.

Molly walked like a full grown woman of fifteen, but looked twenty-five. Fred had a stockier build and looked at least fifteen. Then there were normal kids like Frankie and Sammie, and then me – all aged thirteen. We always stopped at Fred's house because he had a pool table and it was cool to play pool. There was no way for me to avoid stopping. What would I say? My parents need me home because my dad's drunk. I have to help prevent my mom from having sex with everyone in town. Nothing made sense, so I went along with the group. I knew that getting involved with other kids was dangerous. If they found out the truth, then my private invisible world would come crumbling down.

Fred's pool table was in his basement, so we were left alone. His mother was upstairs. On a long, dirty green couch, I leveled myself on the end and tried to stay as invisible as possible. I did not want to play and hated the thought of it. I would feel guilty if I won and ashamed if lost. Games were nothing but trouble, best to stay out of it.

The trip to Fred's house became a regular thing, so one day, he said, "Let's start a club."

Molly who was by far the coolest and most adult of us all took a side pocket shot, missed and said, "Clubs are dumb."

Everyone relaxed into the better idea of not having a club. Sammie and Frankie rubbed their cue sticks with chalk and shrugged their shoulders. It was a collective, "*Yeah, clubs were dumb.*"

Then I shocked everyone mostly myself by saying, "We could make a club c-c-cool."

"How are you going to make it cool?" Molly asked, leaning over to make a corner pocket shot she missed. She looked at me with beautiful blue eyes and she swept long strands of blond hair out of her face so she could see me better.

"By taking our clothes off, stealing stuff, and making b-b-bombs," I said.

Molly froze for a moment as if the world had stopped, not only because I was speaking for the first time ever, but because of what I said. "You're not going to take you clothes off."

I stood up and began unbuttoning my shirt. I pulled out the tails and put the shirt on the couch. "It's the one thing that can make us s-s-special."

"Keep going," she said leaning back on the pool table with the cue standing between her legs. "I don't believe you're going to go all the way."

Fred and Sammie and Frankie all had their mouths open in complete shock.

I had seen so many naked people screwing my mom that it meant nothing to me. Soon, I stood on the cold concrete basement floor naked and as hairless as a new born baby.

"Nobody else is going to do that," Sammie said.

Then Molly began unbuttoning her blouse. "I don't see why not," she said.

Molly wore a pleated red and black skirt, a white blouse with a red ribbon around the neck, white socks with little ruffles, and back patent leather shoes. Fully dressed, she reeked of sex and all of the boys in school felt honored just to be in her presence. Nobody talked about her lustiness, least of all to her. To stand next to her, however, made us all feel like men.

Slowly the buttons revealed a white bra that connected two round cups. You could see her cleavage revealed between the folds of her blouse. Better revelations were ahead, maybe the best ever. We were afraid to move, less we break the spell.

Unafraid, she pulled the blouse out of her skirt, freed her arms and then placed the garment on the pool table. She stood there for a moment, killing all of us with the slow march of time, then reached behind her back and unclasped her skirt, unzipped the zipper, and let the dress fall to the floor. She stepped out of the skirt, picked it up, which revealed more of her cleavage, and then put it next to her blouse. Her panties were lacy white. Next, she leaned against the side of the pool table and took off her shoes and socks. This was a disappointment because we wanted her to get down to the important stuff fast.

Then, she reached back and did the unthinkable. She unclasped her bra and let her full breasts spill out to feed our hungry eyes. She pulled her panties down and stood there naked and gorgeous blond and pink. Dressed Molly was beautiful but undressed she was perfect. We all stared at her in awe.

"Your turn," she said to the other boys.

The boys looked at each other with fear and uncertainty, but Molly and I stood there naked and waiting. There was no escape. In heaps and droves, the clothing melted away. Soon, we were all naked and feeling thrilled but, amazingly, comfortable. We had been afraid of showing our nakedness, but once we were exposed, it was as if we were all dressed. It was the same, but no more secrets. No one had to wonder what Molly's breasts or crotch looked like. You could see them plain as day. Her nipples were round pink and pointy and her pubis was blond and curled.

Molly looked at me with a new softness, "You said something about stealing stuff and making bombs."

"The businesses in town leave their windows open," I said. "Late at night we can take anything we want. The hardware store has twenty-five pound kegs of blasting powder and rolls of dynamite fuse. I've never found the dynamite but it's probably there."

"We can take anything we want?" Molly asked.

"Don't have to worry about a thing," I said. "We can pick out anything we want, and they won't miss a thing."

Sammie sat down on the couch, hiding his bald penis between his legs. "Why do you want blasting powder?"

I spread my legs exposing myself even more to give the idea that we had nothing to hide. "I want to build rockets and bombs."

"Sounds like fun to me," said Molly.

Everyone nodded in agreement. Official: the mission had started. We were to become crazy, naked rocket builders and bombers. This was no ordinary club and each of these facts proved it. I pulled out a package of Dentine gum and gave each of us a piece. This small event, naked and chewing gum together somehow sealed the deal.

Because of this one moment, I became one of the most popular kids in school, still invisible but popular invisible. Word spread about our club but none of the details, and everyone wanted to be a member. But our club was secret and this made it even better. We were doing something exciting and only the club members knew it. What teenager doesn't want to see everyone naked? We were very careful to tell no one. We were going to steal stuff and we didn't want to get into trouble. In a gang, if someone talks it would bring everyone down. We had a pact and the pact was good.

With my newfound notoriety, making friends became easier for me. I always smiled and was accepting of other students. I was never confrontational. In time, I became a leader because my ideas were exciting and original. Most years in high school, I was chosen to be a class officer. Of course, the students were not crazy enough to elect me to an office where I had to speak, because they knew I wouldn't speak. So, they made me vice-president – a position with no speaking.

One time, however, it did happen and I tried my best but failed. I stuttered, stammered, and sweated through the fog of trying to get my point across. The advising teacher chastised the class saying, "You elected him. It's your fault. Look at what you did." Despite the teacher's misgivings, we got through the meeting and the kids were satisfied.

During this time and after occasional stays with different families, my mom and I came back home for a while so she could try life on her own. The club members and I immediately began our host of activities, which always included every meeting, everyone naked. This helped to keep everyone honest and the club secret. We called the club the "Nor Club," which was my first name spelled backward. Because this was my idea, everyone assumed I was the leader and even Molly deferred decision-making to me. I advised them which stores had open windows: the grocery store, department store, gas station, and hardware store. The drugstore was locked.

We prowled the streets at night only in the summer. It was too hard during the school year and it was easier during the hot southern nights of our youth. Because I had to scrounge for food, the rest of the year it was only me. I didn't tell the other kids I ate from the dumpster. I pretended always that my family was normal. We all had our family secrets lined up like good little soldiers. Family talk was taboo and that was fine with me. A river of secrecy was more precious and darker than a river of shame.

The first time we stole, we met at my house at three a.m. and walked east up South Main Street toward the center of town. Crossing over the railroad bridge, I could tell the kids had the spooks. It was their first time up late at night. I tried to keep a sputtering running dialogue to calm their nerves. "I told you, no people, n-n-no cars, and no p-p-police. It's only us. We own the night. Nobody knows we are here or what we are doing. We can do anything we want but its n-n-not a good idea to go into anyone's house, even if we know they are out of town. People take their personal space as private and sacred. The worst thing you can do is invade someone's place of safety. If we do that, they will hunt us d-d-down."

"How do you know all this?" asked Molly.

"I just do." Out the words flew. We crossed the railroad bridge. "Look at those stars, billions of them with people looking down at us while we look up at them," I said.

"You're giving me the creeps." Molly shivered and rubbed her arms as if she was cold.

"If you don't believe me, look up. Some of the stars move," I said. We all stood on the bridge for a long time and looked up at the starry sky. I knew the Russian Sputnik satellite flew overhead every ninety minutes. I had watched it the night before feeling excited and fearful because it was sent up by a Soviet intercontinental ballistic missile. "See, there's one," I pointed at a star that moved slowly across the sky. Then a shooting star flashed by. "There's a faster one," I said. I did not tell them that the slow ones were planes and the fast ones were meteorites. I left it to their imagination. I loved to weave a spell of the haunted and mysterious. No one could resist the fear of the unknown. We had been watching TV about vampires, the walking dead, and aliens. Teenagers love to be spooked.

Standing in a tight circle, we watched the stars for about an hour. "If we get into trouble, we have to stick together. Tell people we just went for a walk late at night just for the thrill. They will understand that."

"I don't want to get caught," said Fred.

I tried to comfort him and the group. "Businesses take inventory of their products each m-m-month but they lose a lot to shoplifting, accidents, and m-m-misplacement. A lot of stuff just gets lost. If we only take only one or two things at a time, they will just chalk it up to business as usual. If we take something valuable, they will suspect that someone stole it. The secret is to take a little, just what we want and n-n-no more."

"I want a new bike," said Rusty, who was one of our new members.

"Worst thing you can do," I said. "All bikes have a distinct look, color, and brand. Steal a bike and we go to jail."

"So what can we take?" asked Hardy, another new member

"We take one or two things when there are a lot of them and they all look alike. Like candy bars, Cokes, or twenty-five pound cans of blasting powder."

"You keep talking about gun powder," said Fred.

"Exciting isn't it," I said. "It's right this way."

We walked by the department store with its mannequins staring out from the front windows, then turned left past the drug store, and then stopped square at the front door of the hardware store.

Sammy pulled on the front door. "You said it was open."

"The front doors are locked," I said. "But in the back the windows are open."

We all traipsed carefully down a little alley and stopped before a panel of large windows. The glass was white with lines of white metal crisscrossing it for security. I bent down and pulled the window up. "These are always open." I bent down and stepped into the dark store.

Everyone else paused and looked scared.

"Come on," I beckoned. "The first time is scary, but no one is in here and no one is going to come. There are no alarms."

Everyone climbed in and we searched the long rows of basement merchandise. "The blasting p-p-powder is down here." The building was quiet and very dark. All you could hear was the shuffle of our feet. The group stayed tight behind me.

Down on one of the lower shelves, there were about twenty black metal kegs of blasting powder. I took one of them and handed it to Fred. Then I got a roll of orange dynamite fuse. "Remember, we only take one."

"Then why not take two?" asked Molly.

"Because, we only need one," I said.

The next day we began our experiments – making rockets and bombs. We filled Coke bottles full of blasting powder, put the fuse in, enclosed the fuse with toilet paper, and the bombs were ready. For the rockets, we filled the cardboard part of a paper towel roll up with powder, tapped it in with toilet paper, put a cone head on the top and cardboard wings on the tail. When we had six bombs and two rockets, we were ready. We walked out of town to an old sawmill down by a creek and set up our detonation site.

With us hiding behind pallets of lumber, the bombs exploded. We had all watched rockets takeoff on television, so we were excited to see our own birds fly. We set one of the rockets up with a stick and lit the five-foot fuse. When the fuse hit the blasting powder, there was a great roar of smoke and fire. The rocket tipped over and shot along the ground for about fifty yards then sputtered out.

Over the next several weeks, we never got a rocket to take off, so we used the bombs. We bombed a creek once until I saw little minnows float to the top. "We killed those fish," I said, looking at the little bodies floating down the creek.

"Relax, they are just fish," Molly said.

I wouldn't be comforted. "Life is too precious to waste."

"It's just a fish," Sammy said, with everyone nodding at his truth.

Still not comforted, I said, "A fish is just like a person. It eats and breathes just like us. If aliens come to earth, maybe they will kill us and s-s-say we don't matter either. How would you feel about life and death then? Best to treat all life as precious, believe me animals know a lot more than you think."

With that, our gang left the riverside. The fish haunted me for many days. I remembered a plea for help, our burning house, and Baby.

# CHAPTER 6

We kept our club very, very secret. One night among many, I decided to take the gang to my favorite place. A place I visited for hours when I was alone.

"This better be good," said Fred. "I was counting on picking up a new pair of tennis shoes."

We sauntered across the street from all of the stores, and then skipped passed the old courthouses and down a little grassy hill. As usual, the back windows were open in the small, stony building and we all climbed right in, no longer afraid of getting caught. The room was calm and still and the long shelves lined up in every direction.

"What is it?" asked Joe. "Looks like books."

"It's the library," I said.

"Let's go get my tennis shoes," said Fred. "I can go to the library at school."

"Why your favorite place?" asked Molly. "It's just books."

"Information is power, when you have the f-f-facts, you can go anywhere and do anything you want. People want you around when you know lots of s-s-stuff and you are not excluded. Information is power and power means money."

Fred shook his head. "That's a bunch of crap."

I put my hand on Fred's shoulder and said, "What does your dad do for a living?"

"He sells insurance."

"Why do people go to him for insurance? Why don't they buy insurance on their own?"

"He knows a lot about insurance," he said.

"Why don't people find out about insurance on their own?"

"It's too complicated."

"They need an expert. Your dad studies insurance and with a lot of work he can make a very complicated subject simple. He tells you what is the best insurance and if you trust him you buy it. That's information and that's power. This is the most powerful place in town. Here you can gain wisdom. No one

43

can take your e-e-education away. What you learn is your future."

As we walked home, Molly caught up with me and took my hand. "I'm babysitting tonight at the Johnson's house maybe you could come over and help me. They are never home until way after midnight and the kids go to sleep around nine. I've got something important to tell you."

This was a dangerous sign, but if she needed to talk to me, I was willing to listen. A stutterer is a wonderful listener because most of the time they don't speak. People have always told me secrets and stories they would never tell anyone else. Somehow they secretly knew I would not reveal their truths or untruths because to tell was to speak and to speak was painful. To my mother, father, and friends, I was the listening post. I tried to smile and encourage people no matter what they told me, always. Besides people's lives are fascinating. I was never bored of the drama.

Later, the safety of night came with a belly of hunger pangs. I steadily traversed up to the supermarket hoping for something fresh to eat. As I was standing in the dumpster digging through the spoiled fruit and vegetables, I heard a noise behind me. I froze. The night was hot and humid and moths were flying circles around the streetlight. Intently, I listened but didn't hear anything accept the patter of moths against glass. *Probably a dog or cat,* I thought. I knew cats jumped in the dumpster, I had seen them here many times, but dogs couldn't make the leap.

I slowly went back to my selection of tomatoes and put the good ones in a plastic bag. Then, I heard a noise again. This was too heavy a sound. It was definitely not a cat – maybe the police or the owner of the market? I stood still with a pounding heart. "Who's there?" I asked, holding my breath.

A child's voice said, "Me." I could see a shadow of a figure moving behind a stack of boxes.

"Step out of there!" I was filled with shame. Now everyone would know I ate garbage. "Let me see you."

From behind a pile of boxes and trash cans, a black boy about my age stuck his head out. He was wearing a torn tee-shirt, jeans, and no shoes. "I'm sorry," he said, walking slowly toward me. "I'm Ben." Then he hesitated as he recognized me. He said, "Do you remember me?"

This wasn't the owner or the police. This was the raggedy black kid whose father had given me a ride home from my lost trip in the woods and the frog gigging.

"My momma sent me for food. We are in some hard times." He was short with thin arms and legs and his face appeared rusty and dusty. He cocked his head with curiosity.

"You came to the right place," I said. "You got a bag?"

He shyly walked up the dumpster. "They got plenty of bags here."

"Yeah, but they're dirty, you need to come here with clean bags or wash out some of these." I handed him three bags and began to hand him some of the best fruits and vegetables. "Tonight you can take some of mine. I use them over and over again." I still felt ashamed of getting caught but I didn't think Ben would tell anyone. He was doing the same thing and probably felt the same way. For a time, we sat together and ate peaches and tomatoes while listening to the crickets. "First time here, right?" I finally asked.

Ben hesitated, but then said, "This is the first time."

"I come here at least once week."

"You looked like you knew what you were doing," he said, then smiled.

"I'd appreciate it if you would keep what you saw a secret. If people find out what we are doing we could get in trouble."

"You got to do what you got to do." Ben bit into a peach.

"That's how I see it."

We lived in the segregated south of the fifties and sixties. I didn't agree with the racist argument and never believed in the inferiority of black people. At least Ben had a family. With my father being the town drunk and my mother screwing everybody, I knew I was at the bottom of the ladder—like a saltwater fish feeding off the bottom of the ocean.

Ben and I talked a long time. He told me about his large family and their struggle since their father hurt his back and lost his job. Ben thought his father wasn't taking his job loss with appropriate concern. It had been six months, and he didn't seem to be looking for work. "Sometimes he comes home drunk," Ben said.

I never told anyone about my parents drinking and all the problems in my home. If I confessed the truth, my family might go to prison. "My dad's looking for work, too," I said.

"Now, I know why you're out here," Ben said.

From this night with Ben, I saw that we would be friends. Our kinship laid in our mutual familial hardships—it's what bonded us together and it felt good and true.

After we said goodbye, I walked a few miles through the dark streets to the Johnson house where Molly was babysitting. The ranch style home was dark except for one window that lit up the west side of the home. Through the front window, I could see Molly sitting on the couch watching television. Quietly, I knocked on the door, fearing the Johnson's might be home.

She opened the door and I gingerly stepped into the family den. The room smelled oiled with leather and furniture polish. There was a long leather couch, several night tables, and a large recliner.

"I was afraid you wouldn't come," she said and latched the door behind me. She wore a matching blue sweater blouse and skirt, and her fluffy blond hair curled down her back to the middle of her back. She went to the kitchen and came back with two Cokes and a plate of cookies. "Sit over here," she said, patting the couch.

I took the Coke and sat next to her feeling the heat of her body. I began to sweat in the air conditioned room. She bit into a cookie and took a sip of her drink.

"I know, let's have a real drink." She walked behind a bar and came up with a bottle of Bacardi Rum. "This makes a rum and Coke. It's a famous drink."

I didn't resist even though I'd sworn to never take a drink like my parents. "You said you needed to talk to me." I took a sip of the drink. It burned and tasted awful. Momentarily, I wondered why people liked the stuff.

"I know," she said, and took a large swallow. "Why don't we have a meeting with just you and me? So what I say will remain secret." She took another gulp of her drink and pulled the sweater over her head.

"That's not a good idea," I said feeling beads of sweat breaking out on my forehead. The booze felt warm. "The other kids aren't here so it can't be a formal club meeting."

"Sure it can," she said, taking off her skirt and putting it on the back of the couch. "Come on. Let's have a full meeting."

"Okay." I began to remove my clothes.

Soon we were sitting on the couch naked, drinking our drinks. I could feel the warmth of the booze coursing through my veins, my face and body relaxed a bit. "You said you had something to tell me?" I asked.

She took another slug and moved closer. "Can I really trust you?"

"Sure," I said.

"I think only you can keep my secret." She moved closer almost touching me. "You know, the girls talk about you."

"Yeah," I said. I knew girls never talked about me but I remained agreeable.

"They say you're smart. Now, don't be scared okay? Trust me. I've been thinking about this for a long time." Her long earrings danced with the movements of her head. "I'm not like the other girls. I have needs that I haven't told you about, like a weakness I can't control." She inched closer until her leg touched mine.

"I don't have those n-n-needs." I heard myself say this as if I wasn't in the room, but floating somewhere round and round in outer space.

Her hair touched my legs—everything swirled.

I could feel the universe pull all of its joy into this one moment. I was stunned. She wanted to have sex with me. "Molly, this is n-n-not right," I stated.

"It's more right than you will ever know. I'll show you." Her fingers stroked the inside of my leg. "Do you want to feel my breast?" She took my hand and cupped it to her breast. Her skin was soft and moved like jelly. Her nipple tightened.

I stood up and backed away. "I can't." Her body was too much to resist and it took all of my strength to pull away.

"You want me as much as I want you. I can tell by the way you look at me." She slid her hands through her blond hair and smiled.

My mouth was so dry I could hardly speak. "Molly, you are the most beautiful girl...to be with you is the most wonderful thing...but I know something you don't know. Sex can get you killed." There, I had said it. The most wonderful feeling can kill you.

"What are you talking about?" she asked.

"My mother has sex with everybody—"

"I know that. Everyone in town knows about your mother." She stood.

My body got tense and my face got hot. Humiliation filled every cell. I felt utterly destroyed. *Everybody knows!*

"Your best friends have sex with your mother. Don't you know that?"

Stark naked, I grabbed my clothes and bolted out the door running as fast as I could for as long as I could. The rocks and gravel cut my bare feet yet I sailed through the pain. When I got far enough away, I fell, knees first, into the grass sobbing uncontrollably. "*Why! Why! Why!*" My family is the town's joke. I could hear my friends laughing at me as they had sex with my mother. I pitied myself but it was my mother who I felt the worst for. There was nothing I could do to protect her, my family, or myself. I would always be the child of a whore. I was a good-for-nothing worthless human being. All I could do was become invisible again and live in the darkness. When a person has nowhere else to go a coal bin can become their home. Inside there you can feel safe.

Exhausted, I fell asleep and awoke in the grass with the humid smell of honeysuckle and the dying sound of crickets. I walked home in the early dew, but I wasn't me anymore. I was someone I had never known. Molly was right. I had needs that I had never known. I wanted her so bad I could feel myself fall into her safe warm arms. But, she was too good for me. Being with her the night before had made me a new person and this person understood life as never before—as if the air had cleared. The croaks of frogs, songs of birds, and the mating swarms of bugs, all blended: a new meaning. Sexual need and the meeting of that need was the driving force behind all life and it was more powerful than I ever imagined. I understood my mother and my father like never before. They weren't crazy like I thought. They were caught up in a delicate dance of sexual desire and love—as lost and confused as the rutting deer.

For the next few days, I tried to think of other things, but my mind and body kept coming back to Molly. Her smell, her touch, her transcendent beauty and how her soft watery blue eyes pierced through me. I knew she cared for me or at least thought she did. She was everything I ever wanted, how she felt and how her fingers were smooth and welcoming. I couldn't wait to see her again. I knew she didn't really love me, and I didn't love her, she was just trying to meet her needs and teach me mine.

Regrettably, I never touched her again but once—many months later— I asked her if she had ever had sex before. She got quiet and said, "Don't ever ask me that again." It felt like someone had forced her, and taught her, or maybe she had made a young girl mistake. Either way she had a need that overpowered her.

After that night and the revelation with Molly, I walked up the street toward home. As I drew nearer, I heard my mother's terrifying scream. My father was beating her up again. It was a regular occurrence to release himself from the pain of his own responsibility and shame and guilt. As long as he had someone to blame, he could be insane without feeling guilty. I ran up to the front porch hearing her scream again and again. The hairs on the back of my neck stood up. This time I was afraid he was killing her. I was used to hearing the thuds of his shoes on her head and body and her pleading for him to please stop. But when I got down to her bedroom and walked in, she was lying on the bed alone.

"I saw a baby being born," she said tenderly, as if she was watching the miracle of birth. "Isn't it beautiful?" Then she screamed again, a scream that made me think everyone in town would hear.

"What are you screaming for?" I asked.

She screamed bloody murder again from the deepest part of her. "He's going to kill the baby."

"Mom, there's no one's here b-b-but you and m-m-me," I said.

"He doesn't love the baby even though he's the father," she moaned the words.

I was confused. It was like she was talking about herself as the baby and my father as the killer. She was seeing things that were not there. It meant my Mother was more insane than she had ever been.

"Don't you see!" she kept screaming. "It's right over there!" She pulled up her legs as if someone was grabbing her foot. "Get away!" she wailed at it or him—I don't know what.

"Mom, no one is here but you and me. Everything is okay." But she wouldn't listen and she couldn't stop the paralysis of her guttural screams. She was restless, irritable and wild-eyed, like a captured animal.

I couldn't call dad on this one so I called my mother's sister, Ruth, and told her what was happening. It took my aunt about an hour to get to the house with my mother screaming the whole time about the baby and the murderer.

It didn't take my aunt long to figure out mom was insane and called for help. Another hour passed before an ambulance came and carted my Mother away. I hoped that someone would help her. Secretly, I hoped she would never come back. I would rather live alone. My parents were too crazy. I was sick and tired of picking them up passed out in the yard, cleaning up their vomit, and changing the urine soaked sheets. It was exhausting. It was rare that I had time to take care of myself and at school I had to sleep. The teachers didn't have the heart to wake me. Everyone knew.

Later, my aunt called me and said my mother was being sent to a mental hospital. I hoped they had a permanent bed for her because I knew she wasn't going to get better and my father needed a bed there, too. "What about Dad?" I asked.

"He's going to take care of you," she said, not knowing he was even more insane. "I called him and he said he was on the way."

Great, my father was on the way. My lovely days were to begin again. My transformation I had encountered with Molly and the night was now going to be stilted by my drunken father and his life-long love affair with alcohol.

Later that night, I went to the dumpster and Ben was there wearing the same torn cloths and no shoes. "Are you waiting for me, Ben?" I asked. A smile spread across my face.

"I got no friend but you," he said.

"Looks like you need some clothes."

He took on that shameful look that was so much a part of him.

"Don't look like that, Ben. You'll make me start crying. It's no shame to be hungry. It's not your fault. How many kids are there in your family?"

"Six," he said.

"How old are they?"

"Twelve, ten, eight, seven, six and five." He counted them off.

"I'll bring you some clothes next week."

"You don't have to do that. All I want is to talk." Ben walked closer to me and picked up a stone and tossed it.

"Everyone needs clothes."

He looked at me questioningly and tossed another stone. "Where are you going to get clothes? If you can't afford food how are you going to get clothes?"

"Never mind, I'll have you some clothes in a week. I have friends who will help me." I picked up a stone and tossed one with him.

I took on the mission and by the end of the week had enough clothes for his siblings. It was like a birthday party and Ben was delighted.

I handed a few shirts to Ben. "I thought about shoes, but you'll have to measure their feet. Here's a foot measuring device from the department store to get the right sizes," I instructed him. Then I taught Ben how to measure the length and width of each foot.

"You got to help me," he said. "I'll mess this up. You can measure and write it down."

"Can't you write?" I asked.

Ben said matter-of-factly, "Never had time to learn, never been to school. You can come to my house tomorrow. My mom is dying to meet you. I told her about you."

The next day, Ben took me to his frail-looking home that looked barely strung together by wooden boards and introduced me to his mother. She was an enormous round woman who had pearly white teeth and when she grinned, her whole head seemed to smile. To me, she had nothing to be happy about. She had a slew of children, a drunken husband, and no money to do anything.

"Ben told me about you," she said. "I appreciate how you helped him find the right food and thank you Lord for the clothes and if you could see to it that the children got some shoes I would be most grateful." She opened her mouth again and her smile brightened the room.

"No problem," I said. "I just need to draw an outline of each foot, yours too, so I can get the sizes right. I'll bring the shoes to Ben over the next several weeks. I can't bring them all at once. I can get you come clothes, too. Ben says you need a coat for winter?"

"I don't need anything," she said, "If you can help the children that will be more than enough."

I observed the children and Ben. "Everyone needs a coat. I'll get one for you and the kids but it will take me awhile."

Drunk and mean, my dad came home later that night. He was yelling and carrying on at nothing, so I snuck out of the house and went back over to Ben's house to sleep on Ben's porch. Ben's mother found me the next morning next to a big pile of new children's clothes. "You got nowhere to go?" she asked kneeling down next to me. She then lost that wide smile and replaced it with something I had never seen, a mother's love and compassion.

"I just fell asleep," I said.

"Shure you did," she said with her black southern talk. "You can sleep in my house anytime, honey. You always welcome here."

I couldn't believe it. She was offering me a place in her broken down home. And, it was more of a home than I had ever known. None of the white people in town had recognized I needed help, but this black woman had recognized instantly. She saw right through me and my dilemma and even my invisible shield. From that time on I could never fool her. As our time together went on, if I would try to be invisible (which was most of the time) she would look at me with a loving smile. All at once, it was infuriating and impossible to resist. Like it or not, I had a new home: a place of refuge whenever I needed it. She made me a bed and no one disturbed it. They treated me good and I felt like a king.

One day I was helping her shell some peas. We could hear the children playing outside. I couldn't help but ask her. "Who is the Lord you all keep talking about?"

"You don't know who Jesus is, child? He died on the cross to save us. You been to church haven't you?" she asked sweetly. Then she put some peas into a large black pot.

"No." I peered over at two of the children playing jacks on the floor with new shoes on their feet. This made me happier than I had ever been. It seemed like giving to others was the key to living in peace.

She paused. "Well, we'll correct that problem this Sunday morning. You come along with us and we'll show you who the Lord is."

The next Sunday, sure enough there I was walking with Ben's momma and the kids up to a little white church just off a dusty street. Way before we arrived, I could hear the music. I had heard about God before but dispelled the idea as a myth.

I was the only white person in church, but that was fine with me. Prior to this, the only caring people I had ever encountered were my brother, my grandfather and maybe Molly. The rest of the human race, I was sure, did not care about anything other than what they wanted to take from you. I wasn't sure, but I figured good people cared for other people, too. Ben's momma cared about me for no reason and that was confusing. I could tell she didn't just care about me for the food and clothes I gave her; it was somehow different. What that was I did not know.

The little white church was rocking. People were swaying, clapping, shaking tambourines, jumping and dancing in the aisles. They were singing about Jesus and how good he was. "Jesus!" they kept shouting. "Jesus! Jesus! Jesus!" Whoever this Jesus was it was as if he could hear them shouting his name with such happiness. I knew he would like it.

After about an hour of music, shouting, clapping and dancing, the preacher came up to the front and gave a talk. He had stood in the front row with his wife and two little girls and clapped along with everyone except he did not shout or dance. He was subdued until he began to talk. Then gradually he got more and more excited until he shouted, begged, and pleaded for Jesus to help us and for us to understand and tap into his power.

I knew the world needed help, but I didn't know if Jesus was available. If I had known this I would have called on him a long time ago inside a coal bin, or in a boat with small crabs skittering around my legs, or trying to help my screaming mother from going insane. My shouts would have been like these church songs: loud and long.

"Jesus loved you so much," the preacher said, "he died for you on the cross." This sounded crazy, but I was to find out more about the story.

After a few Sundays of preaching, I got the story. God had come to earth to save his children from the sin that would send them all to hell. Hell was a very bad place filled with fire and pain, kind of like my house. If you didn't make God happy he would send you to hell where you would burn in the fire forever.

This did not sound good and I didn't want to go to hell. My hell on earth was bad enough. A worse place would be intolerable.

The preacher said God loved his children so much that he sent his only son to take the punishment for everyone's sins. This seemed crazy but it also seemed possible. Apparently, God was three people in one person, the Father, the Son and the Holy Spirit. It was very confusing and didn't make a lot of sense. But there was definitely something real and good in this church. I felt the love in the music and the prayers. The preacher prayed for everybody— the black people and the white people. I didn't think the white people were praying for the black people, but I didn't know.

When we would sing love songs to God, I cried from something unknown moving me deep inside my heart. Ben's momma smiled wide and handed me a tissue to wipe my eyes. I didn't believe all this church stuff— but there was something here that was good. I sensed that God, who I didn't even think existed, somehow loved me. But all the time a painful truth—like a gaping wound— was too much to ignore. If there was a God, where was he when I needed him? Where was he when I was locked in the coal bin? If there was a God why did he let me suffer? Those facts of mine made me stare hard into the eyes of the preacher and hard into the heart of his stories. Then, I would look away from all of it by virtue of my own doubt and shame.

My mother stayed away in a mental hospital for a year and my brother was sent off to a military school for troubled boys. I didn't know exactly where my mother was so I couldn't contact her even if I wanted to. My brother was four years ahead of me, so he moved to another town hundreds of miles away. I rarely heard from him but longed to hear his voice that made me feel safe.

In high school, I still tried to stay invisible and to do that I had to make grades that were exactly average. If your grades were too low, people paid attention to you because you needed help; and, if they were too high people paid attention to you because you were smart. It took patience and good math skills to stay exactly average. This was me, the invisible boy.

When the Vietnam War began to pick up, this idea of staying average became a problem. I didn't want to kill anybody and I didn't want to be killed myself, so I wanted to stay out of that war. The war in my house was bad enough, I didn't need another one. In order to stay out of Viet Nam, I had to go to college. To do that, I had to make better grades. I decided to increase my grades exactly enough to get into college and no higher. I talked to the school counselor and he said I had to increase my grades in the last two years of high school from a C average to a B average. This took some work but it wasn't hard—mostly I just had to stay awake.

The year sailed by and I was getting ever closer to my senior year—ever closer to college

and my escape from this God forsaken place of a town.

# CHAPTER 7

In my senior year of high school, I had to take a speech class. It was required and I was terrified. I could not be invisible while giving a talk in front of the class. So, I thought of every way to get out of it—puking, breaking my own leg, or pretending to have some unknown disorder like brain cancer. I even considered telling the teacher the truth in hopes that she would pass over me because I had a speech handicap. I knew nothing would work. I would have to give speeches to pass. I was forced to face my greatest nightmare, my monster fear, my biggest shame, stuttering in front of a class that I knew would laugh at me and see me as a cripple. I began to have recurring nightmares of standing in front of the class in the grip of a stuttering block, not being able to make a sound, everyone snickering and laughing, being able to say a few words and then blocking into defective utterings. It was like a sentence of certain death. From the first moment of entering that classroom, I was a pile of fear and sweat. Every sweat bead was full of anxiety, panic and terror. Each second would be in slow motion while the rest of the class laughed—all knowing I was crazy.

When it came time for me to give my first speech, I had not prepared because I had gone numb with the paralyzing fear. My fear had taken my body hostage. There was no way out of the humiliation. The teacher called my name and I walked up to the front of the room and stood there like a deer in the headlights. My fate was sealed, death as certain as being executed.

As I walked to the front of the room, the room got quiet and the students all stared at me. Time stood still, the earth stopped rotating, the stars faded, the God of the preacher disappeared. There was no hope, only shame. For a moment, the truck lights closed in on me and I waited for death. Death would be quiet and still.

"Jesus...was...a...good...guy," I heard myself say.

Some of the kids snickered.

Then a slight pause, I said, "Jesus...was...a...really...good...guy."

Now all of the students giggled and some laughed out loud.

"His...Dad...sent...him...to...earth...to...die for our sins." I said every word very slowly because it was the only way I could get them out.

"Jesus... didn't...think... that ...was.... a... good...idea. In fact, he thought it was a stupid...idea. Maybe God had eaten...a bad pizza."

Now, the teacher started laughing and I suddenly knew they weren't laughing at me because I was stuttering. They were laughing at me because I was funny. I was making them laugh. This moment changed my whole life.

"What...do... you...say... to... a...God...who...is...crazy?" I paused a long time. "Dad...did you eat a bad pizza?"

The whole class roared with laughter. Half of them bowled over as if their stomach was hurting. They were hysterical. I was internally elated. I kept on. The pauses became fewer as I released the words from my stomach and lungs.

"I don't...want to die. Particularly for a bunch of bad people I don't know." I was not only talking funny but my facial expressions began to contort to the humor of what I said. The speech was hysterical. A number of my friends almost passed out from lack of oxygen. The delirium danced on the precipice of each word I let out.

"The world will love you for it, God said."

"Jesus said I don't want to be loved like that. I want to be loved for other stuff, like buying everyone ice cream."

I finished the rest of my story without stuttering once.

"It's all planned, God said. You will die on a cross to save the world."

"Dad, you've lost your mind."

With that, I concluded my short yet funny comedy sketch. When I sat down, the kids all were lost in laughter. I was hysterical. My certain death had ended up a huge success. From then on, the class waited in anxious anticipation for my talks. I would take a simple topic and make it funny, like brushing your teeth or picking your nose. It had to be something that everyone did and thought about but with a twist to make it funny. I chatted about our peculiar behaviors. Why do people brush their teeth in private? Why be embarrassed when you have white stuff slobbering over your lips and oozing down your arm? From then on, I knew I could take any topic and make it funny. I was still terrified of speaking, but I had found a way to get through it successfully without humiliating myself. I could speak and be more successful than anyone else in the class. People loved my sense of humor. I still had to stay invisible but I could talk if I had to.

To pull my grades up, for the first time I began to study. I did not want to draw attention to myself, so I studied just enough to get it the way I needed it. When the grades were just right, I applied to college and was accepted at East Carolina University.

During that last year of high school, the routine at my house in the small Virginia town remained much of the same. Mother and father were never sober. From time to time, my older brother would come home. But he left as soon as he could.

Molly got a boyfriend and we lost touch. From time to time, I thought of her and the moment of truth we shared at the Johnson's house. I learned about gossip and small towns and how nothing is ever really a secret.

The summer after my senior year, I became free from the shackles of my family—the memory of the coal bin, the memory the beatings, and the memory of the men and the whoring. My childhood was something I wanted to forget but I never could. History stays the same even if you want it to be different. When I went off to college I never saw Ben and his family again but I will always be grateful for their presence in my life. The one redemptive hope from my childhood lay in a seed planted in their small white church. Maybe there was a God and maybe he loved me like everyone else. At least I knew some people were good. If one person can be good to you this means that another one can be good to you too. This opens a new world full of hope.

When I got to college in the fall, my cloak of invisibility came with me. In a college environment, I had to start my life all over again. So, to ensure protection, I donned my invisible cloak and embarked on the new ways of college culture. With it, I walked around campus, went to classes, and worked at the library. I tried never to be seen. In class, I sat in the middle and did not move or say anything. On time and on schedule, I walked in the classrooms with the rest of the students and smiled my little "I'm all right smile." I did not make eye contact with anyone. If I rushed along at the same speed as the other students then no one ever noticed me. In the library, there was a desk way in the back of each floor where it was quiet and no one walked by.

I had a roommate named Bill. He was overweight with short blond hair and a round kind face. He thought I was great. I will never know why. He liked me so much he began to stutter himself. He mimicked my gestures when trying to get through a block, like hitting my leg with my hand. We became close friends and he tried to become invisible like me, but he failed. He didn't really want to be invisible. He just wanted to copy me. Bill was a wonderful guy and he became a dear friend.

I went through my first two years doing in class what I'd done in high school. There was lots of shrugging and I stuttered out a long painful stutters to a teacher who asked me a question. It never failed that this would give them cause to never, ever call on me again. Perfect.

During my second year rooming with Bill, we decided to apply for a summer job. We wanted to work so we could travel. We applied to many different employers in the United States and abroad but we got only one offer— as housemen for the Yellowstone Park Company in Wyoming. The job was at the Mammoth Motor Inn as a male maid—they called them housemen. I had never worked before but was willing to take the chance. Then after we saved up enough money to buy a beat up car, off we went.

When I crossed the Virginia state line going west, I felt a tremendous weight lift off of me, like what a baby bird must feel like when it flies for the first time. From this point, no one knew my family and I didn't have to take care of my parents anymore. I just had to take care of me and maybe Bill. Coming across the country, camping all the way, and feeling freer with every mile, I realized the size of the United States. It was huge. We traveled about 300 miles a day. When we got to the Black Hills of South Dakota, we camped in a campground that had just opened for the year. It was in early May, so there was snow piled up and it was cold. We froze in our cotton sleeping bags. With a little hatchet, I tried to chop some wood but the altitude made this simple task physically insurmountable. It was hard to breathe out west.

Over the weeks of traveling I learned a lot about the wilderness and survival. The first rule was you had to stay dry and warm and that took equipment that Bill and I didn't even know about. But outdoor store owners were more than happy to show us what we needed: Gore-Tex wind jackets and pants, down coats, polypropylene underwear, wool socks, and hiking boots. We even bought a two-man climbing tent that weighed three pounds. Before we got to Gardiner, Montana, we were equipped and ready to go through the famous Roosevelt Arch and enter Yellowstone National Park. Once through the small historic portal, I felt yet another surge in me that I was free, on the right track, ready for what lay ahead in my life.

We checked in and went to our dorm room. It was much like our college room but more rustic. The dining room was across the way and the food was amazingly good, food, wonderful food. Since entering college and, even now, I was never hungry again. I didn't have to eat from a garbage can anymore. Starvation and the coal bin were imprinted permanently on my brain but they were in the past and the past can't be changed. You had to live in the moment you had and that was enough. I was so grateful to be out of the pain. I also didn't think I could ever tell anyone about those childhood experiences. No one would understand. To me, it seemed most people lived with food and shelter—even the homeless were cared for.

I worked hard in Yellowstone and after only a few weeks as a houseman, I was promoted to one of the best jobs in the park, bellman. The job was fun because you met people from all over the world, took up their bags and, on the way, taught them about the park. The tips were abundant and I saved every bit of it. I found that if I had on a bellman uniform I could talk because I was something else. I wasn't me I was a bellman and bellman had to be visible.

Like the heaven that the preacher talked about at Ben's church, Yellowstone was a paradise—elk, deer, buffalo, and bear roaming along the roads. There were deep forests and crystal clear lakes and streams full of fish. With fourteen million acres of lodge pole pine forest spotted by an occasional meadow, Yellowstone stood with more grandeur than my heart could hold. It was a natural wonderland. It was the risk-takers who flocked here who became my brothers and sisters. They were fearless and could leave family and friends and travel thousands of miles across the country to work in a place they had never seen. It was as if we had the same genes and we weren't afraid of anything. Bill and I were risk-takers, too, and it was all so good.

In college, I had begun learning the guitar. So, I entered the talent contest at the hotel with a girl who also sang and played the guitar. Amazingly, we won first place. For the first time in my life, I felt good about myself. It was a new hope growing inside of me. I had the best job in the park and I had won the talent contest. All by myself—I did it all by myself. A normal life was upon me as long as I stayed away from my parents and their history. I had a chance to live and to leave my childhood behind me like a ghost.

My second summer out west, I decided to work at the historic Lake Hotel which was the most beautiful lodge in the park and it faced Yellowstone Lake. Here I met my future wife, Betty. She was a sweet girl from Mississippi with tense green eyes and shoulder length brown hair. She did not trust me at first because she had been mentally abused by her mother, but over the months she learned to love me. I loved this woman more than anyone I had ever known and I trusted her completely. Going back home to East Carolina University became depressing, so in order for us to be together, we decided to transfer to a college in a mountainous state. To do that, I had to pull up my grades again. I did just that and Betty and I transferred to Colorado State University where I majored in psychology. Having grown up in a family where everyone was crazy, I thought I had a leg up on the other students who were studying mental illness. The next four years were devoted to studying the diagnosing and treatment of mental disorders. We even worked with some clients toward the end of undergraduate school. To help people with their problems gave me a tremendous feeling of worth, and that feeling of hopelessness and worthlessness began to disappear.

During my senior year at Colorado State University, my desire to further my education landed me in graduate school in clinical psychology at Eastern Washington State University. This longing stemmed from a concern and compassion to "be there" for others. Long ago, no one was there for me. Even though no one had loved me, less a few fleeting strangers, I still wanted to love everyone who crossed my path. In my studies and clinical sessions with patients, I tried to give them everything I had missed. I wanted to become like Ben's momma, loving, tender, understanding and kind. Ironically, in the process of work as a neophyte counselor I began to heal myself. This was a miracle. The first of many I was to encounter.

Everyone's life story I learned quickly was better than any novel. And, the study of the mind and human behavior was totally fascinating to me. I found that my speech disorder was an advantage, like a ghost call from my childhood. *Stutterers were the best listeners; everyone wanted to tell me their stories.* I didn't like to speak but I loved to listen. I sat for hours and listened to a client talk about their lives. People loved to talk about themselves more than any other subject, particularly when I was fascinated by every single detail. I was into the intimate details they revealed.

I read everything I could get my hands on, mounds of reading, that fed my mind and I was hungry for every morsel. I wanted to understand people and how I could help them be a better person. I couldn't get enough of Plato, Aristotle, Pavlov, Freud, Jung, Adler, Fromm, Mower, Hall, Eysenck, Bowlby, Watson, Maslow, Perls, May, Thorndike, Skinner, and Rogers. These heroic visionaries became my soul mates--the stars of psychology. They were heroic because they were compelled to understand why mentally ill people did what they did, how they had gotten mentally ill, and how they could get them better. If only my dad and my mom had worked with these men, I might never have lived in such pain. During those long hours of studying, I awakened to a knowing from the core of me. I knew there were invisible boys and girls all over the world living in the same shame that I had gone through and it was going to be my job to find as many as I could set them free. It sounded like healing the world was an impossible job, but I dedicated my life to it.

It then became my lifelong dream to be a psychologist.

I shared my dream with my advisor. He was a very good man who took me into his office and bluntly said, "You can't be a psychologist, Ron. A psychologist needs to talk to his patients. You can't do that because you stutter." He meant that I couldn't be a psychologist because I had a speech defect. "You might be able to do research but you can never work with people."

I knew this was his truth, not the truth. I smiled and pretended he was right. He didn't know that I had survived the coal bin. He didn't know I had walked many times lost out of the forest alone starving and alive. He didn't know I had fought grown men with guns as a little boy. He had no idea who I was or what I had endured. The idea that I couldn't do something as silly as become a psychologist was ridiculous—completely off. The only way I was alive at that time had been because of my stubborn determination to fight for myself. I knew I could do anything I set my mind to. And, if anyone got in my way, then I was going to go under them, around them, or through them—including him. My advisor was a good man trying to do a good thing but he didn't know what he was talking about.

Betty and I moved to Eastern Washington State University to get my master's degree, and then to Utah State University to get my Ph.D. It was in my doctoral program that I met the most wonderful people in the world, my fellow students and faculty. These people were natural born healers who loved people, and truly tried to help the wounded and broken. They weren't interested in money because there was little money in working as a mental health professional. These men and women were tender, gentle, kind, patient, and supersensitive. With practice, they taught me that we could be ahead of a client's thoughts and feelings and then lead them toward the truth. It was the truth, of course, that would set them free.

Some people grew up believing they were stupid, ugly, broken, sick, shameful, and bad. These lies were told to them or acted upon them by their primary caregiver, a peer group, or even a community. They were repeated like a drum until the wronged person believed these lies were the truth. Once someone knows he or she was worthless then the sky was the limit. Someone could hurt him or her or use drugs and alcohol, or have unprotected sex, or commit suicide or murder, still others, like me, became invisible.

It was amazing to see what I considered to be the best people in the world accept me as one of their own. Then, I became a leader in my group, a role model. The best mental health workers have an almost magical ability to get people to trust them. This is called the therapeutic alliance that is based on love, trust, and commitment. I was uniquely gifted with this. People had no problem talking to me, and I was amazed at the ease with which it all came to me. Sharing secrets with a trusted ally changes everything. At the time, many of my clients had never tasted success, many had never heard they were beautiful, and many had not heard, "You did a good job. You have talent and with your talents you can change the world."

If a person has never been loved, then love is never expected from anyone. Resigned to the fact that it will never happen, they journey through life, loveless. However, I advised that if love happens with one person, it can happen again and then everything changes. Question may arise: what was this person like? How can I find other people like this? Can it happen again? Yes. I would love them and they would feel loved for the first time. They were more than patients but brothers and sisters in pain.

To work with these patients, students and teachers, these wonderful healers was a great honor. Throughout my master's and doctorate programs, the students and I were constantly participating in our own group and individual therapies. We learned a lot about ourselves, how we perceived ourselves and each other. We studied and learned from the maps of our own childhood. Much of this came as a surprise because some of the seeds of our personality and character are unconscious.

I learned that character was infused into a person in early childhood but could constantly change as the person matured and learned about the mechanics of life; especially, what worked and what did not work to ease one's way in the world. Most of the clinical and counseling students learned that helping others made them feel good about themselves. Most of the experimental students learned to test the validity of everything. Clinicians, as a whole, cared deeply about how other people thought and felt. With this, I developed a more deeply evolved sense of caring. Experimental students developed the skill of working in the behavioral lab—at times with animals. They progressed and excelled at learning theory and development. Working side-by-side, each facet was able to discover the truth of their experiments and the validity of their studies. I found that working together was always better.

Along this course of learning and discovery, I had teachers in the experimental faculty who thought I was a joke because of my stutter and clinical teachers who thought I was wonderful because I was sensitive and almost magically empathic. Even though they laughed at me, I learned tons of things from the experimental professors like the theories of learning and behavior. They were great people who knew how to run experiments and find what really worked in psychology. The science of psychology manifested itself from the tireless efforts of these people. I wanted to learn everything from everyone because the more I could learn the better I could get. I knew that every person, student, professor or patient had something to teach me that I needed to learn to make me flourish.

The secret, I found, was to be open, to actively listen, and to filter and remember. I discovered I had an unusual ability to get people to trust me almost instantly. They unraveled their mysteries for me that they wouldn't tell anyone else. Somehow, they sensed I accepted them no matter what they had experienced or even done themselves. This ability of mine was and has always been a mystery to me. What could they see in me that even I couldn't see? It was an air of trustworthiness and caring for them as if they were my own family and that's exactly how I felt. Carl Rogers called this "unconditional positive regard" and this became my mantra.

Years were spent training in mental hospitals, prisons, clinics, and jails. I worked with career criminals, drug addicts, pedophiles, and murderers—some of them had killed their own children. These were people who could be helped. The trick was to get them to see the truth and then decide to live in the truth. Then they would get better. I never excused their bad behavior but I could understand it and offer tools to make it less likely to happen again. Each of my clients was a part of me, and I felt and believed to my core that by helping them, I began to get better myself.

Much of mental illness has a genetic floor, which means it is rooted in our DNA. This means the possibility is there for mental illness to rise to the surface and develop under stress. That doesn't mean it always happens, but it can happen if the right genes are present along with the right factoring triggers. There are also protective genes in place in one's DNA to secure and almost guarantee good mental health. With these genes a person can go through a terrible trauma—like the death of a child or the suicide of a friend— and bounce back to a sense of normalcy over due time and due mourning. These people have a certain gene. They can get knocked down, but it is extremely difficult to keep them down.

In training, I learned the critical importance of how a mother looks at her child in the first three years of growth and development. Most mothers carry their children cradled in their left arm; imprinting from their right eye to the baby's right eye and keeping them close their own heartbeat. The "mommy look" says to the young child, *you bring me joy where ever you go.* Babies, by and large, then grow a healthy brain that says *I'm important and people like me.* It's in the imprinting. A dancing toddler in a store demonstrates what a healthy child looks like. The child knows they are adorable.

For the first three years of life, most children have a dominant right brain, the side of images. This is how they can recognize emotions and friendly faces. Faces are supposed to be like their moms, so if a child here sees a man with a beard for the first time it can be terrifying. Around year three, most children change from right brain to left brain: the brain of words and logic. Then, of course, there is the interaction between the two hemispheres. To the above point, however, the "mommy look" is critical to growing a healthy brain. If the mother is sick, abused, depressed, numb, or angry, the child is imprinted with this emotion and behavior on the brain. If one observes mothers interact with a baby, they are constantly modeling, even mimicking, after each other. The baby yawns and the mother yawns, the baby smiles the mother smiles, the baby pouts the mother pouts. When the mother feeds her child she opens and closes he mouth to show the child how to eat. They mirror each other and watching the mother's face teaches babies who they are.

It is sad to say that I don't have one pleasant memory of my mother or father. I could never have a healthy brain but I could get better and I did with every heartbeat that passed.

When I learned of this mother-to-baby interaction in school, I was amazed and crestfallen all at once. My mother never looked at me as if she loved me, so I grew up knowing I was unlovable. If you surround a person with love and joy, I learned that this can change. Even the most damaged of people grow healthier in a loving environment. The lesson for me was clear—it was my job to look and give my patient's with the "mommy look"—*you bring me joy*—and by doing this my clients healed.

During school in Washington, I had the first of my three children, Robert, who became my best friend. Robert was extremely intelligent so as a three-year-old, he talked like a thirty-year-old adult and he was so beautiful. Everywhere Betty and I went, the eyes of the crowd went right to him. Time after time, we would be in a restaurant and he would lean over the booth and talk to the other people sitting in the booth next to us. They were always shocked and amazed to hear a three-year-old adult who wanted to discuss national events. He never made anyone mad, just charmed them with his child-like magic.

By far, having kids was the greatest thing that ever happened to me because I had the opportunity to become a child myself—to fill up a place in my heart robbed by my youth. I played with my children: Robert, Nyshie, and Shane—as if I was one of them and I promised myself that my kids would know they were loved. I tried to give them everything I missed, particularly time. I spent time with my children and made up long stories. They were epic and some even lasted years. I played fireman, ambulance driver, policeman, commander-in-chief and doctor. We went camping, fishing, hiking, mountain climbing, canoeing and just about everything we could think of. My wife and I were home and available most of the time. As I raised my children, I continued to heal from my childhood. Raising them helped me to heal.

My last year in my doctoral program, I asked to intern as the juvenile court psychologist for eight counties in southern Utah. I chose this internship because

I wanted to work with the program director at Cedar City Dr. Sheldon Prestwich. He was the most remarkable psychologist I had ever met. Like a miracle worker, he did things with clients that seemed impossible. Instantly, he could get people to trust him and tell him their darkest secrets. No one did therapy as fast as he did. His work was stunning because he got to the real problem so quickly. I watched every move he made. For the first time in my life, I was important: a doctor who people wanted to talk to, to listen to and to trust. To have people come to you every day for help was very different for me. I didn't have to be invisible all the time, at least not as a doctor. My patients didn't care about how I talked and they hung on to every word I said as if they were hearing from God. I listened to Sheldon and copied everything he did.

My first patient was a twenty-three-year old woman from Saint George, Utah. She was one of four wives of a polygamist family. She did not want to discuss the other wives but a recent event that had just occurred in her young life.

"My son drowned," she said with no expression, tears, or despair, just an emotionless statement. She sat there with a blank expression on her face as if she was discussing the price of corn. It was nothing I would have expected from a recent death of a child.

I was silent for a long time. Then, uncontrollably, I began to cry. I knew what she needed to do and she couldn't do it. So, I did it for her. "How old was he?" I managed to get out through my tears.

"Eighteen months," she said.

I said nothing but tears streaked down my face.

"He was just a baby."

I nodded.

She stayed stoic and said, "My little baby boy."

"That's terrible," I said.

"My husband found him in an irrigation ditch and brought him home. He laid him on the kitchen table, limp and cold.

I reached out and gently took her hand and she began to sob. We both sobbed so hard we did not speak for a long time. I cried for her child, my plastic Baby, the gigged frog and all of the unresolved pain in the world. The darkness seemed to close in and cover us in the pouring rain of tears.

"My husband never cried," she said and wiped her nose on her sleeve. "He said this was no longer our son, just a body. His spirit had gone to heaven."

"I'm so sorry," I said.

She closed her eyes and went inside of herself, somewhere deep where no one could go. I tried to stay with her down there in the dark, desolate pits of hopelessness.

"This never should have happened," I said. These were the words she needed to hear. That someone understood her pain.

For the rest of the hour, we sat and held hands. Nothing else needed to be said. When the truth is shared you don't have to carry the burden alone and this makes the pain more bearable. People heal when someone listens and understands—when someone truly sees them and their plight. A therapist has to be there with the patient in their pain. They don't have to have the right thing to say they just have to be present.

She visited me every week for seven weeks. She told me all about her son and how wonderful he was. How his smile warmed her and his laughter filled her heart with joy. He would fall sleep on her chest and she knew he was safe in her arms. She blamed herself for losing track of him that day. She knew, however, that Utah canals were famous for taking young children.

"Where do you think he is?" I asked.

"He is with Jesus," she said.

I nodded my head. "Walking with him and talking with him?"

"Yes."

I said, "I bet he'll tell Jesus all about you."

She smiled for the first time since her son died. "I miss him."

"And he misses you."

I traveled eight counties in Southern Utah and saw patients eight hours a day. It was a great honor to have them share their life with me. Using cognitive behavioral therapy, I would try to see how their inaccurate thinking was hurting them and help them to get their thinking accurate. Often, mental illness is caused by automatic unconscious inaccurate thinking. Once you help the patient test the thinking for accuracy the lies that hold them trapped are revealed and patients get better. It takes a lot of work and practice but even patients who are severely mentally ill can recover.

Later in that internship year something happened that changed my life. My beautiful wife, whom I trusted completely, poured her love into another man.

Weeping, she sheepishly admitted to me what she had done, feeling unimportant as the wife of a new doctor.

But suddenly, I was thrown back, kicked back, chided back into being unlovable and worthless. This was a complete over reaction, but I was humiliated and terrified. Instantly my wife became my mother and I became my father, and no one, not even Sheldon, could bring me out of the darkness that enveloped me. I was devastated. Her behavior was understandable in light of the situation; however, I was too wounded to cope with this new revelation. I had seen too much of the ugly side of life and this opened the door to hell and I walked right in.

I handled the pain like my father had. I began to drink myself to death every night to medicate the anger, the frustration, and the resentment that had arisen from the betrayal. No amount of booze I drank could quiet the terror of living through my childhood again. Of course, my wife was a good person who made a simple mistake. Yet, I was so traumatized by the past, I went backward. I could feel myself waiting for the men for my wife like they had lined up to have sex with my mother. My bones shook with the thought—once they found out my wife was vulnerable, even my best friends would come creeping around. My past reared an ugly head and I armed myself with whatever I could find. It was useless in my mind, nothing would keep them away. Once they had tasted the forbidden fruit, they were addicted.

I returned to the locked coal bin and to the forgotten forest of my youth. This is what psychologists call spontaneous recovery, like old highways in the brain springing back to life as if nothing had changed. Thrust into the misery again of mortal combat with no one I could trust, I spiraled downward. People who are trauma survivors do this all the time. This is post-traumatic stress disorder, they have trauma that is unresolved, something triggers the memory, and the person is thrown back into the pain as if it were happening again in real time. Men and women coming back from war can be thrown back into the terror of combat by the backfire of a car or a bad dream. You are transported back to the cliffs of disaster and you are in the exact same pain.

I could not assuage myself. The tormenting anxiety of my misfortune came back and I could not fling it into a lake, nor flush it down the toilet with one square, nor could I drink it away. I couldn't stop those old feelings from taking control, and I felt terrible and knew it was wrong. I tried every therapy I knew and went to the best but I couldn't stop the terror. I knew I loved my wife and I knew she loved me, but I watched my life turn around and go backward at full speed. No longer was I able to feel confident in myself so I became the invisible boy.

I would always be a totally worthless human being.

My mother's betrayal and my father's homicidal rage were too overwhelming—I would never recover from them. I became my past and lost my future. I took on the role of my father and cheated on my wife. It was not about getting even but a crazy attempt to deal with my insecurity. Like I'd learned in school—if I could find a woman to love me, maybe I had some worth and maybe I could feel safe and loved again.

Because I broke my own moral laws, I then drank myself to sleep every night and lied to everybody about everything. No one knew the extent of my drinking. A few years of this and I was a hopeless alcoholic. I remembered as a child looking at my father's drunkenness and saying to myself, "*I'll never be like that.*" Ironic, because now I was a weak drunken coward just like he was. As a clinician I knew this would never work, but I began a search for happiness in other women. I didn't care as long as I stayed drunk. Amazingly, these women fell for me over and over again. It was like driving a roaring train knowing you were going to run off a cliff but I didn't care. These were good women who deserved someone better than me. But these women saw something that they wanted and trusted me even if I was lying all the time. It was not love, but it felt like love to me, and that's what I thought I needed. To further compound my lying, I traveled and used another name and identity in my escapades to make sure I wouldn't get caught. As often as I could I drove hundreds of miles to another town and became another person.

Finally, my wife discovered what I was doing and we were divorced. My oldest child was in high school and had given up on me for a long time. My girl was in junior high and was tearful to see me leave the home. My littlest son was in kindergarten and didn't really understand what was happening. I couldn't blame my wife. I gave her no choice. A few months after our divorce, I dragged myself into treatment for alcoholism. This treatment center had the philosophy that the staff had to "break" the addict down in order to get them well. This is an old technique and it does not work but it was the treatment of the day. The counselors tried their best to shame their patients into recovery but this approach has never worked. I was so used to shame that their attempts to shame me even further didn't work. But for the first time in many years, I learned to live without alcohol. Three months after treatment, my brain fog cleared.

I was divorced but never lonely. I always had women calling me and wanting to be with me. Even to this day, I have never understood why anyone would want to be with me. A few months after treatment, the executive director of Keystone Treatment Center, in Canton, South Dakota called me.

"I understand you're looking for work," she said in a gravelly smoker's voice.

I will never know how she found me, but a recovering doctor is a jewel in the addiction treatment business. Professionals in recovery have a unique way of understanding addiction that you can't get any other way other than walking through the illness yourself.

In the dead of winter, I traveled to the small town of Canton, South Dakota. The land was completely flat and covered with ice with no trees nor noticeable streams, brooks, or rivers. I felt like I had landed on the moon. This was my second visit to a chemical dependency treatment center, the first being my own treatment. But this staff was markedly different than my own treatment of the shaming of "let's beat them up to help them." There were some staff members like that at Keystone, but there were also professionals who respected the patients and wanted to help them. As a psychologist, I knew the best way to change behavior was through positive reinforcement not through punishment. Love would restore patients to health not beating them up.

As a recovering alcoholic, I fit in easily at the treatment center. Even the old time recovering staff, who hated mental health workers, had to accept me because I was working the same 12-step program as they were. I was one of their own. After a few months of watching me work, the executive director made me the clinical director. I learned never to tell people what to do. Instead, I gently reinforced the staff's good behavior and taught them why their old harsh confronted ways didn't work. It took me a few years to make the staff gentle and kind. A positive atmosphere is what works with all who are mentally ill. You have to respect your clients and walk with them to improve treatment outcome. Surround your patients with joy and they will recover.

# PART 2:
# GOD'S VOICE INSIDE ME

# CHAPTER 8

On January the 9th 1990, I was in my office in Keystone Treatment Center, feeling lost and alone because my girlfriend of the last two years was leaving me. I was afraid that I was going to spend the rest of my life alone. My ex-wife and children were no longer with me. I sat full of fear in my Lazy boy chair and said, "God, I'm so afraid I'm going to spend the rest of my life alone." God then began to speak to me in a tender voice inside of my own thinking. This was not an audible voice but it definitely wasn't me and I was positive it was God. I was frightened and God had come to comfort me. I knew I wasn't crazy and I knew this was God. There was no doubt. From that time onward God has spoken to me in a tender voice inside of my thinking. I have had many doubts about the authenticity of his voice but God has consistently dispelled my skepticism. I know it is God. The number of encounters is innumerable.

Honestly, I have doubted God all of my life so this was difficult for me to accept. When I first read the *Big Book of Alcoholics Anonymous*, I read the chapter on "How it Works." This includes what A.A. calls the ABC's: "(a) we were alcoholic and could not manage our own lives; (b) probably no human power could have relieved our alcoholism; and (c) God could and would if He were sought." When I read that for the first time, I knew the 12-steps wouldn't work for me, because I knew there was no God. My history of growing up made that crystal clear. If there was a God where was he when I was in pain? It would seem like a loving God would have done something to help me.

But because there was no other recovery option given in A.A., I began to seek a higher power of my own understanding. Additionally, I began to attend a church pastored by Judy Shaw. Her spiritual direction was filled with exuberance and talent and I was quickly drawn to her. I listened to her carefully and felt myself moving closer to believing. My disbelief still hovered over me, but I was desirous of connecting to a divinity or a spirit or something that felt right.

One Sunday morning, I went to church and the people I'd come to know were gone. They had moved and another body of believers was there instead. Judy was gone as well, and she was vital to my journey. My path took a big turn and as it turns out, it took me several years to find her again. In the meantime, I began to attend a Mennonite church pastored by one of Keystone's clergy, Pastor Dave Waldowski.

For four years struggled with the concept and idea of God. I sought God every way I knew how— in books, 12-step meetings, and churches. God eluded me at every turn of the page, every discussion in a meeting, and every "tried" encounter inside a church. He was just outside of my reach. Maybe the truth was he didn't exist at all.

On the day I found out my girlfriend, Peggy, was cheating on me with another man, God talked to me. Terribly hurt, frightened, and angry, I felt the old fear rise up inside of me after she told me. Here was the old fear again, my mother and my father's hell revisited. I escaped to my office which is quite small but comfortable and sat in my chair feeling helpless and hopeless Why? Why was this happening? Then I began in earnest to beat myself up. *Nothing was going to work for me— not even giving up alcohol.*

I tried to relax myself using an imagery exercise I had used many times before. I imagined a green hill covered with wildflowers. The petals brushed against my legs as I saw myself effortlessly climb up the hill. On the summit, I imagined a church. The church was old and white. Standing there on the beautiful spring day, I felt the warm sunshine on my face and arms. The sky was crystal cobalt blue. I walked up to this church and opened the door. Inside, it was cool and dark. No one else was there but me. Sunbeams were shining through stained glass windows. There was a soft thick red carpet and oak pews. My footsteps made no sound as I walked down the aisle and sat down. In my mind, I imagined God walking into the church. I was terribly afraid, vulnerable, depressed, and hurting. I told God the truth. "I am scared I'm going to spend the rest of my life alone."

Then the God's voice spoke again from inside of my mind, in that tender thought process, *"We want Peggy to come into the Spirit."*

I was shocked. Up until this point, I was taking myself through a meditation exercise. Now someone else had taken over, and it was God. No question. How did I recognize God's voice? I don't know, but I instantly did.

"What is the Spirit?" I asked.

*"Open the Bible," God said.*

I had a Bible on a bookshelf in my office. I was up quickly, quite curious.

Randomly, I opened it. The word spirit was written three times: "As soon as Jesus was baptized, He went up out of the water. At that moment heaven was opened, and He saw the *Spirit* of God descending like a dove and lighting on Him. And a voice from heaven said, 'This is my Son whom I love; with Him I am well pleased'" (Matthew 3:16-17).

In the next verse, I knew, instinctively, that I was to replace some words. "Then Jesus was led by the *Spirit* into the desert to be tempted by the devil" (Matthew 4:1). For my welfare, the passage was supposed to read differently. "Then Peggy was led into the wilderness to be tempted by the devil. The last verse was "Blessed are the poor in *spirit*, for theirs is the kingdom of heaven" (Matthew 5:3).

In the first moment of my contact with God, I had a joy I had never known. I knew that there was a God. The epiphany was overwhelming. The wonderful story I had heard in Ben's church was true. In those few seconds, I was convinced and I was overtaken with indescribable joy. All doubt was removed. Along with the voice, there came a tremendous feeling of acceptance, love, and peace. I was in the presence of God, and I knew I was beginning the greatest adventure of my life. Of course, God was speaking to me from my experience, which was Christian. If I was raised in another culture he would have to speak to me from that religion.

The next day I went to the church where I'd come to trust Pastor, Dave Waldowski. When Dave spoke to me in person or from the pulpit, he always rang of authenticity. I never wondered with Dave because he always meant what he said. He was a good man. When I saw Dave, I was so filled with joy that he immediately knew something big had happened to me.

I walked into his office and said, "Boy, have I got something to tell you," I said shaking his hand. Some fellow church-goers lingered about the foyer near the front entrance.

"What is it?" He stepped back and we had quick conversation.

"It's too complicated to tell you now," I said. "I'll tell you on Tuesday." Tuesdays for lunch was a regular gig for us. I knew we would have a special time then to discuss my experience.

He was genuinely excited for me. I could feel his warmth. "Sounds like something big happened!" he said.

"It is the greatest thing that could ever happen to anyone," I said grinning and beaming like I'd just seen the sun for the first time.

After church, I rushed back to my office to see if I could reconnect with

God. Using the same exercise, I visualized myself in the same church again.

"God, are you there?"

*"Yes, Ron," God said.*

"Are you really God?" I questioned him in our internal dialogue.

*"Yes, Ron."*

"How are you?" I didn't know what else to say. After all, what do you say to God?

*"Fine, Ron. Let's go for a walk."*

I was so excited. This was incredible. I was going for a walk with God. Wow, I put on my coat and walked outside. It was January, but it was a relatively warm day. I stepped slowly and talked to God. As I reached the city park next to Keystone, God said, *"Ron, you are such a good man. I have been waiting for you for so long."*

To hear something like this from God is astounding, because it is true. God does not lie. No one is manipulating you or trying to get something from you. It is nothing like that. The true message sinks in and stays with you.

In one instant and in ways I didn't understand, God had become my closest friend. I had never talked to God before, but it was as if we had been friends forever.

"Am I always going to hear your voice?" I asked.

*"I am never going to leave you, Ron. You belong to me. We are together through all time."*

"Is there a heaven?" I asked.

*"Yes."*

"What's it like?"

*"You are with me."*

"What is it like exactly?" I asked.

*"It is joy. There is no pain. There are multiple Universes with multiple dimensions; there is no death. There is a sweet smell and a mountain."*

"Is there a Devil?" I asked.

*"Yes."*

"Why?"

*"I wanted to give my people a choice."*

"Is there a hell?"

*"Yes."*

"What's it like?"

*"It is without me."*

"Does it hurt?" I asked.

*"There is no light, no love and no truth. The pain goes on forever. It breeds hate."*

"God, I don't want Peggy to go to hell. She doesn't know you. Help her to find you."

*"I sent her my son. I sent her the message."*

"Keep trying," I said.

*"I never stop trying. I will wait. I am patient."*

"Peggy is a good person God. She does not know that you exist. Why don't you be more persuasive?"

*"I only want those who want me. I don't want the others."*

"Was Jesus Christ the Son of God?"

*"I was Jesus."*

"So who are you, Jesus or God?"

*"I am God. I am Jesus. I am the Holy Spirit."*

"Jesus, God and the Spirit are all the same thing?"

*"Yes. Ron, do you see how the clouds catch the sun over there? Isn't it beautiful?"*

The afternoon sun caught the swirling clouds in a canvas of color. "Yes it is beautiful. Thank you."

*"It's for you."*

I began to understand God a little. God wants to love everyone. He is totally accepting—even when he knows all the bad we have inflicted on others and on ourselves.

God asked, *"Do you see the contour of the land over there?"*

"Yes, I like how that looks, thanks. God, why do bad things happen? Why are children killed in accidents, and why do young people die of cancer?"

I could feel God smile. *"Life is life. I am here forever. No child dies without being welcomed into my arms. They live with me, in joy, for all time. Death is not important. The choice is important. The choice means everything."*

"What choice?" I asked.

*"The choice to love me is the decision around which everything turns."*

"I have made the choice," I said.

*"I know, Ron. We will walk through time together."*

"God, what can I do about Peggy?"

*"Let Peggy go. She is not good for you. She is lost in the wilderness."*

"I do not want her to go to hell!"

*"That is her decision."*

"But she does not realize the importance of the choice."

*"Yes, she does."*

"God, you have to help her."

*"She must choose."*

"It's so sad," I said then felt my knees weaken.

*"Yes, it is sad."*

The idea that I'd made an absolute connection to God moved me. My eyes fell on the landscape differently. My eyes opened in new ways and it was the sweetest knowing I had ever known. There was more to come. I danced with pleasure and I danced in uncertainty, too.

Abruptly, Peggy moved out the next day. "I don't want God in my life," she insisted. Just like that, she was gone and my home was empty of a girlfriend and full of God. God was much better.

Peggy just didn't know there really was a God. For a new or old believer, this was and is one of the most difficult situations to comprehend about non-believers. We have found the answer and we want to give the answer to everyone, but some people are not ready. Most importantly, the level-playing ground of life does not make them better or worse off than you are. Their spiritual journey is just different. Maybe they need to spend more time lost in the wilderness before they move toward the truth. Most of us have to be crushed before we turn over our wills and our lives to God. Martin Luther once said, "He whom God decides to use, first he batters to pieces."

On the Monday after Peggy moved out, I had the opportunity to tell one of my friends, Carol Regier, about my conversations with God. Carol is one of the best people on earth. She genuinely poured out information and encouragement when I asked about the spiritual journey. At that time, she also knew I'm not the kind of a person you can push.

I told Carol my experience with God's voice. At the time, I was unaware that Carol checked what the voice said against scripture. Christians are advised to do this. As I shared more and more of my conversation at differing times, she became convinced that I was speaking to God. This particular time—the first time—was a special moment for both of us. Carol had wanted me to come to God, she had helped me, and now I had arrived. Carol was beaming at me and overjoyed that I was in contact with God.

As Carol left, Dave poked his head in my office. "Got a few minutes?"

"Sure come on in," I said. "I've got something incredible to tell you."

"I could tell by the look on your face Sunday.

"Dave, God talked to me."

Dave started laughing. He did not mock me. He was delighted. "That's great!" he exclaimed.

He sat down and I told him the entire story.

"Don't take this lightly." He leaned forward. "This doesn't happen often. I would also warn you that other voices can seem very much like God's voice. Don't be deceived. Sometimes Satan can come like an angel of light."

I crossed my arms. "You mean that Satan can imitate God's voice?"

"I think so."

"How do you tell the difference?" I asked.

"For one thing, God will never say anything that will disagree with scripture. God's message is the same today, yesterday, and tomorrow. You can always check out what the voice says against what is in the Bible. You can check it out with other believers, too. The Holy Spirit gives some people the gift of discernment. They can distinguish between good or evil spirits."

I listened intently to what he offered. Then I asked, "Dave, do you have any questions you'd like to ask God?"

"Ask God what I should do about this church. Should I stay here in Sioux Falls, or move?"

"If I get an answer, I'll get back to you." I smiled and he did, too.

Carol poked her head in the door and handed me two books, *The Holy Spirit* by Billy Graham and *Something More* by Catherine Marshall. "I think you will enjoy these," she said. "Let me know what you think."

After I said goodbye to Dave and Carol, I closed the door to my office, and relaxed, preparing myself. "God, are you there?"

*"Hi, Ron."*

"God, what do you think about Dave? Should he stay in Sioux Falls or move?"

God laughed. *"I love Dave. He thinks too much sometimes. It gets him into trouble. When he is ready to move, he will get itchy feet. If he doesn't move, it will get worse."*

"God, I miss Peggy," I gently implored.

*"Peggy was not good for you, Ron. If she were, she would be here. I know what is good for you. I know what you want."*

I could feel God smile again.

*"I have a woman for you. She is blonde. She is special. She will meet your every need."*

"When is this woman coming?"

*"Don't spoil the surprise."*

I laughed out loud. This was incredible. God was becoming more of a person all the time. Why shouldn't He enjoy a surprise? "Forgive me for being angry at Peggy. I love Peggy, and I want what is good for her. I want her to come to you. I want her to be saved," I said to Him.

*"Ron, I have a woman for you. She is wonderful. Trust me."*

"I'm angry at Peggy. I can't help it. She lied to me over and over again. I was honest with her." I felt anger rise in me like a surge.

*"Peggy is not good for you Ron. If she were, she would be here. I know what you want. It is coming."*

"When is it coming?" I asked.

*"Soon."*

As my conversations with God continued, I slowly began to realize, much to my surprise, that God had chosen me to speak his words to others. The message that God wants me to bring to you is God loves you and he is speaking to you all the time. God wants you to know that you can hear his voice. It is this simple and this magnificent. God is talking to you and you can hear his voice inside. It is all inside of you.

It has been my experience that even many religious people don't listen for God. To this point as well, if they believe they encounter God, and then he is often experienced as a powerful unapproachable force. But God is not unapproachable. Nothing could be further from the truth. God is the closest friend you will ever have. He is the perfect parent. He will speak to you about anything no matter how small. God is interested in everything you do. He is never too busy to communicate with you.

# CHAPTER 9

"God, are you a male or a female?" I tuned in.

*"I have male characteristics. I have female characteristics, but I am not male or female."*

"Some women are angry at the Bible. They think the Bible is sexist," I said.

*"All are my children, male and female. All are equal."*

"But, the Bible seems to have some sexist passages in it."

*"Man wrote the Bible."*

"So the Bible is not perfect?"

*"My perfect message is in the Bible. Man wrote the Bible. Man is not perfect, only love is perfect."*

"But the Word of God is in the Bible, right?"

*"Yes, my message is there."*

"If love is perfect, what is love?" I asked.

*"I am love."*

"Is love a feeling?"

*"No. I am love. When you come to me, you love. If you bring another to me, you love. I fill you. I live in you. Love lives in you. I belong to everyone. You have chosen and I have come, have I not?"*

"Yes, beyond my wildest dreams." I was thrilled.

*"I will come to all who ask. It is my promise. I wait for all of my children."*

"Is asking the only requirement? Suppose someone asks casually, or suppose someone asks in jest. Would you still come?"

*"I am seeking love, Ron. I come to no one in jest. I am like you. Would you be someone's friend, and give them your gifts, if they made you a joke?"*

"No," I stated.

*"They have to mean it. I am deciding who will walk through time with me. It is no joke."*

"God, why did you make people?"

*"I am love, so I wanted people to love. I made men and women like me so we*

80

*could walk through all time together. I have so much to show you. Love necessitates freedom of thought and choice. People have to be able to think and act independently. I knew that some people would not love me some would even hate me because they do not understand. I call all of my children and everyone hears the call. They may deny it, but no one can say I have not touched their heart. The purpose of life is to show my lost children the truth: there is a God, God loves them, and God's love will set them free. No one will feel whole without me. No one will be happy without me. I am love and love is calling everyone home. I have a place prepared for you.*"

"What about scientists who believe in spontaneous creation?"

*"They live in terror."*

"But they don't know you."

*"Everyone knows me. I live inside of them."*

"They believe you do not exist," I continued inside of my mind.

*"To live in a mistake is to live in terror."*

I relaxed, enjoying God's company and then I felt upset again. "I'm still angry at Peggy. I can't seem to help it. Help me to get rid of my anger."

*"Don't be angry with Peggy, Ron. Be angry at her sin. Peggy is weak. Evil is strong."*

"I should be angry at Satan?" I asked, puzzled.

*"Yes."*

I inquired, "If Satan causes you problems, why don't you get rid of Satan?"

*"He helps me divide the sheep from the goats."*

"You need Satan?"

*"No."*

"Then why not destroy Satan?" It seemed logical to ask.

*"It would break a promise."*

"I don't understand."

*"I promised the angels eternal life."*

"What about people? You promised us life and we're dying like flies!"

*"I promised death if you ate of the tree."*

"So to kill Satan would break a promise. Satan will live."

*"Yes, I am sad for Satan. His hate tortures him."*

"Would you forgive Satan?"

*"It is my promise. I am love, remember."*

"Don't you hate Satan?"

*"I hate sin."*

81

"But Satan is sin."

*"No, Satan is Satan. Sin is sin."*

"Jesus said that only those who come to him would be saved. Does that mean if you don't believe in the actual name of Jesus you don't go to heaven?" I asked.

*"I am God. Jesus is God. The Spirit is God. All who come to me will see paradise."*

"What about the people in the world who have never heard of Jesus?" I was trying to figure it out.

*"If they love, they know God. The name is not the issue. Love is the issue."*

"What is the best way to love?"

*"Love is an action. You commit yourself to your own or another person's growth. Ask yourself this: Is this act going to help someone grow and reach his or her full potential? If it is, it is love. Love gives growth. Love is difficult. Love necessitates action in truth. Love is the greatest challenge and the greatest gift."*

"Why do so many marriages break up?"

*"Lies destroy love. Relationships are nourished through truth. Most relationships fail because of lies."*

"It is hard to tell the truth. We are taught from the time that we are children that if we tell the truth we will hurt people. We are taught that truth is selfish and self-centered. If someone has on ugly clothing, we are not supposed to tell him or her they look bad. We are supposed to be nice, polite." I was interested to see how this response would turn out.

*"You can't solve problems without using the truth. Satan is the father of all lies. He does not want people to solve problems; he wants people to suffer. It is a trick he plays. Lies keep people from loving. To lie is to sin. Satan's trick is that it is sometimes good to lie. I tell you, it is never good to lie."*

I looked for more clarity. "Shouldn't people withhold information if it hurts someone's feelings?"

*"It is another trick. Satan whispers, 'If you tell the whole truth, no one will love you. You must keep this, or that, secret.'"*

I listened for more of this…

*"I tell you if you do not tell the whole truth no one can love you. Secrets make love impossible. Bring yourself into the light. I forgive all sin. There is no reason to hide."*

I enjoyed the wondrous presence of God. He is pure love—full of infinite wonder and infinite awe. God was the best friend I ever had. I felt incredibly alive and I was inspired to spread the word about him. It, frankly, was too amazing to hold in.

*"Ron, share your gift. Do not keep quiet."*

I asked, "You mean tell people I talk to God?"

*"Yes, I want everyone to know."*

"If I do that, people will think I'm crazy."

*"Some will, some won't, give them the message that I love them. I am talking to all of my children. They are choosing not to listen. Teach them to hear me. You are my light. I shine you on the world."*

"God, I stutter, I can't talk to people, I want to stay invisible, I don't want to be an evangelist. I wouldn't be good at it. Billy Graham is an evangelist. He is good at it." I felt awkward, slightly afraid.

*"I have great plans for you, Ron."*

"You don't want me to be an evangelist do you?"

*"No."*

"What do you want me to do?"

*"Don't keep quiet about the voice. People will come to you. They will find the truth."*

My fear rose up a bit. "People will think I'm crazy. I don't want people thinking I'm some kind of a religious nut."

*"Was Abraham crazy? Was Moses crazy? Was Paul crazy? Was Jesus crazy?"*

"God, listen, if I start telling people that I talk to you, they are going to think I'm crazy." I pressed the issue.

*"I talk to everyone, Ron. You carry that message. Teach them how to listen. If they listen, they will hear. If they hear, they will believe."*

"Why me?" I was a bit worried now.

*"You are chosen."*

"Yeah, but why?"

*"You are sensitive. You were trained from the beginning. Your walk through hell made you humble and humility is essential to faith."*

"Did you put me in the coal bin?"

*No but I allowed it to teach you how to listen. You have to learn that you need me and only me to be happy, joyous and free. It is from hell that you first glimpse heaven. Humility is essential to a connection to me. You suffered as a child but I was always teaching you, loving you and guiding you. You saw me through the eyes of Ben and Ben's mother. You saw me in your love for Baby. You have to be willing to know me and follow me blindly. Would you be willing to go back into the coal bin for me?"*

"Yes."

*"Good, then you are learning to be happy in all circumstances because you know it's my plan. Without the painful walk you took you wouldn't have learned to be humble and without humility communication with me is impossible."*

"Is anyone else chosen like me?"

*"Many."*

"Who are they?"

*"They will come to you. I want them to come."*

"I'm willing to do anything for you God. You guide and I'll follow. I will try to talk even thought I don't think I can do it." I was assured by my own words and God's gentle guidance.

The next morning, I sat in my office meditating on the incredible fact that Jesus died for me, so I could get right with God again. God is right and just and the penalty for my sins was death. To save my eternal life, however, Jesus took my place at the execution, the crucifixion. He died on the cross in my place. He gave up his life for me. This was a monumental miracle. Then, I was thinking about how horrible it must have been to be crucified when the voice came quickly into my mind. I tried to write down everything that God said.

*"I was so scared. I was terrified. Drops of sweat like blood fell into the sand. I prayed please take this cup of suffering from me. The Father was silent. He stood still. I knew the will of the Father. I gave myself to him. It is in the Book of Luke."*

I got my Bible down from the bookshelf and turned to the New Testament to find the passage. I had never read the book of Luke before, but it was in chapter 22 verses 42-44, just like God said: "'Father, if you are willing, take this cup from me; yet not my will, but yours be done. 'An angel from heaven appeared to Him and strengthened Him. And being in anguish, He prayed more earnestly, and His sweat was like drops of blood falling to the ground."

I had always imagined that Jesus was not afraid at the crucifixion. After all, he knew that he was God. He knew he was going to heaven. But now I knew the truth. Jesus was as human as I. He knew he was going to suffer. He was terrified of the torturous beatings, terrified of the nails penetrating his flesh and the unbearable crown of thorns. He was terrified of death. Yet all the time, Jesus knew he could escape God's plan and go his own way. God gives all of us that terrible choice. Jesus even begged God to spare him. Then God did something that remains beyond comprehension. He sacrificed his son for you and me. Jesus suffered the penalty for our sins by suffering and dying on a cross.

Someone—Jesus— had to pay the penalty, because the penalty for sin is death. God loved us so much that he sent his son to die in our place.

This sacrifice shows you how important you are to God. You are God's child, His perfect work of art. Once you are accepted into God's arms then there is nothing you will ever do that can separate you from God's love.

I closed the Bible and prayed, prayed for the past, prayed for the present, and prayed for my new future unfolding. If God wanted me to speak, I would have to learn how to speak.

# CHAPTER 10

*"Ron, go to a printer and get some business cards. Print 'God wants you to come' on them in raised gold. Use fine-quality white paper."*

"Want to tell me what they are for?" In my communications from God, I was beginning to get guidance on my life and my new mission. I was far from the shackles of my childhood and was evolving into a new kind of life.

*"We are going to do something."*

I was not sure what God was going to do, but it was my job to do what God asked. I was beginning to find that if God wanted me to know more, he would tell me.

On a balmy winter Tuesday, a week later, Dave came in the office. He was fidgety and he had a hard time settling down. "Would you mind sharing what happened to you in church sometime?" he asked nervously.

"I don't want to just stand up and tell people God talks to me. They'll think I'm crazy." I leaned back in my chair and clasped my hands around the back of my head.

He paused momentarily. "Then how about teaching a Sunday school class?"

"Sure, I could do that. They need a class on love?" I asked. *Where did I just get that idea?* I thought and inwardly smiled.

"The next Sunday school quarter is coming up in March," Dave said. "Let me think about it and I'll get back to you." He was still nervous.

By now, I had been using my meditation imagery exercises with my patients in an attempt to get them to help them make conscious contact with God. I used my own voice to direct them in the meditation and to see if they would connect. So far, the results were undeniably powerful and I was glad to be a guide for many on their journey to God and recovery.

Another week went by and Dave arrived more himself on the following Tuesday. He now wanted me to teach the Sunday school class.

"God has got plans for this class," I said. "I don't know what it is, but I think God is on the march."

Dave leaned toward me. "Since you and I have been meeting, I have been feeling closer to God. I haven't felt like this in eight years."

"Go for a walk with God, Dave," I suggested. "Talk to God as if he is actually there beside you. Look at the clouds and the trees. Feel the wind in your hair."

Prior to his leaving, I explained to Dave about the guided meditation exercises I had begun taking the patients through where they made conscious contact with God. Then I took Dave through the same meditation. Dave envisioned an image of God that was very clear to him. "Seeing Jesus next to me was very powerful," he said. There, however, was no verbal communication,

I was excited, elated. God had shown me a way to connect people to his voice via the meditation exercise. His voice and presence had affected me deeply and profoundly in my own life. Now, I was seeing it affect lives of others. Dave, a preacher, a dedicated Christian for many years, was powerfully stirred by this experience as my patients were. Apparently, this kind of meditation was not just for drunks and addicts but for everyone. Never had I heard of using this kind of exercise in church.

When I saw Dave the next week, he was concerned, afraid even, that I might have trouble with some of the conservative people in his church. I handed Dave the messages the patients had anonymously written down and given to me. It was empirical evidence—testimonials. It was their communications from God. "That's all I'm going to do," I said. "If God talks to a bunch of drug addicts, he should talk to a bunch of Christians."

Dave was still unsure. He looked at the notes then said, "In many ways alcoholics are more ready for that kind of communication. That's why Christ spoke to the poor people, prostitutes, and tax collectors, the common people of his day. They had nothing to lose and were willing to listen. The religious people were not ready for Christ. Christian people are often resistant to this kind of thing. Many have heard that meditation is a part of the New Age movement. You have to go slow with these people. They will not be as open as your patients."

I moved closer to Dave. "I'm not going to do anything with them," I said. "God is going to do it. I can't convince the people in your church to trust me. God is going to ask them to trust Him."

"All right," said Dave. "But I'm a little frightened for you."

I got another quick communication from God for Dave, and I spoke it directly to him. "Dave, let God do this. This is God's plan, not mine."

"What is the plan?" he inquired.

"I'm going to teach a course on love," I said. "God is going to teach it. He is going to use my voice. I have no idea how this is going to happen, how I'm going to do it, or what God is going to say. I just know that this is what God wants."

Dave crossed his arms and looked down for a moment. Then he looked at me and said, "I'm going to say one more thing and then I'm going to stop raining on your parade. These people are used to learning from scripture. If you can use scripture you will have it easier," Dave squirmed in his chair. "See, now you see what I'm really like." Dave looked at me helplessly. "My real personality is to doubt."

Doubt was okay. Everyone doubts. I was beginning to doubt the blonde woman would show up. I felt ready. Still, I wasn't sure.

# CHAPTER 11

While I waited for the mysterious blonde woman to come into my life, God began to speak to me in my office about the upcoming Sunday school class.

*"Ron you are going to start a movement. You will write books and develop a webpage www.godtalkstoyou.com to show people how to connect with my voice. You will tell people that I am speaking to them and put them in direct contact with me. We will teach them about love. The church you are speaking to is a loving church. They will help you to carry the message. They are chosen. They have not chosen me. I have chosen them. The cards you had printed are for you to seek out the other chosen ones. You must use the Spirit to show you who should receive a card. Do not use your own judgment. Let the Spirit point them out to you. On the back of the card write the address and time of the class. Bring my people together. I have something to say."*

A little beside myself, I then asked, "God, you're not going to let me down are you? I can't talk very good so you are going to have to teach this class, not me. All I have to do is show up and you will take it from there, right?"

*"Don't worry about the class, Ron. The people are ready."*

I exhaled. "Dave is not sure about that. He's scared I'm going to make a fool out of myself."

*"Doubt is like a wave on a troubled sea. It tosses a man and gives him no peace. It divides the mind. There is no rest for men who doubt."*

"God, I'm going to turn this whole thing over to you," I said.

*"That is the way, Ron. You are the light. Illuminate the way. Most of my children are struggling in the dark."*

Later that day, Dave called me at home. "Ron, the class is arranged. You will start on March the Fourth at ten a.m. I am still scared, but I feel this is the right thing to do. Remember, the more you can use scripture and the name of Jesus Christ, the easier it will be for you."

"That's good information, Dave. Thanks," I said. I was glad to have the information—he was helping me and that felt wonderful.

After a momentary pause, Dave said, "You know, I was thinking, there is a woman here at the church, Angela, a good Christian woman. She's our choir director. She is sensitive and you are, too. Why don't you ask God about her? I'm no matchmaker, but I was just thinking that you are two good people, you know. She did have this boyfriend, but he was not good for her. She's attractive, striking actually. She has long black hair. Why don't you ask God about her?"

"Have her come to the class," I said. God had said blonde hair not black—I was confused. "We'll let God take it from there," I said, finally.

Dave's spirit sounded lifted. "That sounds good to me."

This new information was a bit mysterious to me, so I hustled to my office eager to make contact with God. I knew that this Angela wasn't the person God had in mind for me. Angela's hair was black. I asked God about her anyway. "God, what about Angela?"

*"That's a good idea, Ron. Explore a friendship with Angela."*

There seemed to be a smile in God's voice. I couldn't see it, but I could feel it. "Is that all you're going to tell me?"

*"It is all you need to know."*

One thing I've learned is that you can't press into the answers too much. So, I went about my daily activities of running the facility and guiding patients through the meditations. One day at a time is the key to a lot of answers and a lot of healing. I was patient.

A week later I got more.

*"You will have a relationship with Angela."*

"Romantic?" I asked. I could feel the butterflies in my stomach.

*"Yes."*

"God, I don't know this person yet." This was getting scary.

*"I know her. She is wonderful."*

I was thrilled. So, I intently began searching for this black-haired Angela in church. As far as I could see, there was no one near my age with black hair who happened to be near the choir or in the congregation. I was miffed.

In my office a week later, I got more from God, this time, more than I wanted.

*"Angela will be your wife."*

"Slow down, God!" I screeched. "I have never even seen this person!"

*"She is everything you have dreamed of. She is beautiful, honest, loving. She is a good woman. She is mine. You will experience a joy with her you have never experienced with another. She is wonderful. You will marry her."*

"God, I have never met her!" I bellowed.

*"I know her. Don't worry about it."*

"Well, look," I said, feeling a catch in my throat. "I don't want to get involved with someone I don't know! I don't want to think someone is going to be my wife before I meet her!"

*"I thought you were in a hurry."*

"I am, but I want to choose," I begged.

*"You will choose."*

"Can I say no?" I begged in the form of a question.

*"Yes, but 'no' is a mistake."*

Shortly thereafter, my friend Carol was in the halls of Keystone. Frantically, I waved my hand at her and she stepped into my office. "Carol, help me, God just told me I'm going to marry someone I have never met."

"Oh, who is that?" She seemed disgustingly composed.

I told her what happened in my conversation with God. The whole story spilled out.

Carol had listened with both ears on. Then, she said, "Well, you know, Ron, when I was at the dentist's office the other day, I had heard that you might be interested in Judy. But Jesus told me it wasn't Judy. I was concerned with it being Judy because of the age difference between you two. So, that is confirmation for you."

"But I have never met this woman!" I threw my hands up in the air and then dug them deep in my pockets.

She wrinkled a smile. "You don't have to marry her right away."

"Well, I know that," I said. "But still, this is really strange."

Carol put her hands on her hips and then she said, "We can always say 'no' to God if we want to, but when I have done that, it's always been a disaster."

Later that day, I geared up and went for my usual jog through the streets and side streets of Canton. Further confirmation from God was upon me as I'd gotten into the habit of stopping by the Catholic Church for meditation. No one is ever there, so I had the sanctuary to myself. A large lifelike crucifix hung over the altar. Sweating, I went inside, sat down and asked, "God, what about this Angela?"

*"As surely as I shed my blood for you, you will marry Angela. She is wonderful."*

I was not sure if I was scared or excited. Sometimes it's difficult to tell the difference. I was scared that the prophecy was incorrect. I thought if it wasn't right, then the whole thing about God was a mistake. Maybe I had deluded myself into believing I was talking to God. As I pondered over it, that conclusion did not make much sense. God had pointed out passages in the Bible that I did not know were there. How could that have happened without it being God? On the other hand, if it was God, God had chosen a woman for me. This had to be the right woman, because God was doing the choosing. I swirled in a sea of momentary doubt. It was too much to comprehend.

Back at the office after my run, I ran into a patient who was back for chemical dependency treatment the second time. He was a large man with a broad face and a wide, warm smile. But none of that was evident now. Back in on a relapse, this patient bore the scars of being beaten by life. He looked defeated; his eyes downcast with humiliation, guilt, and shame.

In the hallway, he leaned against the concrete and spoke in a quiet deep voice. "What I can't understand is why I drank. I was going to two AA meetings a week. I was working closely with my sponsor. I just stopped at a store, and while I was waiting for the clerk, I picked up two six packs of beer. Later, I was arrested for drunk driving. Then I grabbed my wife by the throat and threw her on the bed. I told her if she didn't leave me alone, I would kill her. I think I have ruined my marriage. Why did I do something crazy like that?"

"Because the illness is stronger than you are," I said.

"What?" He said with a puzzled look.

"You say you don't understand why you did it. I don't think you wanted to drink and hurt your wife. Question is if you didn't want to, who did?" I asked.

He looked at me, confused. "I did."

"That's not what you just told me. You just said you didn't want to drink. You didn't want to hurt your wife. My question is, if you didn't want to do it, who did want to do it?"

"You mean my illness?" He looked at the floor.

"Exactly, it is important that you learn how the illness works. You didn't want to drink, but another part of you, your illness, wanted you to drink. You didn't want to hurt your wife, but your illness did want to hurt your wife."

"That's exactly how it feels," he said, starting to brighten. "It feels like something else took me over."

"Come to my office. I want to show you something," I said. Side by side, we traversed the corridor. When we got to the office I got out *The Living Bible* and looked up Romans chapter 7 verses 15 through 25.

I handed him the Bible. "Read this out loud," I said. "Let's see if you can relate to what Paul says. He was struggling with sin just like you are."

He had a deep beautiful voice that made the passage come alive. "I don't understand myself at all, for I really want to do what is right, but I can't. I do what I don't want to. I do what I hate doing. I know perfectly well that what I am doing is wrong, and my bad conscience proves that I agree with these laws I am breaking. But I can't help myself, because I'm no longer doing it. It is sin inside me that is stronger than I am that makes me do these evil things. I know I am rotten through and through so far as my old sinful nature is concerned. No matter which way I turn I can't make myself do right. I want to but I can't. When I want to do good, I don't, and when I try not to do wrong, I do it anyway. Now if I am doing what I don't want to, it is plain where the trouble is: sin still has me in its evil grasp. It seems to be a fact of life that when I want to do what is right, I inevitably do what is wrong. I love to do God's will so far as my new nature is concerned. But there is something else deep within me, in my lower nature that is at war with my mind and wins the fight and makes me a slave to the sin that is still within me. In my mind I want to be God's willing servant but instead I find myself still enslaved to sin. So you see how it is: my new life tells me to do right, but the old nature that is still inside me loves to sin. Oh, what a terrible person I am in who will free me from my slavery to this deadly lower nature. Thank God! It has been done by Jesus Christ our Lord. He has set me free."

After reading the passage, the man was quiet. Then he slowly asked, "You mean it wasn't me who did those things?"

"It was you, and you are responsible for your behavior but the Bible says it was sin, or evil, or whatever you want to call the addiction that lives inside of you. The disease tempted you. The choice about what you did is yours, and you are held accountable for your behavior. You want to live and be happy, but the illness or evil wants to destroy you. The illness seduced you into drinking and then to hurt your wife. The illness tempted you, but you ultimately made the decision. See how slick it is. Evil gets you both ways. It seduced you into drinking and then shamed you for what you did. It tells you that you are drinking to do yourself a favor, but look at what happens when you drink; you hurt yourself and others. You drive drunk. You risk your life. You threaten your wife. Alcoholics Anonymous says that probably no human power can remove this illness, but God can and will if He is sought."

Satisfied with our conversation, the male patient left my office. In my heart, I began to feel that the people God put in front of me were ones who I was to help guide and in that guidance the spirit of God was revealed to me over and over and over again.

Years had passed and my roots in the small town in Virginia were gone. My father had died and my mother had finally gotten sober and lived in Richmond. Despite my three-year struggle with alcoholism, my children had developed into people of character and importance. My oldest son, Robert, was a history professor at the University of Hawaii, Nyshie, my middle child, was a producer for MSNBC, and my youngest child Shane worked for USAID at the state department. My brother was in recovery from alcoholism for ten years and had made peace with himself, his children and God. My family was now intact and we enjoyed vacations together.

My next move in South Dakota was to prepare my heart for God's word and the Sunday school on March the 4th. Pleased to be in God's hands, I prepared no notes—nothing. I just kept smiling inwardly and trusting the path set before me.

# CHAPTER 12

We called the class, "God's Love for us and Our Love for Each Other." Dave looked relaxed, but I knew he was nervous underneath. I wasn't nervous because God had promised me that things were going to go well. I had no reason to mistrust God's judgment. God had promised to take over the class. God was going to use my voice to speak his message. I was very excited, but I had no idea what God was going to say of if I could say anything at all. No idea at all.

The classroom had folding chairs and some old tables sidled up next to the windows. The Radiators cracked and whistled. Pastoral pictures of landscapes hung on the walls and there were many pictures of Jesus depicting miracles he'd performed. A few stragglers walked in and bowed in a reverent "I'm sorry" and sat in the back. Twenty people filled the room of all walks of life: farmers, businessmen, home makers, attorneys, plumbers, construction workers, policemen, and people from my treatment center.

At the small lectern, Dave introduced me. "Dr. Ron is a psychologist and the clinical director of Keystone Treatment Center. Dr. Ron and I talked about his giving a class for the church and he has agreed to give us a series on love. I find that Christians come in many forms. Some are into moral issues, some are absorbed into the Scriptures, and some are into prayer. I find that Dr. Ron is into prayer. He is the one who is always trying to get me to take a walk with Jesus. I would like to say that I believe in what Ron is doing. My association with him has been very beneficial to my spiritual growth. Enough from me, I'll turn over the class to Ron."

I stood and God began to speak through me as I addressed the class. I found that I did not stutter.

"This class is going to be a lot of fun. I promise that if you extend yourself you will learn to be happier. I also promise that you will suffer. Love necessitates a certain amount of risk. You have to walk into the raging waters and the fire. Jesus said, 'Unless you change and become like little children, you will never

95

enter the kingdom of heaven.' So reach down and get a hold of that little kid inside you. That child needs nourishment and he or she needs to feel joy."

A few of the class members crossed their arms—many looked ready to hear what came next. There was a palpable intensity as I spoke. Most of them had anticipation on their face as if they were ready for communication from God.

I went on. "This morning I want you to touch your spirit, I want you to touch the spirit of someone else, and I want you to touch the spirit of God. Most of you are used to hearing the voice of God, but some of you are not. I promise you that God is going to communicate with you this morning.

"King Solomon was the King of Israel. He had all of the gold and money anyone could want. He had all the best food and drink of his day. He had lands that stretched as far as the eye could see. He had a harem of four hundred women. This is what he said: 'I denied myself nothing my eyes desired; I refused my heart no pleasure! Yet when I surveyed all that my hand had done and what I had toiled to achieve, everything was meaningless, a chasing after the wind' (Ecclesiastes 2:10-11).

"King Solomon," I continued, "was feeling the emptiness of being without God. Alcoholics Anonymous calls this the hole in our soul. All of us have a hunger for God. God made us for a relationship with him. That is why we were created. Only God can fill us to completion. Money can't do it. Education can't do it. Power can't do it. Marriage to someone wonderful can't do it. Our children can't do it. Only God can do it. We have a need deep inside that only God can satisfy."

As I surveyed the eyes of the listeners, I perceived stillness like a pure holiness had come in and hovered over the room. The presence of God in me and God in the room carried my voice forward. The audience was attentive to what I was saying. A man in the second row put his hands on his knees and leaned in.

"It is important for you to touch someone else's spirit today. You need that experience to learn about relationships. I need a volunteer. I promise I will not shame you." There was a slight pause. Then local regular churchgoer named, Kim, was gracious enough to help me.

Dressed in a simple white shirt and brown pleated skirt, Kim stood in the front of the room. The radiator whistled and eked out a pop.

I stood a distance away from her and then I said, "Kim, all I'm going to do is walk up to you. Keep your hands at your side and look me right in the eyes." I turned to the group.

"Now, watch Kim's face as I approach her. Your feelings will change as her feelings change. You will not be able to see the subtle changes in the color of her skin or how she is holding herself, but unconsciously you will experience it as a change in your feelings. Watch her very closely."

I stepped back about twenty-five feet in the front of the room. Then riveted on her in the eyes, I walked up to her. I stopped at arm's reach. I had reached the limit of her personal space. I turned to the class. "What was the feeling that increased in you as I got closer to Kim?"

"Nervous," several people said.

"Yeah, I got nervous," Kim said.

"Let's call it fear. As I walked up to her, Kim didn't know what I was going to do. She was afraid of what I might do. I might hurt her. Now, I'm going to walk up to her again, and put my hands on her shoulders. Let's see what happens to her fear." I walked back the twenty-five feet and stepped up to her again. This time I stopped at arm's reach, paused, and put my hands on her shoulders. "What happened?" I asked her.

"I relaxed," she said.

"The fear went down. This is an important thing to know. Getting closer to someone is scary, but if we get close enough, the fear goes down. This is true of our relationship with everyone, and it is true of our relationship with God. You now know a very important thing about relationships. Getting close to someone is hard, the trip is scary. But, if you get close enough, the fear goes down. If you do not extend yourself, you will never get that experience. If you do not take a risk, you will not have the opportunity to be close to anyone."

As we moved forward in the discussion, Dave visibly relaxed. I used scripture as he had advised. This was a true path for these people—God's words through me and God's words through scripture. A gentleman in the back stood.

"All of us have a hunger for God, and 'God is love' as it is told to us in John one, chapter four, and verse sixteen. I want to define love carefully for you. Love is the active involvement in your own or another person's individual growth. Love is an action, not a feeling."

I nodded to Kim and she returned to her seat. An elderly woman whose hair was in a bun took out a pen from her purse and took down some notes.

I continued in front of the lectern. "St. Paul says in John one, chapter three, verse eighteen. 'Let us not love with words or tongue but with actions and in truth.' God gave us his son so we could receive eternal life. That couldn't have been easy for God. That would be the most difficult thing for any parent to do. God loves us in action.

"If you understand that love is the interest in, and the active involvement in, someone's growth, you can understand why Jesus said, 'I tell you: Love your enemies...' (Matthew 5:44). You don't have to like your enemies, they may be hurting you, but you can pray that they come to see the truth about what they are doing. Now, I have a question for the class: Does God want everyone to communicate with him, or does God want just the good people to communicate with him?"

"Everyone," several voices said.

Then from the back, the standing man said, "How about Hitler, did God want Hitler to come into the Spirit?"

"Yes," several people said. The rest were nodding affirmatively.

The old lady in the tight bun piped in. "How about Satan? Does God want Satan to come into the Spirit? Does God love Satan so much that he'd say, 'hey there, Satan, you've caused a lot of problems, but I welcome you back into my arms.'" People were still nodding their heads.

I paused for a moment. "I agree with you. I think God would be delighted if Satan came back into a healthy relationship with him."

"Why doesn't Satan just come back?" a younger woman with dark hair asked from the back of the room.

"Satan still thinks that he can do things better his own way," the words issued from the voice of God in me.

I got set for the first meditation by explaining the imagery exercise to the class.

I took a deep breath, and then I slowly began to set the tone for our first journey together. "Now, the time has come for God to come to you inside of your own mind. God is going to communicate with you in one of several ways. Some people see an image of something: a light, color, or texture. Most people hear God within their own thoughts. Believe me, you will recognize God. God will not trick you."

Again, I employed some of Dave's advice. "Some of you have heard that meditation is not Christian. It might be a dangerous part of the New Age movement. But if you read the Bible, meditation is encouraged. The first time it is mentioned is in Genesis. It is particularly spoken of in Psalms. Meditation is a God-given skill. Many of you are not used to hearing the voice of God, so I want you to prepare yourself."

"Get in a comfortable position. If you feel like moving during this exercise please feel free to move. Take care of yourself. Put your hands in a comfortable place, and close your eyes. God is coming to talk to you."

Some people shifted in their seats. There were some audible exhales as each person adjusted to how they wanted to sit in their seats, how they wanted to place their arms, and how they wanted to stretch their legs.

My words floated on the air. "As you are still and quiet, I'm going to play some music. Concentrate on your breathing. Feel the cool air coming in and the warm air going out. Focus on your breathing, and as you do, you feel yourself beginning to relax. You feel more at peace. If you do not feel comfortable doing this exercise, please do not do it. You can trust yourself."

"See in your mind, as completely as you can ocean waves. As you inhale, the waves build, and as you exhale the waves wash against the shore of an island. There is no right way or wrong way to do this exercise—there is just your way. God knows exactly what you need to experience. You see a white sandy beach and palm trees. You feel the warm sunshine on your cheeks and on your arms. There is no reason to be afraid. There is a trail on the island and you take that trail. You walk through the palm trees. The leaves twist and turn in a light breeze. You can feel the wind slightly in your hair. You are not in a hurry. You have all the time in the world. Walking up the trail, you pass a large rock that is cool to your touch. You go past the rock and you come to a clearing and reach a hill. As you climb this hill you begin to feel tired. Your arms and legs begin to feel heavy. You reach the top of the hill, and you overlook a lush green valley with waterfalls. It is gorgeous. This is the valley of the Holy Spirit and you must ask before you can come into this valley. So if you want to come into the valley of the Holy Spirit ask three times in your mind if you can come in."

I waited for about ten seconds.

"The Holy Spirit says, 'Yes, all who ask can come into this valley, all who seek will find, all who knock will have the door opened to them.' You tip over the ridge and walk down into the valley. As you descend, you walk alongside a clear stream that tumbles over rocks. There are waterfalls along the stream. The Holy Spirit descends upon you. You feel the Holy Spirit. The air seems fresher and cleaner. You feel a powerful draw to God. You are led to a hill. The Spirit of God coaxes you along. The hill is covered with wild flowers of every imaginable color and hue. Some of you will see this very well. Some of you will see it not so well. Do not worry about how you see it. There is no right way or wrong way to do this there is just your way.

"Walk up the hill and feel the wild flowers brush against your legs. You are drawn to the top of the hill. You do not know why. You climb, and as you come higher, a steeple comes into view, and then a white church. You feel drawn to that church. You come up to the church, open the front door, and go inside. There is a soft thick red carpet and rows of oak pews. You walk down the aisle and sit in the third pew. You call out for God three times. You hear the door of the church open. You turn and over your right shoulder you see a person walk down the aisle to you. His robe is very white. As he reaches you, you instinctively stand up and come into his arms. You somehow join in, and blend in, with him. You turn, and through the eyes of God, you see yourself, because you are still sitting in the pew. You see your whole life flash before your eyes. You see all the good things you have ever done, and you see all the sin. Now, you understand how much God loves you and how completely God forgives you. God shines his pure light of love into every dark corner and recess of your mind, body, and spirit. God purifies you of all sin until you are his perfect child again. You come out of God and take his right hand and walk outside and sit on the hill, a gigantic field of wild flowers. You sit down and cross your legs, and God sits across from you, and crosses his legs. He takes your hands in his hands and looks you right in the eyes. You ask God a question. God, what is the most loving thing I can do for you? I am going to give you five minutes to receive the communication, and then I will ask you to write it down on your paper."

During those five minutes, I was filled with the Holy Spirit and I sent images of love and affection to the class who was seated before me. I glanced at Dave and he was meditating. I closed my eyes and let the stillness of God sweep over me and the class like a silent song. The rhythm of his love infused the air. Glorious.

After the meditation, I had the class write down their communications with God and then they passed their messages to the front.

There were a few questions; however, God wanted me to ask. "Now turn to the voice again, because one or more of you will be given the number one from God. One or more of you are the number two, and one or more of you are the number three. Close your eyes and turn to the voice. Are you given the number one, a number two, a number three, or no number? Most of you will have no number. Who is a number one?"

This was the way to test the spirits and collect many individual messages into one message for the group as a whole. I did not know if anyone would be given a number, but God came through.

An elderly person raised his hand. "I'm a one," he said.

I told him to stand. Dave said he was a one. Several people were two's and three's.

I had them all stand.

"These people have been given or will be given the spiritual gift of discernment. They will gather what God has told each of us individually into a message for the group as a whole."

The class ended and I felt fortunate to be there. Dave shook my hand and then Nancy, Dave's wife, asked me to have lunch with them after service. Social gatherings weren't typically my cup of tea but I said, "Yes." Later that day, my youngest son, Shane, who was visiting from out of town, and I followed Dave, Nancy, and their two daughters to their home.

Driving up to the house, I recognized two people from the class who were standing outside near the front door. I had noticed both of them in church that morning. They were both attractive, one had brown hair, and one was blonde. No Angela in this pairing—no black hair. I wasn't crestfallen, just paying attention. I did recognize the blonde woman who played piano in the church. I loved her music. Shane and I got out of the car and greeted them.

"I'm Sandy," the brown-headed woman said.

"And what is your name?" I said to the blonde.

"I'm Angela," she said.

I could have dropped in my tracks. My knees buckled. This was Angela! Her hair was not black like Dave had said—it was blonde like God said. Glory to God. I could not believe my eyes. This had to be the person. This was the woman God said I was going to marry! I took a very long look at her. Angela was about 5' 7" with golden hair that fell well past her shoulders. She had high cheekbones, greenish brown eyes, and a smile that made my heart sing. By looking at her, I could tell that she was a gentle and had a tender spirit. I felt God radiating out of every cell in her body. Standing next to her was like standing next to God himself. She had a trustworthy deeply honest quality about her. Angela's facial features were fine and delicate. She was very attractive, and when she spoke, she was intelligent and not afraid. Her voice was like something distant and deeply hidden peace from my past. I recognized she had the same voice quality as Ben's mother, clear, compassionate and with a mother's love.

After lunch, I asked her for her phone number. I did not know if this was a set up or not, but I trusted Dave.

Later that day, I called Angela and asked her over for dinner. I was going to explore a relationship if she was interested.

Angela said, "Okay," and we made a date.

When I picked her up at her apartment I brought her a single red rose. She smelled the rose tickling her nose and placed it in a vase and put it on her kitchen table. When I took her to a restaurant for lunch, I found out that Angela had been a Christian all her life. She was committed to God. It sounded as if she had wonderful parents and had thoroughly enjoyed her childhood. My childhood had been a total catastrophe.

I felt relaxed with Angela and she was relaxed with me. So, I told her about the experiences and communications with God and me. Dave warned me not to do this, but I did it anyway. I believed Angela could handle it, and besides I did not think it was fair of me not to tell her. God tells us to love in action and in truth. If I withheld the facts from her, it wouldn't be honest. I told Angela the simple facts. God had said she was going to be my wife, and we would be very happy together. Then I was quiet. It was up to her.

She would either stay or run. I was sure she was going to run.

"Let me tell you what has been happening on the other side of things," she said. "When I first saw you in church," she paused, "You gave me a peaceful feeling. I'm usually rushed, and really into things, so that was different for me. I asked someone who you were and they said you worked with Dave. I enjoyed looking at you." She laughed, mainly at herself.

"What are we going to do?" I asked.

"I don't know," she said. "God doesn't talk to me the way he talks to you."

I was surprised that she was not totally shocked. It's not every day that some stranger tells you that you are going to be married to him. I would have been flattered, but I would not have taken it seriously. "Why don't you think about it and most of all pray about it? Then, give me a call."

With that, she was gone. I pondered the entire day—the Sunday school class, church, and Angela. Most of all, I pondered God.

Later, I took a picture of Angela that same day beside the rushing waters of Sioux Falls. When I had time to study the picture I could see she was in love with me. This seemed impossible but it was truer than the sky or the water. She was totally focused on me as if we were one person and not two anymore.

"Angela you are stunning," I said, but I felt more than this. I felt that I had met the one person who could heal me of my past. She clearly loved me, even if our relationship had been brief. There was no doubting that photograph or that feeling I had inside of me, that we were one person not two, joined somehow by God's magic. Only God could have done that and that's what he had done. What was it about her that was so compelling? It was as if she was dropped off by a passing cloud or even a sun beam. What was it about her that that made me so incredibly happy as if all of my dreams had come true?

# CHAPTER 13

The next Sunday in the small Mennonite church at the edge of town, Dave spoke about God's voice. I was thrilled. He appeared anxious so I prayed for him.

"For Sermon time," he began in the pulpit, "I want to direct your attention to the sixth chapter of Genesis verses nine through twenty-two. I'll be reading from the New International Version of the Bible. This is the account of Noah. Noah was a righteous person, blameless among the people of his time, and he walked with God. Noah had three sons: Shem, Ham, and Japheth.

"Now the earth was corrupt in God's sight and was full of violence. God saw how corrupt the earth had become, for all the people of earth had corrupted their ways. So God said to Noah, 'I am going to put an end to all people, for the earth is filled with violence because of them. I am surely going to destroy both them and the earth. So make yourself an ark of cypress wood; make rooms in it and coat it with pitch inside and out.

"'This is how to build it: The ark is to be four hundred and fifty feet long, seventy-five feet wide and forty-five feet high. Make a roof for it and finish the ark to within eighteen inches of the top. Put a door in the side of the ark and make lower, middle and upper decks. I am going to bring floodwaters on the earth to destroy all life under the heavens, every creature that has the breath of life in it.

I opened my Bible to the passage he was preaching from and followed along. For a fleeting moment, I thought of a childhood trip on a vessel with my father that had been saved from certain peril by a larger boat.

"Everything on earth will perish. But I will establish my covenant with you, and your sons and your wife and your sons' wives with you. You are to bring into the ark two of all living creatures, male and female, to keep them alive with you. Two of every kind of bird, of every kind of animal and of every kind of creature that moves along the ground will come to you to be kept alive. You are to take every kind of food that is to be eaten and store it away as food for you and for them.' Noah did everything just as God commanded him."

As Dave spoke, his anxiety lessened, and I allowed the words to come into me as if they were tactile. The congregants were listening to him with their full attention. As the light from the window illuminated the altar, it then refracted and gave way to a colorful prism on the tapestry behind him.

"Now, this is really an incredible story. And here's what happened in our story today. God spoke to Noah. God, somehow, through thoughts or through a voice, spoke to Noah, and Noah was able to hear the voice. Of course, the passage says that Noah walked with God. Noah was in the habit of walking with the Lord, and listening to the Lord, and talking to the Lord, and communicating with God. God spoke to Noah, and Noah heard it, perceived it, and then he did something. He built an ark because God told him to do it.

By now, his connection to my teaching the class was clear and I appreciated the support. It was good to hear and I was intent on hearing the rest.

"Now, obviously, that would be a crazy thing to do. Build a huge ark in the middle of the land, and I can well imagine there were many people who began to mock Noah. All the people around might have said 'what in the world are you doing Noah? What are you building a boat for?'Then Noah would respond, 'Well, I hate to tell you this, but God told me to build a boat.' And then the mocking would begin. 'Did you hear what he's doing? He thinks God told him to build an ark. He is a religious nut who thinks he's hearing God's voice.'"

"There were probably times when Noah wondered, *did I lose my mind?* But then when the waters began to build up and the people started running up the mountainside and the water was getting deeper and deeper, they stopped mocking Noah. Now they were calling out, 'Noah help us. Noah save us.'"

"Now this story is in some ways repeated in our day today. Sometimes, we as Christians, when we try to take a stand for the Lord, and try to be faithful, many times we will be mocked. Can God really be real? Can God really communicate with us? But it's a dangerous business to mock God and God's people."

"Now, I was thinking that if I had been Noah, here is probably what would have happened. If I had been Noah, and I heard this voice or some kind of a communication, and I felt very strongly that God was saying, 'Dave, build an ark,' I would have thought, Lord I really believe you told me that. I'm going to get out there and build that ark. Then after three or four days, and I started to think about it, I would have started thinking, now wait a minute here. I'm not so sure about this. Boy, this is a strange idea. People are going to think I'm strange, and one thing I don't want to be, I don't want to be a religious nut. I fear that about as much as anything. I don't want to be a religious fanatic like Noah. So I would start to think about this, and then I would say, well, gee, how could I really be sure that God told me to do this? It's probably something that I just dreamed up, or maybe I had a bad pizza or something like that."

Audible laughter erupted from the congregation. Bad pizza—Dave was funny.

"Then I would say no, 'no, I'm not going to do this.' That's what would have happened if I was Noah. And I may have drowned in the waters because of my fear and my unbelief. Now, the question that comes to me from all of this is this: Does God speak to us today in the same way that he spoke to Noah? Or at least does God speak to us in a similar way? That's the question that's been ringing in my head for a while. It came to a focus this week. We know that God spoke to many people in the Bible. We could list hundreds of people that God spoke to."

Dave looked up and out from the pulpit and began to reel off examples. "I'm thinking now of Abraham. God spoke to Abraham and said, Abraham I want you to leave your home and leave your country and go, I'm not telling you where you're going Abraham, all I'm telling you is to leave your home and then I'll show you where I want you to go. He obeyed God and changed the course of history.

"I'm thinking of the little boy Samuel in the temple. And Samuel learned how to listen to God and how to communicate with God and he became one of the most powerful prophets and leaders that the nation of Israel ever knew.

Then, Dave brought the message to us and how we need to become better listeners. I thought of my own training as a youngster and the stutter and the coal bin that had gifted me with the ability to be a good listener. *Stutterers and people trapped in a box made great listeners*, I remembered thinking. Listening was a skill I learned from my earliest memories—I think God began training me to listen in the coal bin, listening for screen doors and footsteps, listening for the voice of my father or mother, listening for the motors of cars, listening for sounds of nature and the animals of the night, and listening for the footsteps that might bring death or freedom from bondage.

Dave continued his sermon, "God may speak to us in many ways. The first and primary way that God speaks to us, if we are Christians, is through the Bible. This is the most important way and that's why it's important for us to be students of the Bible, because God speaks to us through the word, through the message of Jesus.

"But God can speak to us through other people. God can speak to us through silence. God can speak to us through thoughts, dreams, in a still small voice. God can speak to us through prayer and meditation and through visions. One person said to Billy Graham, 'How do you know God exists?' and Billy Graham said, 'that's easy, I talked to Him this morning.'"

Dave went on to discuss that God's voice is not on the cusp of every little thought or imagining in our heads. This was not true and people who thought this were in error.

"The truth is; God is not in every voice. God is not in every little thing that comes along. We can hear the thoughts and voices of our own mind. There can be the thoughts and the voices of the Devil. There can be the thoughts and voices of the Holy Spirit. "

Then Dave discussed how we need to differentiate between the two different voices. He said that God is love and that any thought that crosses God's law is wrong. Additionally, he mentioned that a more common error with God is we tend to be overly cautious in that sometimes we are afraid to hear God's message—we aren't listening to Him. He then discussed meditation and quoted more than several passages from the Bible that discussed the benefits of meditation. His intention was to show the congregants that this was an old way of being with God. Dave was leading them down the right path and it was good.

"Last Sunday," he continued, "in our Sunday school class, I felt uncomfortable as we went through the meditation part of our Sunday school. I'm not used to doing that, and as Dr. Ron guided us through that I was trying to take it as seriously as I could. He told us to meditate on the Lord.

"At first, as I was meditating, I had nothing but silence, but then I thought I could see Jesus sitting across from me. I know this may sound crazy to you, but I saw him sitting there, the most relaxed peaceful, loving expression that I have ever seen. Then I thought–I had a few thoughts in my mind–and I thought it said, 'Dave, slow down. Walk constantly in my Spirit.' That's what I thought it said. Now, since that time, and of course before that, I've been trying to listen to God more carefully. I really sense that God is calling me to spend more time in silence and prayer, talking to God and listening to God. In fact, sometimes I find out that I get about midway through my day and I can't do anything unless I slow down and spend some time in silence. That's my experience."

Then Dave talked about how we compiled a group message and that perhaps God was speaking to the congregation in a unified way. He continued even though he was scared as to what the reaction might be.

"Here is the message that we compiled from our collective notes. We titled it "A Message from God":

*"My love is the greatest gift and the most important thing. Some of you need to receive my love. You need to love yourselves as I love you, and open yourselves to receive my constant love for you. Others need to show my love and your love by being sensitive to family members, reaching out to others, listening and visiting, caring for your environment, being gentle and touching one another. Love as I love, unconditionally. Come unto me and I will give you rest. In My rest and comfort you will find warmth, peace, light, and happiness. My love can cover all the pain and the past. You can be my helpers in reaching out and comforting others. It is good for you to come into my presence even if it is only in silence. I yearn for deep communion with you. Slow down and walk constantly in my Spirit. Let go of fear. Trust and believe. You are my child. Mend your broken relationships. Listen to one another. Communicate with family members. Rejoice, sing praises, and be thankful."*

I cried. The message moved me. And, to my suspended disbelief, I knew now that the movement had begun.

# CHAPTER 14

Later that same morning I taught the class again. This time, there were a few more people in the church classroom. The same radiator eked and popped and I was eager to get started. Dave's sermon had assisted me in my spirit and I was glad for it.

As before, I let God do the talking and set the stage for the class. Twenty-five people attended—some were new; some were from the class before.

"I want you to see that it is not necessary to use a meditation technique to receive a communication from God," I said. "I'm going to play some soft music and this is what I want you to do. Be still and quiet your mind. When you think you are quiet enough, ask God to come into your life. Develop within you an expectancy that God is coming. When you feel God's presence enter your body or mind, go for a fifteen-minute walk with God. God will point to people, to nature, your walkway, or even signposts that have sayings, for example."

I paused momentarily as I caught Angela's eyes and she smiled that smile of hers that made my heart sing. It was a smile of simple loving of who she was looking at as if he was her prince or willing captive. We were joined together into one.

"So, pay attention for God's communication. Would the people who were chosen as number one stay in the room until everyone has gone? Then they can go for a walk."

I turned on the music and waited. Settling in and closing their eyes, the members seemed to relax their collective shoulders. They began trying to connect with God on their own. Then after about ten minutes, people wandered slowly out the door, stepping over a new threshold, I thought: for me and for them. This was my hope but God advised me.

Dave sidled over and sat down with me. I explained that some people in the class were going to have trouble making contact with God. So, he was to go to those people and hold their hand and ask this question: "Do you feel God's love in my hand?" If they answered yes, he was to say, "Go for your walk." After about twenty minutes there were about eight people left in the class. Dave and I both started to give them the help I had suggested. Except one person, everyone in the class felt the presence of God and went for the walk.

All but two people heard the voice of God using my meditation the previous week, but this week, when left to their own resources, over half of them had difficulty. For initiating the first contact with God, meditation directed by somebody else seemed to be a more powerful technique.

Angela, who played piano in church and who had been sitting in the third row for the meditation exercise, did not say anything to me. I began to feel concerned that she was having difficulty with her decision. Worse yet, she could have decided that I was insane. The next few days passed without her calling. I became increasingly concerned, but I was determined not to interfere with her decision. I wanted God to work, not me. After all, this relationship was God's idea, not mine.

But time passed and by Wednesday night I was worried. "God, if you want this thing to happen with Angela and me you've got to talk to her. She is obviously not getting the message."

"*She will call you tonight.*"

"She doesn't have to call me tonight," I said. "But if you want this relationship to work, you have to speak to her."

"*She will call you tonight.*"

I began to be afraid that if Angela did not call this was not God's voice. I did not want to put the voice to a test because I was afraid of what I might find out. "I don't hold you to this, God. She doesn't have to call tonight."

"*Ron, I am God. I can do anything. She will call you tonight.*"

"All right God, but it's not necessary. If she doesn't call, that's fine," I acquiesced.

Seven o'clock came, and then eight, and then nine. It was not going to happen. I had prepared myself, but it was not going to be good. My belief was going to be wounded. Crestfallen, I went to sleep at ten.

The next day, I wanted to fix the injury that had occurred between God and me. God had made me a promise that had not come true and I was distraught over this. The voice was not always right? This was very troubling. I was happy to see that my faith, however, remained intact. The voice was wrong and yet I still found I believed. This was a relief, because I feared that if the voice were ever wrong, I would give up on God completely.

That night my mother called me for the first time in many years. We'd not seen each other in many years and she, herself, had joined in the recovery program back in Richmond, Virginia. We had begun a conversation in recent years and months. She was working the twelve steps and I understood that. My father had been dead for ten years. His alcoholism and drug abuse beating him to death. My mother was suffering from early stages of Alzheimer's disease and she wasn't always coherent. She was living in an assisted living facility so I knew she was being well cared for. I tried to encourage her and to understand her demented thinking. She only says about ten sentences over and over again forgetting that she just said them.

As I was talking to her, I noticed a message in my son's handwriting on the kitchen table. It said, "*Angela called at ten thirty last night.*" I said goodbye to my mother, ecstatic! God was right again! The voice was not wrong. I was jubilant, elated. I called Angela to tell her what happened.

After the social amenities, Angela got to the point of her call to me the night before. "I thought we could get together and I could fill you in on what has been going on here," she said.

My stomach dropped. "I've wanted to call you," I said. "But I have been purposely not calling. I didn't want to influence your decision. If you decide to try this relationship, I'm going to be your cross to bear. I'm divorced, have three children, and am a recovering alcoholic. That's not going to look very good to your religiously conservative family. I'm sorry, but if you are going to do this, you are going to suffer." I was standing in my truth. I had to.

"I have been thinking about that," she said. "I figured that was going to be a part of it. I've decided just to give it some time."

"That's about all we can do," I said.

Angela spoke sweetly, "That's the way I see it." I could feel her pulling toward me and away from me at the same time. The forces seemed equal in power but if this was God's plan He was going to have to make the relationship happen, not me.

"We'll just see where this whole thing goes."

We made a date for Saturday.

# CHAPTER 15

In the next Sunday school class, we talked about the restless sea of doubt.

I started again and hoped progress would be made. "This morning," I began with God leading the way, "we are going to talk about the hurdle that stands in the way of God. The major barrier to experiencing God is doubt. Last week, all but two of you received a communication from God. Two didn't think they got anything at all. But, God promises us that he is always there even when we think we get nothing we get something. God is trying to get through to people who are not receiving his communication. Perhaps this is not your time to talk to God or maybe the silence is a communication. Sometimes silence is the best communication of all. God promises us that in this communication there is power."

Momentarily, I paused. The class was full of people. Just then, a young man meandered in slowly and leaned against the back wall.

"Through belief in God and prayer we can get what we want out of life. Let me read a few of the passages in the Bible that speak of the power of prayer: 'Delight yourself in the Lord and He will give you the desires of your heart' (Psalm 37:4). 'If you believe, you will receive whatever you ask for in prayer' (Matthew 21:22).'Therefore I tell you, whatever you ask for in prayer, believe that you have received it and it will be yours' (Mark 11:24).

For a moment I paused to let them take the words in. I gazed out among my class.

"'You may ask me for anything in my name, and I will do it' (John 14:14). 'If you remain in me and my words remain in you, ask whatever you wish and it will be given you' (John 15:7). 'This is the confidence we have in approaching God: that if we ask anything according to His will, He hears us. And if we know that He hears us--whatever we ask--we know that we have what we asked of Him'" (John 5:14-15).

"Last week, when God spoke, most of us went home and we thought about whether or not God really did come to us and speak inside of our minds. Sooner or later we are thrown into a restless sea of doubt. For the people of Israel, God parted the Red Sea, made it rain bread, made water come out of rocks, and still they doubted (Exodus 14, 16, and 17). It is natural for us to doubt. Doubt is an important part of faith."

There was a comment from the side of the front row. "How are we to believe?" she asked.

"The word, 'believe,' means to accept as true without seeing. To believe has always been difficult, but it is easy to doubt. We don't know exactly what happened in the creation of humanity. We must use our imagination. I can imagine that God did some thinking about our capacity to think and doubt. To help us with our doubt, God decided to send us prophets. God spoke to the prophets and they delivered the message: God is alive, God loves you, love God, love others, and love you, but that wasn't enough. We continued to doubt."

A man from near the radiator interjected, "I doubt even when my mind is clear and I know where the remote control is." The class laughed.

Smiling, I continued. "Then God helped people to write scripture. Maybe if the message were written down, it would be easier for people to believe. God sent us his word in scripture, and we read it, and we were still filled with doubt. Bits and pieces of unbelief stuck to our consciousness like glue, growing like cancer. We doubted God and each other. Perhaps we doubt ourselves most of all."

Then I quoted scripture and said, "'He who doubts is like a wave of the sea, blown and tossed by the wind. That man should not think he will receive anything from the Lord; he is a double-minded man, unstable in all he does'" (James 1:6-8). We all know that to doubt ourselves and to doubt God feels fearful and to believe in ourselves and believe in God feels whole.

"We doubt God, each other and ourselves. It's amazing that we can believe in anything at all. Where do we learn to trust?" I paused for a moment, then said, "How can you learn how to trust yourself, others and God?" I waited. "I can imagine God asking himself the same question. How can they learn to trust me?

"Then God decided to do the most miraculous thing of all. He decided to come to earth as a person. God would deliver the message personally." I slowly walked about the room. "I can imagine God saying I am going to show them just how much I love them. Then they will trust. Then they will believe."

For a brief moment, my high school speech flashed before me. I remembered how the students on that one fall day had laughed at my account of Jesus. Here I was now, recounting the story again. Like a new dream, I felt the words issue from my lips. I had to be more visible to carry God's message but I still didn't feel completely comfortable. I always felt more comfortable alone and invisible but maybe God needed me to be with others and visible. Maybe I was talking for him and he was planting fluent messages in my mouth. God doesn't stutter, I do, so if I talk for him he might do the talking not me. Maybe it was my job to speak for him in his voice and his words.

"Jesus suffered the entire range of human experience. The evening before he was crucified, Jesus cried out to God because he was terrified. How agonizing this had to be, God's child begging for help. But God remained silent. Jesus knew why he was here. He had free will. He could say no. The choice was his. He decided to die for us."

I walked a bit to the right and then to the left and made eye contact with everyone.

"God wants us to bring God into the courtroom of our heart just as Pilate did with Jesus. We all bring God to trial in our own hearts and collect the evidence for and against him." There were some people who nodded to show they were listening.

"We nailed God's son to a cross and he said, 'Father, forgive them, for they do not know what they are doing.' And then Jesus died. But in three days, he rose from the dead. He had a wound in his side and the nail holes in his feet and hands. He walked up to his friends and his friends doubted. 'Unless I see the nail marks in his hands and put my finger where the nails were, and put my hand into his side, I will not believe it,' said Thomas (John 20:25). So Jesus said, 'Put your finger here; see my hands. Reach out your hand and put it into my side. Stop doubting and believe'" (John 20:27).

"When Jesus was preaching the good news, many people asked him to do something spectacular to prove he was the Son of God. But Jesus said I am the miracle. I have come to earth to show you the truth."

For a second or two, I paused. I wanted to stress this to the class. "Now, my friends, the miracle is you because God wants to come and live inside you. We can't be quiet about the good news. We can't keep it to ourselves because there are a lot of people who have not seen the miracle. They have not experienced God the way we have. I held up the messages God had given the class. God didn't give this message to Moses, Jacob, or Abraham. God gave this message to you." A few people shifted in their seats and I saw a couple look at one another. At this point, I moved forward to make my next point. "Imagine that there is a hydrogen bomb in your home town. It's going to explode and kill everyone. You know how to stop it. You know where the cutoff switch is. You can flick the switch and stop the explosion. Are you going to wait for the bomb to explode or are you going to do something to save lives?" I paused again to emphasize my next point. "Let's say a great ship is sinking and all the passengers are struggling in the water. We see the people drowning, struggling in the water, mothers holding up their children to save them. What are we going to do? We are holding a life preserver. Do we throw it? Do we help those in distress?"

Dave and Angela were there. I moved forward with my talk feeling support from them, support from God. The temperature in the room got hotter as I tried to breathe the breath of God into these people through His words.

"There was a recent article in the local newspaper that said that seventy percent of the people in our town don't have a church home. We decided in this group that God wants everyone to come into the Spirit of God. God cannot be happy that all those people are without a church to guide them."

Then above all, I raised the bar and made the challenge. "It's your turn to go into the lion's den, your turn to be afraid, your turn to pick up the cross, your time to put up or shut up and your turn to decide. I told you that the time would come in this class when you would suffer. That time is here. What are we going to do about the people in this town that don't have a church?" I put my arms in the air to emphasize the question.

"I want everyone to take ten cards out of this box. The card says, '*God wants you to come*.' On the back of the card, we are going to put the address and time of this class. Now, this is what you are to do."

I walked through the classroom all the way to the back. "If you listen to God's voice, God will tell you who to give these cards to. Do not use your own judgment—if you do, you will have problems. Use God's voice to tell you who to give the card to. When you go up to that person, the Holy Spirit will speak for you. I do not know what you will say. I assume that it will be different for every person you approach."

People were pulling cards from the box and handing the passing the box to each other. Many looked down and then up to see what was next.

"Now, let's look at what the cards are for. They will give people you encounter in town a chance to come into the Spirit of God. They will improve your communication with God. You will have to listen to God carefully to hand out each card properly. They will give you a way to love God and others. They will give you the experience of facing your fears. They will give you the experience of suffering for God. Will you do it? God always gives us the option to say, 'no.' I know this will be difficult but going to the cross was difficult, too.

"On the new piece of paper I have given you, write a desire of your heart, a desire that you want to have fulfilled this week. Don't be selfish but write down something you want. Write something you believe you can receive. Be careful what you ask for, because if you delight in the Lord, and if it is God's will, you are going to get it." Then I gave each person the time to think of a desire and to jot it down on the paper.

I said a closing prayer, "God, thank you for life. Thank you for the green grass that tickles our feet. Thank you for the blue sky and the sun. Thank you for the tiny touches of snowflakes. Thank you for all of your gifts—too numerous to mention. God, we delight in you. We are going to ask you for the gift we have put on these papers. If it is your will, please grant us these requests. God, each of us has a question for you: Do you want us to hand out this card to people and bring them to this class? Now each of you receives your answer."

I waited a few minutes, and then closed. "God help us to live life the way you want us to. We turn our will and our lives over to you. Take us. Guide us. Use us."

With that, I exhaled and smiled at the group. Off they went into the day with their missions, hopes, and desires. When the class was empty, I sat in one of the folding chairs and became very still.

I often talked to God about doubt. Sometimes I found myself on the waves of skepticism and incredulity. "God, I wish that something would happen to prove to me that you exist."

*"Ron, so much has happened. I have created the Universes for you. Are the Universes not enough? There are more Universes with different laws and dimensions that you cannot imagine. There are other intelligent creatures that look nothing like you but they can have faith like you and doubt. It's all a wonderful and terrible choice."*

I questioned him again. "But God, the Universes could have been created by natural forces."

*"The man who is seeking miraculous signs will not find me. Only those men seeking love will find me. I will not be found by a scientific experiment. I will be found with trust, faith, and personal experience. No one can come into my presence without feeling the force of the Universe in which they live. That is why you are doing such a great thing by teaching people how to hear my voice. Trust and faith are essential to a loving relationship. I will never disappoint you. If you ever feel I*

*have, you have not understood what I understand. I see everything yet I leave certain elements to chance. There is no free will without risk and the element of chance. I could make man believe in me, but I wouldn't feel the joy of the choice."*

At home, I pulled out one of my psychology books. William James, one of the fathers of psychology, states, "If a man chooses to turn his back altogether on God and the future, no one can prevent him; no one can show beyond reasonable doubt that he is mistaken. If a man thinks otherwise and acts as he thinks, I do not see that anyone can prove that he is mistaken.... In all important transactions of life, we have to take a leap in the dark." (James, 1961 p.113)

A few days later I was to take my next leap. I was filled with the doubt monster again. To ease the burden and clear my mind, I went for a walk in Newton Hills, a local state park. It was fall and the leaves were changing colors from green to gold, yellow and red. The sun was warm and the air was crystal clear and still. Walking up the trail, I topped a ridge and stopped by a bench to rest. I was teeming with anxious doubt that I asked God to please do something to show me His presence. I needed a visual sign.

Suddenly, I became very aware that God was going to walk up the trail. I was going to see God in person. Stunned, I sat there in utter anticipation. I didn't know whether to be frightened or to get on my knees in reverence. I listened to the leaves and the wind. Nothing happened for a long time. Feeling foolish, I got up to traverse down the trail.

As I was walking down the hill, I came to a small meadow. Before the trail topped over the ridge, the wind started to blow. I could hear the voluminous sound rushing through the treetops headed for me. The wind got closer, the trees bent in the wind, the leaves scattered in all directions. Then a whirlwind came like a vortex through the trees and stopped in the middle of the trail. Twirling before me, it was six feet high, and twirled before me for many minutes. Then it moved on through the piney trees. Soon thereafter, the omnipotent wind was gone and I was left with a calm afternoon.

I walked down the trail a changed man. A transcendent moment rid me of doubt.

God does not worry about your doubt. He knows the struggle between doubt and faith is necessary. Doubt is like believing you will always be an orphan, an invisible child. You came from nothing and you will return to nothing. Faith is the "inside" voice of God saying you have a family in Him always. This is how God put it to me:

117

*"I long for the flower of your life. I have given myself to you and I expect nothing in return. I want you to stay with me in the garden until you join me in eternity. Your struggle is a common one and necessary for true faith. If faith came easily, I could not use the process to help me decide. You must struggle in the raging sea of doubt. Stay with me, this personal communication is the best way for you to deal with your doubt. It erases all fears that there is nothing in the Universes except life forms of an evolutionary nature. Most of all you must know that I am here I have built this place for my children. You are so much like me that you, of all people, will understand. I want to be loved, but I will not force myself on any creature. This confuses people sometimes. They wonder why I am not more present. They do not understand that without my presence nothing would exist. Why did I create man? You know the answer to that. I created man to love. I wanted to give other creatures' life and joy. When a father sees his child smile, the smile is imprinted on his heart. So it is with me.*

*When you feel joy, I feel joy. When you laugh, I laugh. When you cry, I cry. I do from within you, living as you live, feeling as you feel, touching as you touch. I experience everything you do on the most intimate level possible. Do not take me into sin. I do not wish to experience sin. It would hurt me too deeply. I grieve for you when you sin. But in your love, I can experience you first hand, as if it is you, but it is I. This communion brings me great joy. I am full of the laughter of my children. I am also full of their tears. Each is the expression of life and life is precious, so precious that it staggers man's imagination.*

*My love surpasses your understanding, but someday you will know and experience all of this wonder in full. The greatest joy awaits you. You will join with me in paradise. It is wonderful to see you grow spiritually. I know the struggle. It is essential. I am with you. You will not fail. Nothing can take you from my grasp. Keep walking forward my friend, life everlasting awaits you."*

After listening to God's message, I returned home and decided through my conversations with Him that a study of interpersonal relationships was the next move. The talking and guiding would not be me. God would take the reins through me and my voice.

The following Sunday, God's voice infused the class with guidance. He took over.

After church, we went into the church classroom and got together. There was about twice as many people in the class as before. Dave and I had discussed the elements of his sermon and sat up front with me. The class was filled and three men, contractors from town, stood in the doorway to listen.

I said a short prayer in my head and got up.

"Listen to what the Bible says about love: 'Love is patient, love is kind. It does not envy, it does not boast, it is not proud. It is not rude, it is not self-seeking, it is not easily angered, and it keeps no record of wrongs. Love does not delight in evil but rejoices with the truth. It always protects, always trusts, always hopes, always perseveres'" (1 Corinthians 13:4-7).

"In our society, we tend to have love mixed up with sex. Love is the active involvement in a person's individual spiritual growth. It is an action, not a feeling. Love is God. God is the vessel for pure love."

"I want you to catch on to a trick of evil, it's the great lie. The lie is this: if you tell anyone the whole truth about you, they won't like you. From the time we were children many of us believe this lie. We swallow it hook, line, and sinker. The lie keeps us lonely and isolated. Acting as if this lie is the truth, we wear false fronts, pretending to be things we are not.

"This evil trick of not showing and telling the truth undermines relationships and makes love impossible for husbands and wives, parents and children.

"Another lie of evil is this: the more control you have, the safer you are. Control breeds resentment. The more you try to control people, the more they want to escape. People have a desire to be free to determine their own destiny. The more you inhibit them, the more they fight. This kind of authoritative thinking promulgates this lie: the more power I have, the happier I'll be."

Seeing two more people scratch down some notes, I continued. "Power and control do not mean love. They create fear, and anger, and spark rebellion. They don't work. A relationship cannot nourish both parties unless certain elements are present. Those elements are that both people must be trustworthy."

I emphasized this point. "They must know how they feel and express their true feelings. They must know what they want and ask for it. They must be concerned with each other's growth."

I exhaled—but just for a moment.

# CHAPTER 16

The air in the room was filled with anticipation about what I was, or God was, communicating to them. I surveyed the faces. Each appeared as if they were on the edge of the precipice waiting for what came next. Light and love filled this air of action and when I continued, I felt as if my body was occupied by a mighty presence. The faces I looked out and into were longing for answers and I was giving them the answers.

I marched on with the voice that rose inside of me. Using God's voice, I didn't want to be invisible. I wanted him to be visible and me to be invisible. I do this to this very day. As I go to work every day I tell God to take over me and change me into Him. That every word I say will be His word and every action His action. That people will see Him and not me that they will hear His voice and not mine that they will feel His touch and not mine.

I continued to let God speak through me in the class. "In our culture, we have problems expressing our feelings. As children we learn to keep our feelings secret. We learn not to trust our feelings, that something is wrong with our feelings. We learn that others don't care how we feel. When we cry, someone says there is nothing to cry about. When we are afraid, people tell us there is nothing to be afraid of. When we are angry, people tell us we are bad. Time and time again, we are taught our feelings are wrong, so we suppress our feelings."

I saw people in the front row nod their heads as they looked at me.

I gestured with my hands across my chest. "If you suppress a feeling long enough you forget what it was. The feeling becomes repressed. If we push anger down, for example, the anger is still there in our unconscious, but it is now hidden and kept secret—even from us. We are angry, but we don't feel angry.

"Suppression and repression wreak havoc on intimacy. They are a breeding ground for lies. Let me give you an example." I walked slowly to the right side of the room. The eyes of the class followed me. "Our society hammers at a young girl's sexual feelings. She is taught that these feelings are bad. Learning this, she suppresses her feelings. Eventually, she might not feel sexual feelings at all. It is a sad fact that we do this to most of our feelings. A classic example of this is that most women can't get angry, so they cry. Most men can't cry, so they get angry. Forced to suppress their feelings, men and women arrive at a point where they don't know how they feel. It's like being numb.

"Feelings assist us in directing problem solving by giving us energy and insight. If we don't know how we feel, we can't act appropriately and solve problems. We are unable to deal with problems because we can't use our real feelings to solve the real problems. People will never cope with life like this. They will stay in a hopeless struggle. To correct this problem, we must be committed to live in reality—no matter how painful it may be at times."

The class broke for a quick break.

Dave came over to me. "It's going well," he said. "I think we need to talk more about what you meant by feelings. Thank you for using some scripture. I believe it helps with the connection to some of the older congregants." He paused as a man passed by. Then he asked, "Did you talk more with Angela?"

I nodded. "We are taking things slowly. I want to do what is best for her and for me."

"Gotcha," Dave said. "That's a good call."

"Well, you know, Dave, it's not my call," I pointed upward with my eyes and continued, "it is His."

Dave slapped me on the back. We laughed. The release felt good.

The class meandered back in from the break. I started again as soon as they settled into the folding chairs. "Let's go over the core feelings and come to an understanding about what they are telling us to do. Remember that all feelings give us energy and direction for movement. They direct action. There are eight basic feelings: anticipation, joy, acceptance, fear, surprise, sadness, disgust, and anger. All of these feelings are directly connected to specific motor movement. Fear, for example, gives us the energy and direction to run away from the offending stimuli. Anger directs us to make the pain stop. Sadness directs the movements necessary to recover the lost object. The expression of these feelings is universal. In all cultures, people act in similar ways when having similar feelings. Smiling, for example, is a sign of friendship and approval in all cultures throughout the world.

"Imagine what happens when we hide how we feel. If we feel one way but act in another way, people will judge us using false information. You will be perceived incorrectly. People won't know how you truly feel if you are hiding feelings and showing something else. We must stop this craziness of hide-and-seek or we will never be close to anyone.

"There was an alcoholic man in treatment at Keystone who had a long history of lying. For twenty years, he told his family and friends that he fought bravely in Vietnam. He had long stories of the war that he told to his wife and children. He cried about the stories and he was depressed about the close friends that were killed in combat.

"Now," I continued after a brief pause, "his family felt great compassion for this man and, before this treatment; he was diagnosed as having a posttraumatic stress disorder. He lived his life as a Vietnam hero but, in reality, he had never been to Vietnam. He was living a lie. He was convinced that people loved him because he was a hero. He felt totally empty inside and he filled his void with booze. About three weeks after he entered treatment, we talked about truth. He was convinced that he couldn't tell the truth. He had been living a lie for twenty years. No one would understand. After a few more days of thinking about how lonely he was, he came into my office."

"'I've got something to tell you,' he said. 'You know that Vietnam thing. I was never in Vietnam.' This man watched me carefully, afraid I was going to reject him—afraid I would shame him. The lie was out. Now the consequences would come.

"'I'm proud of you,' I said. 'That took great courage. You are a very brave man.' The relief on this man's face was wonderful to see. You could see the worry lines dissolve. He had been carrying this heavy burden for twenty years and finally he set it down. Later that week, he told his group and in the family program he told his wife and children. Everyone loved him for the truth. He couldn't believe it. People were going to love him for who he was, not for who he was pretending to be. His dreams of acceptance had become a reality.

"A psychological law always holds: the closer you can get, the more you can share, and the more you can share, the closer you can get. You must start telling your loved ones the truth. They need to see who you really are. It is the only way they can know you.

"In this country, the average parent spends about twenty minutes a week communicating with his or her child. The average husband and wife spend an equal amount of time talking to each other. Compare this with four to eight hours the average American spends in front of the television every day. What does this mean? What does it mean to your child when you come home from work and sit down and turn on the television? You have just spent at least eight hours at work. Your child knows that. The child may come to you and say, 'look at what I did in school today–look at the picture I drew.' You might say, 'Just a second honey, the news is on.'

For a split second, I could see a glimpse into my childhood—the dumpster diving, and the face of my friend, Ben.

"I tell parents, 'you do not fool your children. You are not fooling the people who love you. They watch what you do.' I challenge you to ask yourself these questions: how do I spend my time? If you are so busy that you do not have time to love then what do you have time for?

We meditated as a group and collected individual messages we thought we got from God. This is what we believed we received as a group:

*"First, you need to accept my unconditional love. I will never leave you and I am always with you. Pray and love me and you will be filled with my love. Love yourself and let your real self-shine through. Forgive yourself and let go of bitterness and begrudging in your heart. Believe in your inner thoughts. Love yourself then you can love others. Love others by loving unconditionally, telling them you care, sharing your life experiences, being aware of their needs, helping them in time of need, being honest in a loving manner, forgiving them, praying for them, spreading God's gentleness and kindness, smiling, giving friendly greetings, listening, visiting, taking time for the little things, making phone calls, giving gifts, and writing notes and letters. Pray, be humble and serve others."*

The message was like seeing golden lettering in a holy text. The words lived in the people in the class and when they expressed those words, it was like the phrases carried their own spiritual epistle to each other and the world. Everyone was lifted at the glory each had helped manifest for God and each other.

As we left that day, I knew that the next class would be hard.

What was forefront on my mind was one word.

Angela.

# CHAPTER 17

I got into a war with God, and of course I was losing. I had been going out with Angela for three months. She was attractive, healthy, fun, and trustworthy. Everything anyone would want in a wife. But there was a problem. I didn't feel the romantic feelings I wanted to feel. God and I had long conversations about this.

In my office one day sitting in my recliner chair, I asked, "God, I don't desire Angela the way I want to."

*"It's not the time for those feelings."*

"But I don't want to marry someone that I don't have romantic feelings for."

*"Angela is wonderful."*

"I know she's wonderful. That's clear to me. She is honest, loyal, healthy, and fun. But I don't desire her the way I think I should. I have some desire for her but it's nothing like what I want from a wife. I want a wife like Peggy," I almost pleaded.

*"Do you want Peggy back? There will be more lies."*

"No, I don't want Peggy back. I want Angela to be as desirable as Peggy was." I fiddled with a paper clip on my desk.

*"It's not the right time for those feelings."*

"I think it is time for these feelings."

*"You want things your way?"*

"Well, yeah," I said.

*"Ron, I love you. I want you to be happy. It's not the right time for those feelings. Trust me. Be patient."*

"This makes me wonder if you exist at all," I whined. "I could just be talking to myself." The sea of doubt covered me, wave after wave after wave.

*"You know me."*

"Well, I could be fooling myself," I said. "This voice thing could be just an unconscious trick I'm playing on myself. I could get married to someone I don't love or desire and then be stuck with her for the rest of my life. I don't want a marriage like that."

*"I don't want you to have a marriage like that either."*

"Then give me the feelings!" I demanded.

*"Be patient."*

The war between God and me went on like this day after day. One day, I was so frustrated I could hardly stand myself. I went up to the Catholic Church where I often spoke with God. Staring at the life-size crucifix, I sat there fuming. Gradually, as I stared at it, the light began to change slowly. I leaned forward, a tad perplexed yet intrigued. It changed more. Then, little by little, the figure of Christ began to take on a life-like quality. The figure was coming alive with the iridescent light. I knew this wasn't really happening. It was an illusion, a trick of the lights, but it seemed so real. For the first time since I had been speaking to God, I heard his voice sound intense. *"Ron, don't give up now. I have big plans for you. You are like Paul. You are going to carry the message. Angela will help you. These feelings will come. Be patient."*

Now, any stupid fool would have given in then. If you can't trust God, who can you trust? But I still doubted the whole thing. If this was only happening in my mind, I was headed for big trouble. "God, I'm not going to marry someone I don't love!"

*"Ron, I don't want you to do that."*

"I'm not going to marry someone I don't desire either!" I repeated again as I'd done in my office.

*"I don't want you to do that either."* His voice was always calm and reassuring.

Still, I did not leave the church happy even though I had seen a great manifestation of God's presence. But I left that church discouraged. I wanted these romantic feelings, and in a stubborn childlike way. I wanted them now.

This was how I got into problems with God. God told me to do something and I wanted to do it my way. My way was not God's way. My way was not as good as God's way but I had difficulty trusting anyone but myself. In my whole life there was no one I could trust. Every time I tried this trust was betrayed. I learned the hard way to trust myself and only myself. Now this God was telling me to trust Him, that He was my best friend I would shut up and let Him make the decisions. This went down like a chicken bone the wrong way. The fact was I was afraid to trust even God because I had been hurt and disappointed by people too many times. As A.A. says I had to let go and let God. So I continued to trust and mistrust God's voice. The more I trusted God the better my life got and the more I trusted myself the deeper into the ditch I got. It was a slow process of turning my will and my life over to God.

By the time of the next Sunday school class, I decided to talk about this problem I had with God.

"I've got a real problem and I suspect that some of you have got the same one. My problem is, when things don't go my way, I get upset. This is a hurdle that keeps me separated from God."

Then I shared a story about Moses I thought would assist all of us with this struggle. "Many of the Israelites did not understand why God wanted them to come out of Egypt and walk into the desert. Many of them were happy in Egypt. But Moses heard the voice of God and God said take my people out of Egypt, and I will take them to the Promised Land.

I walked about the room. I said, "I am sending you to Pharaoh to bring my people out of Egypt. Now, I ask each of you in this class: what if God asked you do something like this? What if God asked you to build an ark? What would you do if God asked you to do something that you did not want to do? Suppose you didn't agree with God's plan. You thought your plan was better. How far would you go with the voice of God? The commandment that we break more than any other is, 'Thou shall have no other gods before me.' When we do things our way and not God's way, we break this commandment.

I paused. Then I used myself as an example again. "I'm fine in life as long as everything is going my way, but if things begin going against me, I'm unhappy. Then I whine, complain, sulk and pout."

"I think I know what is best for me. But only God knows what is best for me.

Then I asked, "do you think Jesus really meant it when He said in Matthew, chapter five, verses thirty-nine through forty-two? 'If someone strikes you on the right cheek, turn to him the other also. And if someone wants to sue you and take your tunic, let him have your cloak as well. If someone forces you to go one mile, go with him two miles. Give to the one who asks you, and do not turn away from the one who wants to borrow from you.'

I could see from the expressions on the class' faces that I needed to add more.

"What would the world be like if we treated everyone, as we wanted to be treated? God asks us to, 'Love each other as I have loved you.' God knows that our life here on earth is incredibly short. God knows that we are going to live forever. It is with this knowledge that God makes decisions. As it is, however, we go through life trying to meet our needs. Things like time, sickness, and death are important to us. These elements are not as important to God because God can see the big picture.

"If you try to control the people who love you, they will rebel. If you force your will on them, they will resist you. I see this often when a religious parent tries to force a child into going to church. This child will either actively or passively resist this attempt, and because belief is such a private thing, the parent may never know about the resistance. You can't shove religion down someone's throat."

Two people who had been taking notes looked up and nodded when I said this.

"In this class," I continued, "you have received a communication from God. How would you feel about putting this in the newspaper? How would you feel about going on national television and telling the world that God spoke to you? Would you be frightened?

"God has a great plan for you, and you have a plan for yourself. Who do you think you should trust you or God? If God gives you direction, I suggest that you follow God's plan, not your own."

While I struggled, Angela was obedient. She let the whole debacle go and left it up to God. I could learn a lot from that woman. I wondered if this wasn't God, through her, teaching me a lesson.

A week later, I learned that Angela could have doubts. She spoke to me about them and agreed to come over for dinner. Afterward, we walked up to the Catholic Church. I wanted her to overhear one of my conversations with God. As we went through it, I realized that God talks to me in two different ways. One is in normal conversation with each word articulated, the second is in blocks of thought, as if someone handed you a book with many things inside. I don't know how God does this but he sometimes speaks in exact words and sometimes in blocks of ideas or concepts that you get all at the same time.

I asked Angela if she had any questions about the communication.

"How can we get married and not break God's law about adultery?" she asked. "My dad says me marrying you would be the worst thing that ever happened to him in fifty-one years."

"Wow, if I'm the worst thing that has ever happened to your dad, he's had a pretty easy life."

"Let's ask God your dad's question. I don't want to be the worst thing that ever happened to anybody." God's answer came right away.

*"You are new flesh. When you become of the Spirit, you are new flesh. You become a new person inside of God's Kingdom. All of your sins purified. There is no adultery in your new flesh. You are born again into a new person. The old person is dead and the new person is alive."*

I tried to explain the message to Angela. "Apparently, God cleans the slate at conversion. There is nothing of the past life. God forgives and forgets the sin. A new believer becomes totally new in the eyes of God." I could see Angela was still confused. "Did that answer it for you?" I asked.

"It breaks God's law," she said.

God answered again. *"You are confused. It does not break the law. There is no adultery. The new person has not committed this sin."*

Walking back to the house, Angela said, "I've come up against a brick wall with my parents. They say if we marry we will break God's law. We will commit adultery. They are very sure about this and I really trust my parents."

My heart fell a bit but I knew what to say. "I think you should pay attention to your parents," I said. "Your parents love you and want the best for you. What do you think about what God said?" I asked and then stopped in front of her.

"I don't know," she said looking up at me.

I stepped on a stone and then asked, "You mean you don't know if it is God? God said, there is a new person here. This new person hasn't committed adultery?" My question floated to her.

"I don't know," said Angela. She was blinking back tears. I could see she was being torn apart by this decision.

"Then let's just be friends," I said. "There's nothing wrong with that. Maybe being friends would be better for everybody. Your parents can't complain about you having a new friend. To God these laws are simple, but when people get a hold of them they can get so complicated that we don't know what the law means anymore. What are you going to do?" I asked removing my foot from the stone.

Angela surveyed the ground and then looked up at me with those brown liquid eyes of full of love and longing. She loved me it was clear and there was nothing she could do about those feelings, they were too powerful. "I need some time away from my parents and away from you. I need to be by myself." Tears streaked her face.

I felt sorry for Angela, but I was regrettably neither romantically nor emotionally attached to her. I could let the relationship go without getting hurt. Her parents were good people and I encouraged her to listen to them. I knew they loved Angela, but I also knew that people often confused God's laws. I trusted Angela to make the best decision for herself. I thought that this was a good time for Angela, her parents to grow and me to grow, too. God challenged our faith with a crisis such as this. The education through Him was always a time for growth, for finding a new way, or to look at an old lesson with fresh eyes.

Patience let her go and think.

# CHAPTER 18

The next Sunday school class brought a river of tears.

April brought fresh snow and the class came in from church with coats in hand and snow shoes squeaking down the tiled hallway floor. The class held some of the same faces and many new ones, too. I recognized our postal carrier and his wife and gave a small wave. The class was growing every week.

At the lectern, I said a small internal prayer and then I began, feeling the glory of God inside of me and issuing out to the people who had come.

"Write your parents a letter using your non-dominant hand so the writing looks like that of a small child. Write to your mother and father as the child you once were. Write about the things you wanted from them and didn't get, and about how you were feeling. No parent is perfect and all children have unmet needs. When you are through, look at the letter you have written. It will have your unmet needs defined for you."

As I said this, I was transported to a time in my childhood where my unmet needs clung to me like a bad unending virus. My own parents were hallmarks for the imperfect. I remembered the frog, Baby, my drunken parents and my time in the coal bin. I needed to feel safe and loved. The class was to write down some of their unmet needs.

"These things are what you needed as a child and it is what you need today. The responsibility for meeting these needs is yours. You must be your own mother and father and see to it that you get what you want. The most important thing that you can give to yourself is a personal relationship with God. By the end of this class, you will be talking to God and God will be talking to you. This will be the beginning of this relationship. God is the perfect parent. He promises us that He will meet all of the desires of our heart. Our mother and father could not do that, but anything is possible with God.

"Remember that this little child continues to reside in you and still needs all those things that you needed when you were young. Now, it is your job to see to it that these needs are met. What better way to do this than turn over your will and your life to the care of God who loves you.

Many of the attendees surveyed what they had written. I saw some scratching through list items and others enumerating more unmet needs.

"As you work on healing that injured child within you, you must forgive your parents. They were trying as hard as they could. Jesus made it clear in the Lord's Prayer: 'Forgive us our debts as we also have forgiven our debtors' (Matthew 6:12). He spoke of forgiveness again in Matthew six, verses fourteen through fifteen: 'For if you forgive men when they sin against you, your heavenly Father will also forgive you. But if you do not forgive men their sins, your Father will not forgive your sins. All people are children of God. No matter what your parents did or did not do that hurt you, God wants you to forgive them and welcome them into God's arms. Many people hold resentments toward their parents. It's not good. They can be hurt and angry for life. This constant pain is not necessary if we work toward forgiveness. You want to be forgiven, don't you? To be forgiven, you must forgive. The best way to forgive anyone is to pray that they come to see the truth. Sometimes it takes weeks of praying that this person gets everything that you want for yourself. Soon you will find that you mean that prayer and you will forgive the person's hurting you. Refusing to forgive only gives the person power to hurt you even more. Forgiving others frees you from the bondage of the past."

"I have a patient named Joe who was cruelly abused by his alcoholic father. When Joe was fourteen, his father went to treatment and has been sober ever since. Although his father has been loving and supportive since he got sober, Joe was unwilling to repair the relationship. To refuse to honor our parents' results in separation from God's plan.

"Joe's life fell apart. He married, divorced, had an illegitimate son with a girlfriend, and remarkably, found himself repeating his father's sins. Joe became so depressed that he ended up attempting suicide. In treatment, he couldn't sleep and was riddled with anxiety. He blamed his condition on his father.

"Joe's way worked for a while. Alcohol reduced anxiety for a short period, but ultimately he became chemically dependent. Now, Joe had two problems: he had to treat his alcoholism and he had to repair his relationship with his father. Doing one without the other was not going to work. Joe had to repair his relationship with his father so he could repair his relationship with God and himself. In treatment, I asked Joe to pray for his father, every day for two weeks.

"The next morning I asked him how the prayer went. He said, 'It took me quite a while to fall asleep. I went back and forth with good and bad thinking about my father. I asked God to help my dad. I feel a lot better since the first time you talked to me. I don't know what happened. You know, talking to that higher power, I did that going to an AA meeting Tuesday night and I felt really good. I didn't get nervous talking. It was really weird.'

"'So when you clean up some of your resentments, good things happen,' I said to Joe." I continued my slow walk in front of the Sunday school class describing Joe's story.

"Joe went on and said, 'I felt good about myself. Before I went into the groups I felt the fear, but I asked God to help and I felt calm. I was looking at other people and they looked pretty nervous too. It made me feel not so nervous.'"

"'What did God help you see?' I asked him."

"Joe said, 'I saw other people being afraid. I wasn't the only one who was scared.'"

"I told him. 'God directed you to look outside of yourself so you would extend yourself to others. How did you do in the group?'"

"Joe said, 'I talked a lot. I had been to AA before, not using God to help me, and I was too nervous to say much, but this time I could share.'"

"'What happened when you prayed for those people who had hurt you?' I asked him."

"Joe said, 'I didn't feel good at first. I didn't want to do it. I felt like crying.'"

"Then I said, 'God is not asking you to feel good when you pray for people who have hurt you. He is asking you to treat these people the way you would want them to treat you. When you do what God wants, God does something for you. When you treat someone with love, God pours his love into you.'

"Joe then said, 'the war is still going on inside me—the good against the illness.'

"'God can win that war,' I told him." 'Then you will sleep like a baby. Once you learn that the illness is to blame not you, you can forgive yourself for hurting your son, and you can forgive your father for hurting you.'"

The class took a quick break and when they returned, they were as attentive as I had ever seen them. Apparently there were many unhealed relationships causing the group members unresolved pain. I recounted another example through one of my patient's experiences with her father.

"You need to give yourself a gift this morning. This is a gift that you have freely given others and it's time that you give the gift to yourself. God wants you to give yourself the gift of forgiveness. You need to forgive yourself for the wrongs you have committed. This is one of the best ways we can free ourselves from the pain of the past. We make a mistake; own the mistake, ask for forgiveness from God, and make a commitment to try not to make that mistake again. Jesus died on the cross to forgive us of our sins. All we have to do is accept this free gift of God's wonderful grace. It is not earned but a free gift from a loving father."

"When my patient, Cindy, was sixteen years old, she learned that her father was getting married to her nineteen-year-old friend. She was frantic and the staff had overheard her talking about killing herself. Her counselors brought her to me and we sat down to talk. I could tell she was struggling. Her face was red and her eyes were swollen from crying. 'My dad, he makes me so mad. He's getting married to a real bitch.' Hate contorted her face.

"'How do you feel about your father's decision?' I asked."

"'Mad...and scared,' she said."

"I asked her then. 'What scares you? And she said, 'I don't know.'"

"I pressed another question, 'What could you lose?'"

"Her response was, 'I've always had all of my dad's attention.' I then told her that she might lose some of that and she agreed.

"I then asked her, 'What is the worst thing you could lose?'"

"She said, 'I could lose him.' while jabbing at the face of her watch. Her chin quivered and then she broke down, sobbing."

A lady raised her hand from the back of the class. I acknowledged her. "This girl was how old?" the older woman asked. "And she wanted to kill herself over her friend marrying her father?" An air of incredulity carried her words.

"Sixteen—and, yes," I said.

"I knew from Cindy's history that she had all of her father's attention as she was growing up. She was her father's little girl, mother, and lover. She was very confused."

I continued the recap of the story.

"Then I asked Cindy, 'Try to tell me the feelings you are having.'"

"'I'm angry, scared, and jealous.'"

"'That sounds confusing,' I told her."

"Yeah, it is."

"Then I asked her another question. 'You say that when you were a little girl you had all of your dad's attention?'"

"'We went everywhere together,' was her response."

"Then I pressed on. 'From the history you gave me, it sounds like you were everything to him that a woman could be. Did you sometimes feel like his mother?'"

"'I took care of him,' she said flatly."

"'Did you feel like his little girl?'"

"'I still do,' she told me."

"'Did you even feel like his girlfriend?'"

"She nodded her head and I told her that would be confusing to anybody. She nodded her head again to me. And I asked her if she felt all the roles were necessary for her father to love her?"

"'I don't like talking about that sexual stuff,' she said.'"

"'It makes you uncomfortable,' I said."

"'Yes, it does. I don't want to think about it.'"

"'It must have been confusing for you to get that kind of attention from your father?' I inquired and then she nodded."

"She paused and said, 'I didn't want that kind of attention.'"

I stepped forward to make a point and gestured with my hands.

"In a healthy home that's what you would have said to your father. 'I don't want that kind of attention.' In treatment that's what you will learn how to do. You will tell people how you feel and ask them for what you want. That keeps people informed about how they affect you and it holds people accountable for their actions.

Momentarily, I paused to allow that story to sink in.

"I also helped Cindy to see that fleeting sexual feelings between fathers and daughters are normal. It's only when these feelings are acted on that people become confused. She was encouraged to see her father as a disturbed child of God who had been abused himself. He needed to be held accountable for his actions but also forgiven and understood. She would have to work these issues through. If she kept them quiet, it would be difficult for her to have a healthy relationship with anyone."

People held their notes and letters and let their own childhoods express sympathy and empathy for Joe and Cindy. I wiped my brow and thought of Ben and his siblings and my brother. His journey must have been just as confusing as mine.

Two powerful stories had enriched our class on this cold April day. I left the sanctity of the place happy that my communication with God was impacting the people before me. I knew in my heart, however, there was more work to be done.

God is patient. More messages were coming.

# CHAPTER 19

Now that the Sunday school class had experience communicating with God, I asked them to write how God communicated with them. I collected their varied notes and read through each at home on the next Sunday. With an open heart, I was ready to see how God was being revealed in their words. At my kitchen table, I leafed through the notes, restless to see what was to come next in this glorious display of God. Flash: Like the white church in a small Virginia town. I smiled.

This is how the class members responded:

1. God speaks to me through thoughts and feelings. It almost always involves taking a risk of doing something different.

2. I have a great sense of well-being after class. I find myself talking and visiting with God more throughout the day than ever before.

3. I heard God tell me to do specific things for others. I also saw (visualized) a place I was to go, but at first saw no way to get there. Later, a path or bridge appeared that was not visible at first.

4. I felt God move my heart to be more accepting and loving toward my husband and my family.

5. God communicated to me that his love is an action and not a feeling. His love is doing, thinking, and speaking. We are to always use his love and to share it.

6. God communicates with me in many different ways. One way is by a small voice deep within my soul, speaking to me about a situation that I needed to look at more closely. God also speaks to me through being still and relaxing. God speaks through the words of other people. I may be thinking about something and then at that time someone will share a thought or personal experience about the area that I was looking at. God speaks through his word (scripture).

7. On both occasions, I heard God's voice through my own thoughts,

usually a few words of communication. I think this was a good and challenging exercise to wait to hear God speak to me.

8. As I remember, I had a picture in my mind of the Lord in a white robe embracing me. The thoughts I had were about my Dad—that in heaven all his twisted thinking would be righted—it would be right.

9. I have gained more spirituality than before. God has told me to love myself that I am growing and still have a great more to come. I have not seen a vision of him, but I feel and occasionally hear this voice in my head--guiding me, questioning my reasons for actions. It's almost like a louder conscience. I know when I listen and deal with this as I hear it--I feel a peace within.

That night Angela called. She had made the decision to continue our relationship. She was going with what God told her. I decided to concentrate solely on being Angela's friend. My wish for romantic feelings was too frustrating. God had told me to explore a friendship, then a romantic relationship, and then Angela was going to be my wife. It was no accident that I had heard those messages weeks apart. I realized this. God was giving me the relationship in order. Angela was about five feet seven, twenty-eight with a warm athletic body. She was very intelligent and well educated. She taught music at several elementary schools in Sioux Falls, South Dakota. She had a deep passion for her work that I couldn't quite grasp. I didn't know if it was passion for music, her students, Jesus, me or everybody. Even after all of these years together I have never heard her say a bad word about anybody. She was a deep untapped well of passion just like God said. Once in the house she took off her shoes and curled her feet up under herself on the couch. It was one of the most sexual things I had ever seen.

One day Angela asked me to watch her teach her classes in school. It was one of the most incredible experiences in my life. I had never seen an elementary school teacher teach and she taught music to every student in every school where most teachers taught one class at one school. Every time a student would enter her room, and they seemed to pile in all at once she warmly called each of them by name. Remember, there were about two hundred students in each school and she taught at four schools so that's a lot of names. I never could have done it. If one of the students was having a bad day she immediately recognized this and went out of her way to make this student feel more important by thanking them for coming to class and how important it was to have them help her. She often assigned one of these students to do something special for the class, like arrange the musical instruments or hand out the sheet music.

If one of the students came in angry she immediately defused this by saying something like, "James we are not going to have a problem today are we?" James would shake his head and then Angela would say something positive like, "I'm so glad to have you here, you always make me feel better. Now let's get ready to work on our concert." Then she would get the children to sing songs or play instruments for the next hour. They always obeyed her and the music was beautiful even from the first grade students. It was nothing short of amazing to see her work and it made me passionately desire to be near her. I now could understand a part of what God wanted to do with Angela and me. God sent me Angela, this warm loving woman so He could love me through her and heal my childhood wounds. She was the mother figure I never had and God wanted to show me that I deserved a mother's love. Every time she greeted a child I could feel her love embrace that child with the love I so desperately needed. I needed her love more than I could ever comprehend. It was too basic and early. An infant that needed to look into his mother's eyes and see, you bring me joy wherever you go.

When the time was right, God said I would have the romantic feelings and I was feeling them already, but I was more feeling a deep committed friendship. As this sunk into my thick skull, I found I was in agreement with God's plan. And, because I was following God's plan, peace reigned in my world. When you are following God's direction, God's way, the feeling of peace is your affirmation that you are on the right path. Any other way, and you are right back to the path of confusion and restlessness.

# CHAPTER 20

*"People will like this book you have written. I am God and I live inside of you. God lives inside of you. You have all of the spiritual gifts and much more. You have the seed of God. You can trust me, Ron, I am God. You will marry Angela. With all of the gifts you will do great things. You have the power of God that lives inside of you."*

"What will Angela do?" I asked a bit tentatively.

*"She will love you and make the music of life and God."*

"Can this go wrong?"

*"Yes, but you have the power of God. You will make it happen."*

I was elated and honored. A mixture of feelings consumed me.

*"You can count on me, Ron. You will know that this is my plan. It will happen just as I have said. You will see. You will believe."*

"I believe you God. I just have these uncomfortable doubts," I said this and felt the lurking doubt rise in me.

*"Don't worry about your doubts. Just keep coming down the path I have laid out for you."*

I thought about the whole spiritual adventure: the talks with Dave, the lectures during the Sunday school classes, the insights about my life with Angela, Ben's pastor and his sermons. Either this was the most wonderful thing that had ever happened to me, or I was a fool. It was not pleasant to think about the second possibility.

My faith remained strong. In spite of it, I still believed in God. At the end of the workday, and after I was sure the call wasn't going to come, I sat down to reflect. The voice couldn't be God, because God couldn't be wrong. It was probably just my own unconscious. I talked to myself. Did this make me question God? You bet, but my faith wasn't as shallow as I thought. I didn't give up on God. Weeks prior to this, I would have given up. However, I was growing. Then, as an experiment, I asked the voice what had happened. The answer was the same message as before.

*"You will receive the communication on a Monday."*

This was possible. The voice hadn't told me which Monday. It could be a Monday in thirty years. All I could do was trust God's timing and not my own.

On Tuesday, I went for a jog and stopped by the Catholic Church for my normal meditation. I wiped the sweat from my brow and sat in the third pew. I looked up at the cross and this is the conversation I had with God.

"God, please make this prophecy come true. I'm counting on you. I don't know what I'm going to do if it isn't true. You may not be true. I just can't believe that this voice is not God. It is so filled with love. It fills me with love for everything. I am willing to follow you, but I can't do this alone. You're going to have to help me. I don't know what else I can do."

*"You can have faith. The call will come on a Monday."*

The sweat sidled down my brow. "Which Monday are you taking about?"

*"Love is patient and faithful."*

Was God testing my faith? Was He strengthening my faith by delaying the call? Was He teasing me? I didn't know the answer to that. I could continue to have faith, though, and that's what I decided to do. That's all I needed to do to continue on the spiritual journey. Sometimes we have to give up our plan and our understanding and trust God.

I talked to Angela at great length. "I can't marry a person who has been divorced. As my parents and I read it believe that is adultery according to scripture."

"But I have been born again. According to scripture once I am born again I am a new man. The old man is dead. The divorced man is dead and the completely new man has been formed by God. Don't you understand that part of the Bible?"

I began to look at Angela in a new way. She was beautiful with long blond hair and captivating greenish brown eyes that looked at me with such love and passion that she had to feel attracted to me. Just the way she looked at me turned my heart into Jell-O. Even if she had doubts she was hooked. We were bound together as surely as if we were connected by God himself. There was no going back. This was God's plan and not our own and we were connected as powerfully as Adam to Eve. We were meant to be together from the beginning of time and there was nothing we could do about it but submit to God's plan. We could argue and doubt but the commitment was sealed by God himself.

Even though my faith was strong and I needed to march on, I still floundered from time to time. Angela listened with an open heart. I asked her "What if it wasn't God? What were we going to do?"

At my house, Angela said, "Tell me more and I will help you." Her kindness felt like a light in the darkness.

I explained to her that if it was God's voice, our future together was sealed. I had written this book and, according to God, it was going to bring people to God. The book was going to teach people how to communicate with God. God wanted me to record a meditation tape Communication from God and a website www.godtalkstoyou.com that would help people hear God's voice.

"Go for a walk and ask God to ease your worries," Angela advised. "This might help your troubled self. It had always been expected of me to be a farmer's wife like my mother but I've always had different ideas. Farmers are good people who live off the earth but I have dreams of traveling and maybe going back to the seminary to become a music minister. That God is talking to you is wonderful. He doesn't talk to me like that. When he opens a door I have to walk through it."

"Like this relationship," I said.

"Yeah, I've thought about that a lot. When I am with you I feel an incredible peace as if this is the way it's always been and this is the way it will always be. I don't know. It's hard to explain. I've never felt this way before."

For a long while, we sat there. Then she held my hand. For a moment, I was assuaged. I could not help but feel that this wonderful woman loved me. Somehow inside of her she knew her heart belonged to me and my heart belonged to her. There was no doubt about this bond. It was created by God from the beginning of all time and there was nothing we could do to argue it away. It was God's grace and we would have to accept it.

If I lost trust in the voice, then my relationship with God would forever change. If there was no God, there was no relationship. I wouldn't talk to God anymore, and I wouldn't listen for God to talk to me. This felt empty.

T. S. Eliot once said, "Life without God is not even very interesting."

Then I realized the lesson: if the call had come right on schedule I my faith wouldn't have grown stronger. Lesson learned through my own doubtful mind. Eliot was right. My life was growing each day in the interest of God: maybe the invisible boy from the coal bin had grown into God's leader and maybe that was the plan all along. Maybe the coal bin had been how I had learned how to listen and Ben, his Mother and the small white church had been how I had first learned how to love. Maybe God had been training me to be his leader all along. Many theologians think that Moses had a stutter and God gave him his brother Aaron to speak for him if he needed that. But soon Moses was speaking fluently for God and when speaking for God you don't have a speech defect. Why would God choose men with a speech handicap to speak for him? I think this is because stuttering makes you feel little and humble. God needs humility so you will follow Him blindly following God is the only time when you feel strong and at peace.

To date, there have been sixty-eight times when God's voice has predicted the future for me. For example, the voice told me to deliver this message to a Catholic priest: *"Don't be troubled by the sexual problem, it was given to you as a challenge."* When I, reluctantly, approached the priest at the Catholic Church and told him this, he instantly said, "This is the work of the Holy Spirit." I didn't know what the message meant but the priest did.

When my boss, Mitzi Carroll had terminal cancer and was trying to make a decision about whether or not to go on a last cruise with Carol Regier the head nurse, Mitzi, and I asked God what to do. God gave us all the same answer--go. Predictions of the future cannot happen by coincidence alone.

At his house one afternoon, Dave said, "I used to have a lot of doubt. One week I would be a believer, and the next week I would be back to being an atheist. It didn't feel good to struggle with those two elements. I decided that I was ninety percent sure that there was a God and I had ten percent doubt. I made a decision to live my life in that ninety percent."

Dave sipped his coffee,

I said, "There are some things about God that I don't understand. The Apostle Paul said, 'Now we can see only in part, but in heaven we will see fully.' If I didn't get a Monday call, I would think that there was a good reason why I didn't get it. I might not understand the reason, but I believe that someday I would understand."

The next morning, I woke up unexpectedly. I was lying there, and as I usually did at such times, I started a conversation with God. "God, what am I going to do if this call doesn't come on a Monday?" I felt stuck on one day of the week.

*"The call is coming on a Monday. Ron, do you doubt that I exist in your thoughts?"*

"You exist in my mind."

*"I exist in your thoughts."*

"Yes," I said.

*"Do you doubt that I exist in your feelings?"*

"The feeling connected with your presence is very powerful. It is distinct and different from anything I have ever known."

*"Then I exist in your feelings."*

"Yes."

*"Do you doubt the things I have done for you?"*

"No, the things you said you would do, you have done," I said.

*"If you don't doubt me in thoughts, feelings, or behavior, where do you doubt?"*

I thought for a few minutes. "I doubt the things you have done. That's what gives me the most trouble."

*"It is important to build your faith, Ron. When your faith gets strong you will do wonderful things. Faith needs to be tested until it is strong. You are coming up the pathway that I have prepared for you. You are doing the right thing. It was not easy for Moses, Elijah, or Elisha. It was not easy for Samuel or Jeremiah. It was not easy for Paul. They all had to test their faith many times. Ron, don't let your faith rest on a telephone call."*

"Am I going to get this call on a Monday or not?" I asked with a sense of panic. I did not want God to change this prophecy. I was counting on it to seal my faith. This is, of course, the very thing God advised me not to do.

*"Yes, Ron. You will get the call on a Monday, but don't let your faith rest on a telephone call."*

God was right of course. One shouldn't let one's faith depend upon a single event. The religious leaders wanted to test Jesus, so they asked him to show them a sign. They wanted to see something miraculous before they would believe that Jesus was from God. Jesus answered them saying, "A wicked and adulterous generation asks for a miraculous sign! But none will be given it except the sign of the prophet Jonah" (Matthew 12:39).

Jesus would not produce a miracle to prove who he was. To Jesus the miracle wasn't that he could do great things. God had come to earth in human form. This was the miracle.

God was right. I was suffering in doubt over a day of the week and a phone call. I needed to get out of my own head and into my heart of faith.

# CHAPTER 21

The next day, I got up early in my house and had a conversation with God.

*"You are coming along the path. I am proud of you. Your faith is growing. The book will sell many copies. Don't worry about how many, that would be needless worry. Trust me to do this. Keep writing the book. It will help many people listen to my voice. I feel you all day, Ron."*

"I feel you all day too," I said lovingly.

*"I live inside you, Ron. You are not struggling with Angela as much, are you?"*

"No, I'm not. I can see you sent Angela to me to give me a love I never had. I really needed to know that someone loved me and I have never had that mother's love except from Ben's mom. Angela gives me love like that, unconditional love. When she looks at me I see that I am worthy and my purpose in life has meaning and worth.

*"That is good. Just keep coming. Angela will bring you joy. There is a side of Angela that you haven't seen. It's an exciting side. Her passion for you runs deep. This is a deep untapped well of joy."*

"God, she seems to hold back," I said.

*"That's because you hold back."*

"God, I can't do anything with Angela if I don't feel like it," I declared.

*"No, but you hold back. Your lack of faith holds you back. When you have faith, you will not hold back. Angela is wonderful, Ron. She is a deep untapped well."*

The next day, I had another conversation with God. This time He gave me some insight into why I was having a difficult time with my doubt.

*"Ron, you need to hear something about yourself. You are afraid. You are afraid of life. You have been afraid since you were a child. There is no reason to fear, Ron. I am with you. It is difficult for you to trust. It is difficult for you to believe. People have betrayed your trust. I will not betray your trust. There may be times when you do not understand, but a time will come when you will understand fully. My love for you is deep. It surpasses your understanding. Suffice it to say this, I will never*

*leave you. I will never forsake you. I will live with you, inside you, throughout all time. We are bonded in everlasting love. Believe this, it is the truth. My light is with you always. You are mine, and I am yours. It will never end."*

Those wonderful words filled me. Then, I revealed my fear. "God, I'm afraid of my ego. I'm afraid that I might have some desire for power or money or something, which will keep me from following the way you have laid out for me," I said this and then waited.

*"Ron, you are a good man. Your fears are genuine. Love will keep your path straight. Take my love for the Universes and let it shine through you. Love and cherish all things. Love conquers all evil. Evil cannot exist in truth. When you slip from the way you will feel fear. When you are in the pathway I have laid out for you, you will feel peace."*

I exhaled. "I have been feeling a great peace, God."

*"Yes, you are coming, Ron. You live in the Spirit of God. There is a peace and a joy waiting for you that you have never known. Only in death is there eternal peace. It is not the peace of unknowing. It is the peace of knowing. There you will know fully. The Universes are great places. It is teaming with life sprinkled about the stars and planets. Life is a rare jewel among the stars of the Universes, a treasure awaiting discovery. You will walk through all time with me. We will have plenty of time to visit and wonder at all things, particularly life. The life and the light are one. It is I, and I am your friend and lover. We will never part. There are no boundaries between mother, father, son, or daughter in heaven. There is only union. The personalities are separate yet united in the spirit of eternal love."*

At this juncture, I wasn't resisting God's plan. I wasn't trying to hurry things along, like with Angela. I was learning to let go and let God. No longer fighting every moment, there was quietness in my spirit.

I was learning from myself and I was learning from my patients, too.

Let go and let God: this is your (our) challenge. Who better than God who is your (our) best friend? He is the perfect parent and creator who wants to guide your every decision. At the same time, God wants you to have freedom to make your own choices that does not involve God or divine intervention. Then God wishes you well either way. He cannot guide you, however, to the best life possible without your following His plan. If you insist on doing things your way via free will, then you are on your own. By doing things your way, the best you can settle for is second best. By doing things God's way, you can get everything your heart desires. He also wants you to enjoy life in full. Yet, you cannot do that without divine guidance. God will give you love and guidance, if you let him.

To illustrate this kind of divergent road with God and free will was a forty-year-old patient named, Kim. Struggling against herself and her past, she arrived at Keystone. She came from a very wealthy family and had been a brilliant child. Raised in a home where she adored her father, at age six, when her brother was born, she lost her position of prominence. She was crushed as she watched her father focus his attention on her little brother rather than on her. Kim tried to be to regain her position by being better at the little girl things she did. It didn't work. For years, it didn't work.

Finally, she gave up on life entirely, and resigned herself to a hopeless existence. She married a person her father rejected and had a short, but noted career, as a writer. She began drinking to dull her intense emotional pain. Over the years, she increased her drinking to the extent that she lost much of her brilliant mind.

During treatment, Kim didn't do well because she continued to be lost in her fantasy world made up of past abuse and neglect. She believed in God but she had no personal relationship with Him. She didn't feel God was personally interested in her.

"He's too busy running the universe to bother with me," she said. She had transferred her feelings. Her father wasn't interested in her, so God wasn't interested in her either.

I said to her, "What if I could prove to you that God is interested in you?"

"I don't think you could do that," she responded.

I leaned forward in my chair. "Suppose I could prove to you that God is interested in you and is there to help you. Suppose God is and has always been involved in your life. Suppose he has a good plan for you."

"That would be wonderful," she said. "But I don't think God has the time for me."

I said, "Would you be willing to give God a chance to prove to you that you are wrong?"

"Yes," she said with a terse laugh of disbelief.

Taking her to the church and to the field of flowers with God, I walked Kim through the meditation. Step-by-step, I guided her in the hopes she would have a communication that would assist her on her journey.

Once we concluded the meditation, she said, "The first minute in the field of flowers there was a figure in a long white robe. His face was partially hidden by fog. I felt a message, 'Save the child'. I heard distant organ music after the thought. I heard birds outside. Then, I was reluctant to leave the ocean beach."

I asked her what she thought about her experience. I was riveted and happy she'd made a connection to something.

"It had to be God," she said smiling. "I wouldn't say anything like 'save the child'. That's not like me."

"So, you think you had a communication from God?" I asked.

"Yes, I definitely did," she said.

"If God is not interested in you, how is that possible?" I asked.

Amazed, she said, "I guess he is interested in me."

"What do you think the message, 'save the child' meant?"

"God wants me to save myself," she said. "He wants me to save that little girl inside of me." A slight pause and then a slight smile gently appeared on her face.

This patient's first experience with God was the most important experience of her life. From this point on, God was real to her.

Not long after I'd had the discussion with Kim in my office, I was talking to God about a prediction he had made. It hadn't come true yet and, as usual, I was troubled. God used this situation to teach me more about our relationship.

*"Ron, this is your voice, and it is my voice. I live inside you. I am directing you from within yourself. I love you, Ron. I don't want to lose you. Don't let little things stand between us. Would you do that with any friend? Your hope is in me. I have a perfect plan for you but you can't let little things get in your way. Look to today for your reward. Don't lose the point, Ron. When the voice is you and me, sometimes the message can be misinterpreted. Look for love when you are confused. What is the most loving thing to do? Look for consistency in the voice."*

"God, sometimes I feel like a fool," I said. "Like I've been talking to myself and thinking its God."

*"You are talking to God, Ron. Think about the feeling. Is the feeling coming from your unconscious mind, the feeling that you are loved and completely accepted? It seems the opposite feeling has usually troubled you. You have never felt accepted, consciously or unconsciously. This is a totally new feeling. This new experience is from God. It can only come from God. Only I can accept unconditionally. Only I can totally love. It is God you feel. You cannot deny your own experience. The prophecies have come true, as you have understood them. It is difficult for people to understand that God understands them. It makes me lonely, Ron. You are mine forever. There is no turning back. The relationship is sealed."*

The next morning, Kim came back into my office and was exuding some frustration. I could tell by the way she carried herself.

"It's difficult for me to keep my mind quiet. I keep thinking about other things. I have been helping two of the other patients, Bob and Sandy. They have opened the floodgates to me. I don't want anyone to cling to me, that wouldn't be good either, but I think I have helped them."

"To save that hurting child within you, you have been helping others," I said.

"It feels good," she said and sat down.

My phone rang but I ignored it. This was more important. "Have you tried to listen to God's voice again?" I asked.

"It's hard for me to switch off my mind," she said. "I haven't heard the voice again but I'm more comfortable with myself. You know, I have this imaginary room. I'm high up and overlooking the ocean. On each side of the room there are glass walls. There is a wall of books, and a wall with a door. If I want to, I can let someone in to share my space."

"Do you think of this room often?" I asked.

She paused and then said, "It makes me feel safe and at peace."

"Let's use this room in our next meditation. Remember we are trying to tune in to God's voice. God's communication can come in many forms and God may want to teach you something. Be willing to listen for God in every way you can."

I turned on some soothing music. "Concentrate on your breathing. Feel the rhythm of your breathing as your chest rises and falls. See ocean waves, building as you inhale and washing upon a shore as you exhale. You are in the room looking out at the waves while sitting in a chair made of velvet. You are completely relaxed and at peace. There are two walls of glass overlooking the ocean and the wall of books. You want God to come into the room with you. You call out for God three times inside of your mind. God comes into the room, and God has a communication for you. Open yourself up, and receive the communication."

While waiting for Kim to receive her communication, I folded my hands in my lap and waited in quiet reverence.

"There was a glowing golden light," she said after opening her eyes. "Almost like a globe. It floated through the door and hovered over the chair across from me. Behind me there was the ocean. I asked for help and the light pulsed. I asked for help in living a sober life and it pulsed again. I asked if he would show me the way. It pulsed again and moved away, back over the chair and into the sun. The sun began to set and a full moon came out. There were millions of trembling reflections on the waves. It was a pure light. I could feel God's love. All the sparkles of pure light were confirmations of God's love for me. I asked if I would kill myself. A cloud obliterated the moon. The sparkling lights were not seen anymore. The communication ceased, symbolizing death without God. I asked God to come back and the cloud drifted away. I was left feeling peaceful, and my eyes felt burning beneath my lids—as if I were, or had been, in strong sunlight."

I waited for a moment for the air to clear. "What do you think the communication means?"

"That couldn't have been me," she said. "I would never say or think such things. God is there for me. God will allow me to kill myself but that will mean death without God."

"How do you feel about that?"

"I don't want to be without God," she said.

Kim was finding new hope, even instruction, in her experience with God. Her whole demeanor softened through her shoulders and face. Through the communication with God, she had a reason to live for the first time in years. She saw that there was a chance for her to recover. I didn't know Kim was considering suicide, but Kim knew, and God knew. My heart filled with gladness for her. I smiled. She smiled. For the moment, all was well.

Kim left my office and I reflected.

Simply stated, though, illumination can be difficult. You slug things out with God one step at a time. I am stubborn, so God needs to talk to me constantly about my problems. Sometimes, I feel like I am in a wrestling match or a boxing ring.

*"Ron, I cannot communicate with you if you do not believe in me. You will blot out the communication. I love you, Ron. I don't want to lose you. Have patience— the prophecies will come true. They will all come true if you continue to follow the path. The presence of God is a mighty feeling. You cannot deny it. It is your experience. The relationship is sealed. There is no going back. Patience has always been difficult for you. You want things now. You do not understand the whole plan. The plan has been in effect since the beginning of time. All of the elements must fit together in perfection. There will be many Monday calls not just one. I know the plan. Trust me. Perfection will not occur on your timetable, only on mine. The day will come when you will understand fully. Don't let your feelings of doubt influence what you do. It is normal to doubt, but don't let doubt affect your behavior. You are*

*on the path that I have laid out for you. That took great faith. To stay on the path will take great faith. I love you. You know that. Keep coming."*

I believe that God can be found in all religions and in all cultures. If you grow up on an island where there is no religion or culture, you can still find God. Like Mother Theresa said, "I love all religions but I love mine the best."

Throughout scripture, God says he believes in us. If we follow his path you will be happy, joyous and free. God is hungry for your love, and all people have a similar hunger for God. By reading this book, and practicing the steps, you (we) can come home to God again. God is waiting for us, for you.

God and I have had many conversations about Jesus. One day, prior to seeing Angela, I went to the Catholic Church to get close to God. I said a quick prayer and then got quiet:

*You have believed in me from the beginning. The tenderness, goodness, and love that lives in your heart are from me. Christ was and is the son of God. Jesus was very different for mankind. He is not like Moses, Jeremiah, Amos, Muhammad, or Buddha. Jesus is me come to earth in human form. I wanted to experience the human experience. I wanted to live the life of a human being. I wanted to feel a new union with all people. I could not do that without the personal experience of human life. It gave me new knowledge about the struggle that my children face. I understand the dilemma that walks with you all of your life, the uncertainty, and the fear. The war between what you desire in your immediate gratification and what you desire in the pursuit of goodness is a difficult dilemma. It was meant to be difficult. I want those men and women who can do well in spite of worldly desires. Their reward will be great. On earth and in heaven, they will taste God.*

In my quest to know and understand more, I studied scripture and religious history. I needed to be fed with the truth of the stories and the trials and tribulations. Triumph, too.

The Bible says, "We know that we have come to know Him if we obey His commands. The man who says, 'I know Him,' but does not do what He commands is a liar and the truth is not in him. But if anyone obeys His word, God's love is truly made complete in Him. This is how we know we are in Him: Whoever claims to live in Him must walk as Jesus did" (1 John 2:3-6).

That is, we must stand in our truth, God's truth, and walk the walk as Jesus did. To do this is to know God.

Out of His love, God gives the gift of salvation. In Martin Luther's case, he was trying to prove to God that he was worthy of His love. In the following, he discusses his passions on God and the human condition.

"For however irreproachably I lived as a monk, I felt myself in the presence of God to be a sinner with a most unquiet conscience, nor could I believe that I pleased him with my satisfactions. I did not love, indeed I hated this just God, if not with open blasphemy, at least with huge murmuring, for I was indignant against Him, saying 'as if it were really not enough for God that miserable sinners should be eternally lost through original sin, and oppressed with all kind of calamities through the law of the ten commandments, but God must add sorrow on sorrow, and even by the gospel bring His wrath to bear.' Thus I raged with a fierce and most agitated conscience, and yet I continued to knock away at Paul in this place, thirsting ardently to know what he really meant.

Later, Luther read about God's grace and found his own peace, finally. After years of struggling with the message of God, he comes to a crossroads. This is his experience:

"At last I began to understand the justice of God as that by which the just man lives by the gift of God, that is to say, by faith, and this sentence, 'the justice of God is revealed in the Gospel,' to be understood passively, that by which the merciful God justifies by faith, as it is written. 'The just man shall live by faith.' At this I felt myself to have been born again, and to have entered through open gates into paradise itself" (Benton 1978, vol. 11 p. 189).

Martin Luther struggled over and over and over again in his attempt to understand the meaning of God and like an anointing of grace, he finally understands the point. Man is to live by faith. Once this epiphany came to him, then he was re-born into the gates of paradise. His incredible journey encapsulated in a moment of grace.

Like the first time you see a flower, like the first time you experience real love, the experience of contemplation is like rapture, the most beautiful symphony you have ever heard. It is the divine presence of truth, wisdom, and beauty all at the same time. This is God.

My next patient, Joey, a stubborn fifteen-year-old high school student, had been in treatment for a few weeks. After his treatment, he was still determined to use drugs when he went home. Joey had been raised in a home where he couldn't count on his parents. As such, he was allowed to roam the streets and early in his childhood he was in trouble with the law for various drug related charges and grand theft auto. In jail, his behavior got worse and he, eventually, spent a year in the juvenile reformatory. He was not a hardened criminal but a child who needed love. Raised in isolation, no one cared for him and he knew it. He was living his life in a dark well of despair. My own childhood reflected parts of his. I had stolen for the when I was a kid too, not because I was bad but because I was in a small town and bored.

"Why shouldn't I drink?" he asked defiantly. "It makes me feel good."

I rolled forward in my chair. "Because if you continue to drink and use drugs you will die," I said.

"I never had a problem with drugs." He crossed his muscled arms.

"Joey, you are here because you are a drug addict," I said. "If you go out there and use drugs you will be even more miserable than you are now. Is there any reason for you to get sober?"

"None that I can see," he said. Then he looked with boredom out the window.

"Why do you want to continue to use drugs?" I asked.

"Drugs make me happy." He continued to stare through the window.

"Is it possible that you could be happy without drugs?"

Still reluctant, he looked at his hand. "Well, yeah. I suppose."

"What do you have to look forward to if you were clean and sober?"

He shrugged. "I don't know."

Momentarily, I waited. "Don't you see any hope for yourself?"

"I'll be okay."

"I don't think so. If you go out of here and use drugs, you will be in more trouble, you will end up in jail, and you will end up miserable. I don't want that for you."

Joey looked at me in suspended disbelief, almost dumbfounded.

"Don't you think I care what happens to you?"

Returning quickly to his defensive behavior, Joey shrugged his shoulders.

"Has anyone ever cared for you?"

Again he shrugged.

"Do your parents care for you?"

He returned his stare to the window as if he looked at it for an answer.

"You don't feel like anyone cares for you, do you?"

He was still, almost as if he were trying to shrink into himself.

"That's very sad. I had that same feeling when I was growing up," I said.

"You've had that feeling before?" he asked, genuinely surprised.

"When I was growing up, my parents were alcoholics. They were too sick to spend time with me. That hurt a lot, but now I know something that I didn't know then." I caught his stare.

"What?"

"I know that God cares for me and he is my parent. He is always there—never too busy or drunk. Do you believe in God?"

"Yes, I do."

"Have you ever had God talk to you?" I asked then leaned forward.

"No, nothing has happened to me like that." He looked back down at the back of his hands.

"What's the closest you have ever felt to God?"

"One time in the reformatory—I had been reading the Bible, and for a little while, I felt close to God like I do now.

"Sounds like you were feeling God's presence in your life."

"Yeah, it was neat," he said.

"What happened to that feeling?"

He crossed his arms again. "I don't know. It just went away...I stopped thinking about it."

"Did that warm feeling feel as good as you feel when you were high?"

"Yeah," he said as he reflected.

"Was the feeling better than drugs?"

"Yeah, better."

I leaned back. "How was it better?"

Emphatically, he stated, "It was better because it wasn't drugs."

"So there is a way for you to feel *better* than you have ever felt on drugs?" I asked.

"Yeah."

"Suppose you could experience it again, anytime you wanted to?"

"That'd be great." He gestured with his hands palms up and folded them back together again.

"Would that give you a reason not to use drugs?"

"Maybe?" he shrugged with uncertainty.

"Want to try?"

"Well, yeah, I do."

I shifted in my chair as I prepared to connect this young man with God. "We are going to try to connect with God's voice and then you can ask God anything you want. When God comes you will have a feeling. That is the feeling that is better than drugs.

I slowly took him through the meditation—the field, the rock, the images of nature and the church. When we were done, I just waited for Joey to speak.

After a long pause, he said, "It seemed to me that we were talking with our hearts. God said, 'even though your parents aren't there, I will always be there for you! I LOVE YOU!'"

"How do you feel about that?" I smiled.

"It's neat," he said with a new sparkle in his eyes.

"Was the feeling better than drugs?"

"Yes, it was." Joey leaned back and smiled.

"God is there for you, Joey. God will see to it that you are happy. Drugs cannot get you what you want, but God can get you anything."

After our session, Joey left renewed. My hope was that he would continue to connect with God as we'd experienced together. If everyone knew this, the power of connecting with God and the high it created; there might not be any drug addicts at all.

The next patient was a sixteen-year-old girl I'll call, Sherry. Her smile was wide but her actions were laden with anxiety. Underneath her cloak of friendliness, she exuded a constant air of fright. Raised with a younger sister in a small town, her life had been uneventful, until age thirteen. Late one night and without any warning, her drunken father raped her. Too ashamed and frightened to tell her mother, Sherry finally told a school counselor. The school reported the incident. Charged with child abuse and rape, her father and the family underwent a formal investigation. Then Sherry had to go through the humiliation of a trial. Her father was found innocent on a technicality.

Degraded, Sherry withdrew into herself. She drank to deal with the pain and her grades spiraled downward. After she was arrested for possession of alcohol for the third time, she came into treatment. Experiencing flashbacks of the rape and trial was commonplace for Sherry. In treatment, Sherry had a dream. One day after lunch, Sherry described her dream to me.

By my office window, she sat in a folding chair. "I was a beautiful fairy who lived in a village in a wooded glen. All the other fairies that lived there loved me. I was the princess fairy, and as I would walk through the village, the people would smile at me and think about me. I would smile back, particularly at the old people and the children. I was wearing this beautiful pink gown with diamonds and I had a magic gold ring. I was spreading joy as I walked through the village and I did this every day. When I got home to my cottage, the smile left my face. I sat on a long white couch and felt lonely. I gradually turned into an ugly woman, an evil witch wearing black. This was the real me. No one else knew who I really was. I was never the beautiful princess. I was the ugly woman who was fooling and manipulating everyone."

154

"What do you think the dream means?" I asked.

"You got me."

I waited. "Who do you think the fairy princess is?"

"Me, I guess."

"Who do you think the ugly woman is?"

"That's me, too." She sounded defeated—no air in her at all.

"Who do you think you really are—the beautiful princess or the ugly old woman?"

"I don't know." Sherry looked down at her worn shoes.

"Sounds like a part of you thinks you are beautiful and another part thinks you are ugly."

She shrugged. "I don't think I'm a beautiful princess."

"Do you think you are a witch who is manipulating everybody?"

"I don't know." She flipped the blinds with her fingers.

I delved a bit deeper. "Do you pretend to be someone that you're not?"

"I do that all the time."

"What are you pretending to be now?" I asked.

"I'm pretending to be happy." Tears welled up in her eyes.

I handed her a tissue. "But you're not feeling happy."

"That's right," she said. Tears streamed down her face to her chin and she began to weep in earnest.

"How are you really feeling?"

"I don't know," she hiccupped through the words.

"But you know you're not happy."

Breathing heavily, she said, "I haven't been happy in a long—time."

"Then why pretend to be happy?"

"I pretend because people want me to be happy," she said defensively.

"And you give people what they want."

"Yes."

I handed her another tissue. The light streamed through the window. "What about what you want?"

"What do you mean by that?" she hiccupped again.

"You are pretending to be happy to give people what they want, but how are you going to get what you want?"

"I don't know what I want." She rubbed the tissue against her nose.

"Think about it for a minute." A pause lingered in the air between us.

She cocked her head. "I want to be loved."

"How are you going to be loved if you don't act like yourself?" I asked.

"What do you mean?"

I leaned forward to deliver my point. "The fairy princess was loved by the villagers, but it wasn't really her. She was the witch. The princess knew that the villagers didn't love her. They didn't even know her. To be loved you have to be yourself."

"So how do I go about showing people who I really am?"

I put my index finger up in the air. "First you have to stop telling people what you think they want to hear then start telling the truth."

"I don't know the truth," she emphatically stated.

"Sounds like you've been too busy feeling what you think people want you to feel. Why don't we see if God can help you?" I asked. I briefly described the meditation to her and she was willing to give it a try.

After we journeyed through the meditation, this is what Sherry recounted. "I could feel the peace and the happiness. My heart felt really full--like it might pop. I could hear him talking to me in my heart. I know he wants good things for me and that he cares. I felt free from my old self and felt like a new beginning."

As Sherry left, I was suddenly troubled that the voice could be wrong. Was I being misled by myself? Even worse was what if I was turning my patients onto an internal voice that wasn't God. I asked God about my fears. "If mistakes can be made, the voice is worthless. I'm trying to navigate through life. If some of the course changes are incorrect, I'm going to get lost. I will never know that I'm going the right way." I pleaded to understand and to get to the answers. It was like being on that old boat with my father in the middle of the Chesapeake Bay. I was in a channel with no markers.

*"It is the destination that is important, Ron."*

"God, I need to know that I'm doing the right thing. I need to know if I'm following your plan exactly." I asked.

*"You are following my plan, Ron."*

"But, sometimes the voice has seemed to be wrong," I said a bit helplessly.

*"The voice hasn't been wrong. You can misinterpret the voice. You can misinterpret anyone's voice. Communication can be difficult."*

"If I can be wrong, how do I know that I'm doing your will?"

*"Ask me."*

"But, if I ask you, I could get the wrong answer. I could misinterpret again."

*"Ask again."*

"I could get the wrong answer again," I said, getting more frustrated.

*"Ron, you must follow the Spirit. The Spirit will not deceive you. You might misinterpret a certain course change, but the Spirit will not allow you to get dangerously off course. If you misinterpret briefly, the Spirit will correct you. It is the destination that is important, not every single decision."*

"God, that's not what I want. I want the voice to be absolutely correct all the time. I never want to misinterpret the voice. I want to know that I am exactly on course." I was determined to be right and to get it all right.

*"Then you want to be perfect. Only God is perfect. Life—to be free—needs a certain element of risk."*

"I don't have to be perfect but I want the voice to be perfect." I exhaled and waited.

*"The voice is perfect. The receiver is imperfect."*

"So as long as man receives your voice there will be imperfection in the communication?"

*"Yes."*

"I don't like it."

*"People cannot perceive anything nor do anything perfectly."*

"Why didn't you make humans perfect?" I asked a bit exasperated.

*"Because then there would have been no free will or risk. There would never have been the element of chance. I wanted friends to love me freely. I wanted the element of risk, chance, and surprise. It makes the Universes fascinating."*

I pressed on. "So I can never be one hundred percent certain about anything. Is this the uncertainty principle of physics or what?"

*"You can be certain that I love you. You can be certain that you are on the path. If you get off of the path, I will correct your course. You can be certain that you will make some mistakes, but trust in me and I will make your path straight again. I want to be consulted on the course changes, particularly the major ones. It gives me joy to direct your journey. Do not be afraid. I know what you need. I know what you desire. I know where you are going. Trust in me and I will deliver all goodness. You can sail through life in complete confidence that you are in the arms of God."*

# CHAPTER 22

In the past and today, I feel incredibly blessed in my own spiritual journey. God has taught me and continues to teach me about the mysteries and miracles of life. I open myself up each day and am grateful to have the friendship, the parent in my life. Admittedly, sometimes I get frustrated and have a difficult time with understanding what he lays before me, but He never seems impatient or angry—even when I want the world to do things as I want them done.

Remember my Monday call? So far, I've had seventeen Monday calls from people wanting to publish my books. I have published 17 books so far and am working on three others at the present time. The calls didn't happen exactly like I thought they would happen. They happened in God's perfect timing, not mine. Faith to me means that God has his arms around me even when I'm unsure of the outcome.

One step at a time, God is constantly training me. I used to think that hell was a place that harbored the same things on earth but magnified: lies, abandonment, neglect and abuse. However, one-night God woke me up at three in the morning and he said, *"Come with me. I've got something to show you"*. Then he took me by the right hand and we went to hell. In hell, there is no light, no love, no beauty and no truth. Dark, damp, and cold, I could feel creatures like huge spiders with hairy legs scuttle past me and then snakes slither over my skin. It was akin to the cataclysmic boat ride with my father and the bucket of overturned crabs crawling all over me and him and the boat. My hair stood on end. If anyone would sleep in hell, then large beetles the size of your hand would land on your body and bite off large chunks of your flesh. This was horrible but God had me by the hand, so I wasn't completely terrified. God didn't have to show me hell for long. It was a nightmare, and I wanted to get out of there and never go back.

"Hell is a lot worse than I thought." I said and held my arms.

*"It's important that you know the truth."*

I asked, still holding onto myself, "Why do you send people to hell?"

*"I don't send them to hell. They choose to live in hell. People who chose to live without me."*

"No one wants to go to hell."

*"They know what they are doing."*

"How do they know?" I was incredulous.

*"I have placed my law in their heart."*

"People might not understand." I said.

*"The law is perfect. They understand the law in their heart. They make the choice to live without me. All of the laws and the prophets point to this truth. It is not difficult to understand. If people chose to live without me they decide to live in hell. This is the choice around which everything turns. Everyone will stand in judgment and no one can say they didn't understand."*

The more I turn my life over to God, the stronger I get.

I can swim in the sea of doubt with strong strokes. God, however, is guiding me every stroke and step of the way. My compass to life points always to one way: God's way. This is right and good.

By the summer of 1990, I had been dating Angela for a year. Suddenly, something very different happened. The more I learned about Angela, the more I knew that God was right. She was wonderful in every way that I could imagine. Her kindness permeated our talks and she listened as if she absorbed every word I spoke. She looked at me as if I was the most important person in the world. She watched my every move and tried to anticipate my every need. Music teaching and directing was one of her passions and she struck chords of song and love into everyone at home or at church. You just wanted to be around her...all of the time. One morning as I was laying in my bed, God gave me a vision so vibrant and intense and real that I thought I was on an ethereal plane of angels. And, I was.

*"Come with me, Ron, I have something to show you,"* God said.

I felt myself lift off the bed and travel through space, over the stars, through the brilliant colors of the universe. Then, God took me to a room where I saw myself as an old man. I was lying alone in a single bed. Jesus came up to my bedside and took my hand. *"Are you ready?"*

"Yes, I am," I said. Then as if death were the most natural thing in the world, I lifted up and out of my body and Jesus and I rose to heaven. We went up and over something huge, unintelligible. Then we gently went down to a soft, white place—Angela was standing there, smiling her beautiful wonderful smile. I embraced her fully—as I held her in my arms, I felt the greatest feeling of love for her wash over me and through me. This feeling has never left me, not even for one moment. I will love her like that throughout my life and throughout all eternity.

That weekend I asked Angela to marry me. She didn't hesitate for a moment and said, "Yes. I've been waiting for you to ask me and hoping you would. My doubts about us have been answered by God and he has confirmed that you are the man I have been waiting for my whole life. Remember when we had our first date and you brought be a single red rose. All my life I have said to myself, "I will marry the man who brings me a single red rose. This is just a part of it, Ron. You are a man of deep faith and that has always been the most important thing for me. I need a man who puts God first and you are definitely that man."

Just after this beautiful moment in my life, the vision of God and Jesus and Angela, I went once again to being my own worst doubting Thomas. It was as if I was conspiring against myself and the voice and could not embrace fully what was being shown to me. It was exhausting but I continued to question.

Till one day.

"God, how can I be sure this voice is really you, that I'm not playing some sort of a psychological trick on myself?" I asked for the thousandth time.

Then God said something incredibly specific about my boss and friend, Mitzi Carroll. She had been the executive director at the Keystone Treatment Center for a number of years and was looked up to by me and the staff. God said, *"Mitzi will die of cancer on August 28th. This will seal the covenant between us."*

August the 28th was one year away. I was shocked, and I didn't want Mitzi to die. I didn't tell anyone about this because it was too shocking and surreal.

Regrettably, the following winter, Mitzi was diagnosed with lung cancer. Through the spring and early summer, she became weaker. By August, she and our friend, Carol Regier, had decided to go on a Caribbean cruise.

Because Carol knew I had a special relationship with God, she came to me in my office and asked me to pray with her. She was frightened Mitzi would die on the trip. "Pray that she won't die on the cruise," Carol pleaded with me.

This put me in a bind. The cruise lasted through August, past the death date that would seal the sixty-eight promises God had promised me. I didn't want to spoil God's plans and I selfishly didn't want to lose my promises, but, who knows best but God? I was unsure of all of it, but I did know that Carol was frightened and I wanted to protect her. I said the prayer she asked me to say. "God, don't let Mitzi die when they are on the cruise."

*"It will be done," God said.*

Now, I was confused and thought I had spoiled everything—the compact we'd made a year earlier. "God, what about the sixty-eight things you promised me? What about Angela? How can I make sure this is your voice? Mitzi's death on August twenty-eighth was the way you were going to seal the covenant. How will I know that your promises will come true?"

*"Go up to the church and I will show you a sign."*

I did as I was told and I walked to the Catholic Church. Each step of the way, I peered around, expecting to see angels or something equally magnificent descend from heaven to show me the sign God had promised. Curious and a bit flustered I traversed the path hoping to see or hear or experience something.

I was sure as I stepped through the doorway to the church, I would find His sign. With great anticipation, I waited in the third pew. An hour slowly ticked by and nothing happened. The church was quiet and still. Finally, I couldn't stand it any longer. "It's all a big fake," I said. "I was an idiot to think God would talk to me. I'm no good. Why would God call on a cripple to talk for Him?" The old fear crept back. I was going to spend the rest of my life alone after all. After an hour of waiting, feeling rejected by God, and thrown back into the pit of despair, I walked up the aisle to leave.

As I pushed open the front door of the church, I noticed a sign sticking on a post, like a stop sign. It was a picture of a lake with a rainbow. *God Keeps His Promises,* the sign said in bold letters.

Just a sign stuck on a post, the end of my doubt and a testament to how struggles can make one's faith strong. Mitzi died in the fall and I was happy for her because I knew she was going to live with our father in heaven.

Angela and I were married on September 20, 1991. I knew I loved her and I knew this was God's plan for me. In the stillness of our honeymoon and without a sound, the miracle happened; all of the feelings of romantic passion washed into me. I fell in love with Angela in a deeply romantic way, and I have been in love with her like this ever since. We have a passionate love that all lovers wish for and seldom have. We have been married for over twenty years and she is everything God promised me and much more. Shane my son Angela and I have been in a praise band to lead worship at church. So far I have published seventeen books and have several websites that get millions of visitors a year: www.godtalkstoyou.com, www.robertperkinson.com, and www.alcoholismtreatment.org. Every day I get hundreds of emails telling me how the meditation exercises on the webpages have changed people's lives forever.

One morning, God woke me up. *"Look at your wife."*

I cradled Angela with my loving eyes. She was beautiful, sleeping peacefully. I welled up with tears of appreciation—I loved her so much.

*"She is your miraculous sign."*

She had found her way into my heart …and, because of coal bins and frog gigging and parental neglect, I'd tried to keep her from getting to my heart. I cannot keep her out, though, she is too wonderful. She is the most loyal, kind, and loving person I have ever met. I trust her completely. In her every word and action, she shows me the face of my Father God that I have come to know so well. She is always tender and kind. She treats me just like God does and looking into her eyes, I see God look back. God often says to me, *"Ron, I sent you Angela so I could love you. Now, let me love you."* Still, I sometimes try and resist, but I always fail. I am bonded to Angela like I am bonded to my children. I love her more each day.

As I was finishing this part of the book, I asked God if He had anything else to say to you, the reader. This is what God said:

*"Put in the book that I love all life. Life is so precious and rare that it requires special attention. I desire to heal all wounds. I do not inflict pain on my children. Sin is the creator of all pain. I have allowed free will. You must understand the monumental importance of this decision. It brings out the best and the worst in all people. Free will is the mother of creativity and it is the father of sin. Without free will my creatures could not blossom into their full potential. Yet, free will results in much pain and suffering. To allow man freedom of choice was my great gift. I did not have to give it, it was my desire. Love necessitates freedom of choice. Anything else would have been bitter. So in the birth of joy, there was the birth of pain. I am watching. My judgment is pure. I know what is in your heart. On the last day you will meet me face to face. Then you will know me. Then you will see. Then your heart will be opened. There will be no secrets then. The truth will be exposed. You will face yourself as you face me. Those who are pure in heart have nothing to fear, but those who think they are getting by breaking God's law they will reap the seeds they have sown. They have made their decision. They will live with the consequence. My judgment is perfect."*

# PART III:
# GOD TALKS TO YOU

# CHAPTER 23

I thought I might be crazy after first talking to God.

So, in my quest to be educated fully, I decided to research the phenomenon carefully. I needed to see if this had happened to anyone else. After more than twenty years of research, I have come to this well-established conclusion: I believe that God is speaking to me and God is speaking to you. God is personally speaking to everyone, all day every day. Perhaps after hearing my story, you will want a story of your relationship with God. I hope you will listen for God's voice because he wants to talk to you. When I was writing this book, God said, *"Ron, don't you think I want them all to hear?"*

God wants to talk to you. This is no accident you are here reading these words. This is a special moment in time. God has been seeking you for a long time. He wants to walk beside you every day as your closest friend. This is why you are reading this book. God has been waiting for you for a long time and he plans for your eyes, your smile, and your story to change the world.

You know how to pray and how to ask God for things, but most people do not know how to hear God talk back. I believe that God is speaking to you right now, and if you listen you will know it. You thought it was your idea to pick up this book. Truly, it was God's idea. God wants you to read these words. He is talking to you right now and if you will listen you will feel the peace of his presence.

You can put the book down if you want to. That's what evil wants you to do. Evil doesn't want you to talk to God. Evil wants you alone and isolated from everybody like I was. You might feel like you are lost in the coal bin of your own life and that no one understands you. Evil wants you to think that there is no God, or if there is one, God is mad at you. But if God were mad at you, your eyes would not be securing these words with the exciting feeling that is flowing through your heart right now. This is God. This is God encouraging you to read on.

You may have sought God before in a book, a church, or a religion. Yet, you may have ended up feeling empty. God eluded you. God didn't seem interested in you or was too distant. So, you gave up. This could have happened because of your circumstances: a bad relationship, an unforeseen illness, or a death of a loved one. That feeling that God was not present is a universal feeling. But still from time to time, you could feel God—a gentle knock on your heart.

God is going to talk to you. When He does, you will never be the same.

In the next few chapters I'm going to share some of my research with you, but don't stop there. Keep reading, searching, watching and listening for God to speak to you. He may speak in nature, a bird song or a blooming flower. Sometimes you will hear music and tear up feeling God's love for you. Open up every sense and take it all in. Then, walk into the presence of God you will be changed forever. Nothing ever becomes real till it is experienced. To know God is to know that a *part* of God lives inside of you. God will contact you inside of your own thinking. If you want to see one place where God lives, go look in the mirror. God lives inside of you. He has been there all along. You do not have to look for God in someone else or something else. Look for God inside of you. God resides there in the person you see—there in your heart and soul.

As you read this, you will feel a gentle nudge. God wants you to feel this touch. Almost imperceptible, this tap on your heart is so serene and tranquil. God is as real as you are. God wants to whisper into your soul and tell you that he loves you. He loves you more than anyone else can.

God wants to communicate with you, but you have been too busy. Unknowingly, you have been turning away from God's voice. You have been concentrating on the busy aspects of your life: that is, cooking breakfast, working at a dead-end job, running countless errands, wasting time by smoking or drinking, or just being busy to be busy. By this, you have been ignoring God's voice. But God has been talking to you anyway—encouraging you, supporting you, and educating you. Like the remote control to your TV, your God antennae have been on mute. When I was a young child, God was talking to me through nature: the deer, the butterflies, and the wind on my face. He was teaching me in the coal bin to listen and in alcoholic parents how to love a child. He brought me to the home of a beautiful African-American woman who took me to a white church on a hill. God was talking to me through Ben, Ben's Mother and the preacher at Ben's church. That church was so full of love that it was full of God I just didn't know it. The look of compassion on Ben's mother's face was the face of God looking at me. I was looking into the eyes of God but I didn't know it.

God talks to people every day. You may have sought God in another person: a priest, a rabbi or a holy person. That's not going to work in the long run because God wants a personal relationship with you. Richard Foster states, "The history of religion is the story of an almost desperate scramble to have a king, a mediator, a priest, a pastor, or a go-between. In this way, we do not need to go to God ourselves. Such an approach saves us from the need to change, for to be in the presence of God is to change"(Foster 1988, p. 24). What he means is that when we ask for a mediator then we don't change. We don't grow. In order to grow and change, we need that personal relationship with God: between you and God—no one else. This is the key.

Communicating with God is intensely pleasurable. The conversation is like discovering a whole new world. Brother Lawrence states, "There is not in the world a kind of life more sweet and delightful than that of a continual conversation with God" (Brother Lawrence 1963, p. 43). To this point, Richard Foster describes the ease of hearing God. "His voice is not hard to hear, His vocabulary not hard to understand" (Foster 1988, p. 3). What a wonderful way to view a conversation with God. Not hard at all.

To make this voice of God concrete, let's talk about Elijah and the story of how he heard God's voice.

Elijah was hiding in a cave when the Lord said, "Go out and stand on the mountain in the presence of the Lord, for the Lord is about to pass by." Then a great and powerful wind tore the mountains apart and shattered the rocks before the Lord, but the Lord was not in the wind. After the wind there was an earthquake, but the Lord was not in the earthquake. After the earthquake came a fire, but the Lord was not in the fire. And after the fire came a gentle whisper. When Elijah heard it, he pulled his cloak over his face and went out and stood at the mouth of the cave (1 Kings 9:13).

God's voice is a gentle whisper, inside of your thinking. It is not an audible voice hovering outside of you with a hand holding a megaphone out of the clouds. No, instead, it is an "inside" voice.

Charles Stanley states, "I believe one of the most valuable lessons we can ever learn is how to listen to God. In the midst of our complex and hectic lives, nothing is more urgent, nothing more necessary, nothing more rewarding than hearing what God has to say. Only a few minutes of sitting before God who speaks can transform a life, metamorphose a mind, and reset purpose and direction for eternity" (Charles Stanley 1985, p.161). People are tuning in and listening for God everyday—their lives are changed by every divine precious moment.

Two women, who wish to remain anonymous, wrote in the book, *God Calling,* "I lead you. The way is clear. Go forward unafraid. I am beside you. Listen, listen, listen to My Voice. My Hand is controlling all" (God Calling 1978).

If you want to communicate with God, be willing to keep reading, keep trying, and keep seeking. Know that word after word, sentence by sentence, that God is reaching out for you, moving you with His words, step by step on your path. If you have doubts—good! This means that you are being honest with yourself. You are thinking rationally. God can handle your doubts. When God speaks to you, you will know who it is—there will be no doubt.

Imagine the God who knows everything about the past, the present, and the future—the God who knows everything about everyone, the God who has all the power, and the God who can do anything. Imagine this God talking to you, encouraging, supporting, educating, and loving you.

Aren't you excited to find out what God has to say to you?

This is a communication that God left with me for you.

*"I want the world to know how much I love all things. I am the Lord God and I created all. I am going to do something to show the world I exist. I am going to speak to the people. My people must learn how to hear my voice. I yearn for deep communion with all people. I will not remain quiet. Listen to me. I have a plan for each of you, a plan that will bring you to the zenith of your creation. You can only reach this pinnacle of existence with my plan. I love you so much that I give you the choice to reject me. This rejection causes me great pain. I suffer for my children. A great wind is coming. It begins with the whisper of my voice. This wind will sweep the earth and consume the universe with love. I, the Lord God, am coming. I will strike my chord in every heart. I have been doing this since the beginning, but people have not listened. Even good people do not listen to me. People fill the churches and sing songs, and listen to each other. I tell you, the time is here to listen to the Lord your God. If you do not, you will be isolated from me for all time. I will leave you to the darkness. You give me no alternative. In your heart, as you perceive this message, you know it is I. You cannot deny your God, any more than you can deny yourself. Listen to me. I am speaking, even now, to your heart."*

You are God's child, his masterpiece, his perfect work of art. God wants you to be happy just like any parent would want for his child. Did you ever create something that you were pleased with—a painting, poem, story, song or child that you wanted to show proudly to the world? That's how God feels about you.

You do not have to live in pain anymore, because of God's love. All you have to do is ask God to come into your life and help you. At this point, God will free you from your past mistakes and fill you so full of love that it will overwhelm you. Your dreams begin with God and never end.

Be aware, however, that the force of evil can also speak to you inside of your mind. Evil is at war with you. Evil seduces you into sin and then shames you for it. It finds where you are vulnerable then works in seductive ways to bring you down. For example, if you fear poverty, evil will tempt you with you being poor and the need for money. If you have sexual vulnerabilities, evil will tempt you sexually. If you gamble excessively, evil will tempt you into giving in and going to the casino. The goal of evil is to destroy your relationship with God. Evil never wants you to communicate with God. It will laugh at you as you read this book—hoping to fuel your doubts and to get you to put it down. Remember, however, God has all the power. God won the victory on the cross. God offers you a gift—union with him in everlasting paradise, like a trip to a boundless infinite tropical beach.

When you surrender to God, you will undergo a conversion. This can happen in different ways because each person is unique: it can happen slowly, it can happen over many years, or it can happen in an instant. At this cornerstone in time, you are made into a new person filled with the spirit of God. God arises inside of you to live forever with you.

After my conversion, I experienced a total change as a person. I changed from within. I began to see things through the eyes of God, developing a deep compassion and understanding for other people that I had never experienced before. My new vision and lens on life shed light on people in a new and different way.

People in 12 step programs are encouraged to turn their will and their lives over to the care of God as they understand him. Because many arrive with no concept of God or feel abandoned by God, this step is difficult for many patients. Although as they progress in the program, most members begin to believe in a God of some sort. In spite of that, it has been my experience that many still don't have a *personal* relationship with him. To develop that much needed personal relationship, a *direct* communication from God would do wonders. If it worked, it would prove to some that God was alive and available.

With all of this in mind, I decided to try and get patients at my Keystone to experience the presence of God like I had. Several attempts with patients like

Kim and Joey and Sherry had given me the resolve I needed to step into this new phase of development.

In front of thirty or more patients, I described what we were going to do with the meditation that was becoming second-nature to me. There were some who were young and some who were old: all ages and differing ethnicities and cultures lay in front of me. Each was given a piece of paper and a pen. Then, with God's voice directing me, I took them through the transcendent visualization exercise like the one I had taken myself through many times. After five minutes were up, I asked them to write down any communication they received from God. As I sat there, I was amazed as many wrote notes on their paper.

Out of the twenty-nine responses received, here is a few of what we got back." Twenty-five of the patients received an internal communication. Here are ten examples of God's communication:

1. He told me to love and forgive and he gave me a piece of light to carry with me.

2. I imagined all the sweet things, like ocean, beach, path, water, and flowers. I was in touch with God--I was wearing white. I sat under a tree and was whole with God. He said nothing but his face was beautiful and he even wiggled his toes. Forgiveness was so much there. I went off with him.

3. I felt a warm comforting feeling growing within me. As the figure moved closer I could feel the contentment I want or need. As I was embraced, the glowing sensation assured me of love, and took away my insecurities, and left me with a feeling of what it means to feel alive. I can still feel the feeling.

4. I seriously tried to reach 'conscious contact' for the third time since I've been here. For the first time I felt something. I saw my power as a bright and warm light. I asked for help, forgiveness, and strength, for him to PLEASE love me too. I asked for strength--thanked him for the fact that I am alive and here. And that we all are alive and here. Felt, (still feel) a beautiful warm feeling inside my whole body!

5. He sat by me then we got up and went for a walk on the beach and I asked him questions. He asked me what I wanted most out of life. And I said, "I need money to be secure." And he said, "If I lived within you, would you feel secure?" And I thought, Wow! Yes, Yes I would, so he blended into me and I felt the best feeling ever. And then I walked on the beach alone feeling great.

6. God told me that I had to work with my wife, show her love,

compassion, trust, talk to her, share with her, and hold her. He told me to pray for her. He didn't really talk to me much. He is going to help me in my sobriety. My wife and I are someday going to have wonderful, healthy children.

7. I saw myself enter God and see myself, I didn't see me clearly, but I did hear God saying to me after I went back by the tree that he loves me, and that no matter what, he always has. God has chosen me to be his son. I didn't know why. While I was seeing through his eyes, I did see a young man that was very afraid, and lonely, and hurt, and didn't even want God to know how he felt. He had a hard time looking at God eye to eye, and he seemed closed off to the fact that God took the time to even come see him. He just could not believe that God would come and see him.

8. I just felt at peace with my surroundings and myself. I felt loving and loved.

9. As I was sitting against the tree, Jesus sat down across from me and smiled. He spoke no words, but I heard him in my head. He offered me love and peace--serenity. I felt his love and peace flow through me--all the while, he kept smiling.

10. I saw Jesus and after we established eye contact he said these words:
Bless you my son
For the life you have been leading
has been all but fun.
Take those evil feelings that
you've bestowed in your pocket.
Position them to your side
and release them like a rocket.


These shared experiences fascinated me. All but a very few got a message. Those who stated that "nothing happened," did have something different to report after I talked with them. The reason they said that nothing had happened was because they were confused about how to describe their experience in words. Something had happened, but it was beyond their normal experience. This is my conversation with one of them. He was an older muscular man in a T-shirt and tattered jeans.

"You said, 'nothing happened'?" I asked in the hallway after the meeting. Three of the other patients were lingering in a doorway across the hall.

"No," the patient said. He shook his head and looked at his feet.

"Nothing?" I pressed.

"Well, I did feel kind of different." He looked up.

I leaned forward. "What do you mean different?"

"I felt this warm feeling in my body—in my chest."

"What do you think the warm feeling means?"

"I don't know," he said. He put his hands in his pockets.

I asked, "What else has given you a warm feeling in your chest?"

"I feel like that when I'm happy," he said, smiling.

I smiled back. "So you did experience something. You experienced a warm feeling in your chest, a happy feeling."

"Yeah!" he said, smiling widely. "I did." He pulled his hands out of his tired pockets and joined the others.

It was not difficult for these people to tune into God's voice. A simple exercise carried them there. In this sampling of patients, there are liars, thieves, prostitutes, child molesters, atheists, agnostics, and believers. God communicated with them all. It did not seem to matter who they were. God came to them with a message that stated, "I am God, I am alive, I love you, I forgive you, and I will help you." This is what resonated with me.

God did not always communicate to these individuals in words or a voice inside their thinking. A feeling or a visual image sometimes came up. In one case he came as a texture, a tactile feeling. But one thing was consistent: the participants were convinced it was God. After the session, many of the patients expressed their complete and utter joy. There were hugs and smiles and laughter. Many had been so weighted down with guilt that they believed God had abandoned them.

When you are in a dark forgotten land, it is like you've been thrown out to lie on the wet crags and rocks of despair. The wallowing sea overcomes you and your inner child is lost.

The voice of God stretched out to these people and lifted them. I could see it written on their faces. I held the writing in my hands.

# CHAPTER 24

Religion is an organized system of faith and worship. Through the centuries and today, religious leaders and teachers and lay people make up the religious rules, orders, and doctrines. These laws of code and doctrine can sometimes hurt because religions tend to be exclusive. They exclude people who don't follow their rules. Certain religious beliefs and practices can either help you or hurt you along your spiritual journey.

In contrast to this, spirituality draws a different distinction when lined up with religion. By and large, we see the two, religion and spirituality, as separate canons of thought. In Latin, the word spirit comes from the word *spiritus*, which literally means *breath*. Our breath, our spirit, our spirituality knows no boundaries by rules. Spirituality is the innermost relationship you have with yourself and all else. We are all spiritually connected to one another because God is inclusive. God encourages everybody regardless of race, creed, color, gender, ethnicity or sinful pasts to come to him.

During the month after my first large group session I took another patient population through an imagery exercise. The pastoral scene of serenity was laid out before them: a velvety field of green grass with God. The words floated from my mouth as I assisted them in trying to see an image of God walking toward them. Pausing at each word, I gradually asked them to open up to anything God when he arrived. These are a few examples of what they received.

1. Be yourself because I'm your higher power not your alcoholic disease. You will have no more worries if you let this happen to you.

2. He told me to trust in him, and to help others learn to do the same. Help others as he helps me.

3. Have faith and gratitude. He will give strength and will power. I will know when it's time.

4. I'm going to tell people there really is a God for you are here with me now and tell people you are here to help people with their problems.

5. Stay close to me. Love me, for you shall save your soul.

6. God wants me to give him my will, my faith, and my unconditional love.

7. To devote all of myself to him.

8. Stay with the recovery program!

9. Be kind, things are going to work out. You have a future.

10. Accept me into your life again. Keep me near to you and let my will be done.


God's love and forgiveness is the dominant theme that runs through these messages. Additionally, he wants them to serve, to help others. With God's support and encouragement all of this is possible.

Hearing God takes practice.

Certain factors are required to establish contact. It's like tuning in to a radio station, but you are tuning in to God's voice. Once you know where the station is, it's easier to find it again. As you tune in, you will experience God's voice and begin to understand the essential parts of the relationship. God speaks, you learn how to listen, and you receive his communication. There is nothing more wonderful than hearing the voice of your Heavenly Father. He is your closest friend. He knows you perfectly and communicates with you as his perfect created child. He has a mission for you to literally change the world.

To make the connection first, find a quiet place. Little noises may be distracting, particularly at first. It helps most people to close their eyes. Choose a quiet room, get into a comfortable chair or lie down. You want to blot out the world and open yourself up to God. Feel yourself relax. Concentrate on your breathing. Feel the cool air coming in and the warm air going out. With an open mind, be willing to let go and allow the communication to occur. Truly, you don't have to have a deep religious faith. Just be you. Let the words come naturally without effort. Some people try to communicate like pressing their head against a board. Then they say it is too hard and get frustrated. In truth, it is very simple and quick. Ask a question and wait for a word or phrase to come through your mind. God knows exactly what you need to experience.

Say something like this, "God I don't know if you are out there or not, but if you are please come into my life and help me." That opens the door. Then ask God this question: "God, what is the next step in my relationship with you?" Ask this question as if God was sitting in the room with you or you are in a field or a beach under a palm tree. He is there with you. Ask with absolute seriousness. Don't be afraid. God will not let you down. Wait for a word or phrase to come into your mind. It is easy and simple. Allow yourself to let the words flow little by little. Don't be afraid—then write down what you experienced.

This word or phrase is a journey, usually a long journey you are to embark upon. If the word was *believe*, for example, you need to take a journey so you can believe in God. If it was *trust me*, you need to take a journey to learn how to trust God. If it was *faith*, you need to take a journey to learn how to have faith in God. Remember this: it is a journey to God.

Next, confirmation that you actually communicated with God is crucial. Go to the scripture of your choice and turn randomly to a page. As your eyes fall to the words, read it exactly as it is stated until you feel a feeling of peace. The words from the page will echo in your heart and you will experience an "Oh yeah!" moment. This is how God signs or seals or reveals his communication to you—through the scriptures. The reading serves as a signpost to you, much like the one I saw about Angela outside of the church that day. It will tell you the hurdle or hurdles in the way of your pilgrimage to God. It will mark for you what you can do today to begin your spiritual journey.

One step at a time is all you have to take. The millisecond you take that first step with God, the feeling of tranquility will be with you. As long as you stay on the pathway to him, you will keep a continuous flow of peace and serenity. If you get off the journey, you are back to the fear, back to the sea of doubt. There is no fear with God—no threats, no confusion, no shame. God will comfort, educate, support, and encourage you. He will forgive you, accept you, and love you.

Now, look for the next miracle. As a psychologist, I know it is difficult for people to listen. Most of us do it poorly. So, my suggestion to you is to open yourself in every way you know how, every sense, some sort of a communication with God. It is like you are who you are and God joins you as a voice to support, assist, and guide you on life's road to him. The gateway is there. When you receive the voice, it is like stepping over that threshold at the gateway and taking God's metaphoric hand into yours. The words come as if you are thinking to yourself, but somehow you will know that it is not you. You are not creating the words—God is doing that within you, a Voice inside of your thinking.

Ask God some questions and write the answers down. You should ask the questions that seem most relevant to you. Something like this might be a good idea. "God, what is the next step in my relationship with my family?"

The source of these communications has only three possibilities. Either they are from God, from you, or from some other source. To confirm that the communication came from God, compare the communication with scripture. God has spoken in scripture and you can connect with him here. Also, check out the communication with other believers you trust. Some believers are given the gift of discernment, the ability to tell what is from God. A prayer group or clergy person may be willing to guide you, too. Remember: you are not alone.

God's voice is connected with great joy. When you feel this kind of exuberance, you will want to improve the communication. Time is the gift here. Go for a walk with God, take God shopping, or go for a drive with God, even have lunch with him. Anything that is good for you, God will enjoy doing, too. Begin this relationship and soon you will be going everywhere with him. He will be your constant companion, a true friend. Direction and solace will be found in his quiet still voice spoken inside of your mind.

As your body, your temple moves through your day, so do the divine power of God and his words.

What is your next step?

# CHAPTER 25

Prayer is a dialogue with God, a conversation. "Hey, God. Good morning. How are you?" It's like dialing God up and talking about anything and everything. What's new at the office? What is your new baby doing? What is a situation you need help with? You have the digits or the smart phone. Just swipe the right button and you are there. He answers back, "Good morning to you." It is just like a chat you would have with a close friend. You talk with God and listen for him to respond. You talk to God and God talks to you. The sweetest piece of this is God knows the *all* of everything: past, present and future. God will tell you about his plan for you. He will tell you the next step in this plan. Only by following this plan will you reach the zenith of your creation. Your plan is to change the world for the better. All you have to do is use your eyes, your smile and your story. There is nothing more powerful than your testimony.

If you follow God's plan, he will see to it that you get everything that you need. "Delight yourself in the Lord and He will give you the desires of your heart" (Psalms 37:4). He is the best advisor possible he knows what is right for you. By and large, he will not tell you everything about the future. God doesn't want to spoil the surprise ahead. God wants you to experience the joy of new gifts and adventures. Only if it is necessary will he tell you about the future.

God promises to answer your prayers, but sometimes you may not understand why you didn't get exactly what you asked for. I've heard complaints from patients before. They prayed and prayed but God did not come through. There is a course for you and God will give you what you need, but not necessarily everything you think you want.

Martin Luther said it this way:

The granting of our prayer is to be defined that God does not always do what we desire but does what is beneficial for us. For since God is good, he can give nothing but what is good. However, we often ask for our children, often for our friends, often for ourselves, not what is good, but what seems to us to be good. In such cases God grants our prayer even when he does not do what we ask. This is why in the Lord's Prayer we pray for the hallowing of the name of the Lord, for the coming of God's kingdom, and for the fulfilling of his will, before we pray for our own concerns and the necessities of this life, that in such matters God may do, not what seems good to us but what he knows is good for you and the world (Martin Luther 1539 volume. 11 p. 1096).

Prayer should be a dialogue. "If we are to listen to God, we must be quiet and let him do the talking" (Stanley 1985 p. 81). Thinking that God spoke only to the prophets, many believers have had difficulty doing this. It's like believers did not feel as if they were good enough to hear God's voice. This is not true. Would God, who desires our friendship, stop communicating with us? That doesn't make any sense. You want to love you friends and enjoy your life with them. You want to walk with them through the perils, pitfalls and joys of life.

The spiritual life consists of interacting with God explains Dallas Willard in his book, *The Spirit of the Disciplines 1988*. The spiritual side of life is not completely comprehensible. Only God understands this reality. Many individuals have tried to describe this reality but it is elusive. It seems to exist just beyond our senses. This is the arena of the mystic. The best teacher in the spiritual arena is God himself. As you move along your spiritual journey, God will teach you exactly what you need to know.

The goal of prayer is communication with God. It is no mistake that God chooses to talk to us inside of our own minds. It is the most intimate communication possible.

One day, as I was writting my thoughts down; here was a dialogue I received from God:

*Ron, how else was I to come to my children? I did not want to put my face in the sky. People would be frightened, and seek me out of fear. I want my children to seek me in the purity of their thoughts. It is a person's most personal and individual characteristic. I desire the most intimate relationship imaginable. I live inside your mind, inside your body, inside your spirit. I touch you there, where you are you. I know your every thought. I feel your every feeling. I act in every action. It is why I hate sin. I see the pain it causes. I feel the injury my children inflict on themselves. I want all my children to feel joy. It is in freedom that they can love.*

On the other hand, many believers have abandoned meditation and, ultimately communication, out of a fear that they will connect with the forces of evil. But as Charles Stanley 1985 states, "This abandonment is at our great peril, because meditation and its scriptural application are of immense value if we are to listen accurately to God" (p. 93). Likewise, Cho 1984 reports, "The way to hear God's voice is to get still and meditate. If we are too busy to meditate, we are too busy to hear His voice." (p. 129).

Simply stated, the Bible encourages meditation over and over again. A total of fifty-eight times, scripture uses two different Hebrew words to convey the idea of meditation. Meditation is a sound practice. It is a sacred act that places one in union with that which is completely holy, completely wonderful, and completely joyous—an unwavering and unbending friendship for all time.

In contrast to this idea, many researchers have found that experiencing something in mental imagery is psychologically and physiologically similar to experiencing that same thing in real life. Imagery and sensory perception share much of the same physiological machinery, in meditation you direct and are in control of your own thinking. This is not God. This is you thinking to yourself, purposefully causing images or thoughts to form in your mind. This is the beginning technique that is encouraged by most mystics, including St. John of the Cross. (Kavanaugh and Rodriguez 1964).

You will reach a point where you turn over your thinking to God. When you open this door in your meditation to allow God in, then he creates the images and words for you. This is communication from God, and it moves you from the state of meditation to the state of contemplation. Meditation is you talking to yourself. Contemplation is God talking to you.

I have always enjoyed reading the works of St. John of the Cross. He was known for his deep spiritual experiences with God. He taught beginners to use imagination and fantasy in their quest to communicate with God. Later, he taught them to keep an empty mind, opening the total being to God. With the use of meditation, the seeker will draw closer to God. Holy images and words will form (Kavanaugh and Rodriguez 1964).

As you become more proficient at meditation, there will come a point where you let your mind stay blank. It is like an open space between words. Your own thoughts and words and sentences are like the air. Here, if you ask, God will take over your thinking. This is contemplation. God will encourage, support and educate you. Allow God to bring you along. Don't be in a hurry. You will have a unique spiritual journey. While we are all on a similar path, our communications are as unique as we are.

Take a pad of paper and a pen every morning and ask God what he has to say to you today. Then practice your meditation in a quiet place. The words will come: a sentence, a paragraph, or a few pages. You will sense when the message is done. Save these messages and go back and read them from time to time. You will see, hear, and feel that everything God said will come true. It might not come true in the way you thought it would, but it comes true. We are the receivers and we receive imperfectly sometimes.

Do not continue on this spiritual journey alone. You need someone to guide you. A person in this role is called by many different names: spiritual guide, soul friend, spiritual companion, and spiritual director. The relationship is vital. I have chosen the name *spiritual friend* after Tilden Edward's book, *Spiritual Friend: Reclaiming the Gift of Spiritual Direction 1979.*

A spiritual friend is essential to spiritual growth. Thomas Merton said:

The most dangerous man in the world is the contemplative who is guided by nobody. He trusts his own visions. He obeys the attractions of an interior voice but will not listen to other men. He identifies the will of God with anything that makes him feel, within his own heart, a big, warm, sweet interior glow. The sweeter and the warmer the feeling is the more he is convinced of his own infallibility. And if the sheer force of his own self-confidence communicates itself to other people and gives them the impression that he really is a saint, such a man can wreck a whole city or a religious order or even a nation: and the world is covered with scars that have been left in its flesh by visionaries like these" (1949, p. 118).

A spiritual friend should have a genuine relationship with a God that you both respect, whether it is through religion, spirituality or both. A relationship with a spiritual friend is an intimate relationship that leads to spiritual growth. Even with this guide, you will falter at times, never completely understanding the ways of God. God is the perfect communicator, but you are not perfect. Our language is imperfect. Remember the saying, "There are no words to describe..." Sometimes this is true – no word or words to understand fully what God is saying.

St. John of the Cross recommended that a spiritual friend be listened to as if he or she is God. This will prevent you from going off on your own and doing harm to yourself and others. In accordance with this, Thomas Merton writes,

"The abbot or another experienced monk [is] capable of guiding the beginner in the ways of prayer, and of immediately detecting any sign of misguided zeal and wrong-headed effort. Such a one should be listened to and obeyed, especially when he cautions against the use of certain methods and practices, which he sees to be out of place and harmful in a particular case" (Merton 1969 p. 42).

God's revelations to you will not always turn out according to your expectations. In other words, you should not act on them blindly. Double-check with a spiritual friend to make sure you are on the right track. Your spiritual friend will help you. In detail, tell your friend everything you experienced with your communication from God. Often you will make mistakes. You will think God means one thing when he means another. For example, God told Abraham that he was going to give him the land of the Canaanites. Abraham had every expectation that this revelation was going to come true and four hundred years later it did come true. Abraham did not see God's plan evolve in his lifetime, although he certainly expected it to. His descendants, however, saw the prophecy come true. God does things in his own time not in ours. We have to learn how to be patient and trust that God's words will come true, but they will come true in God's perfect time not ours.

Here's another example from the Bible. God told Jonah to tell the people of Nineveh that they were going to be destroyed in forty days. Refusing to deliver God's message, Jonah got on a ship and went the other way. God created a storm, and Jonah was thrown overboard and swallowed by a fish. Finally, after three days, the fish vomited him up and Jonah decided to deliver the prophecy.

The people of Nineveh believed Jonah and repented, so God changed his plan. Jonah was furious that God had changed what he told him was to come true. What Jonah prophesied, he expected to come true. "I am angry enough to die," he said (Jonah 4:9). But the actions of the humans at the time changed God's plan: the original prophecy was still correct. The actions created a compassionate God and he decided not to destroy the city. Jonah just didn't understand why God changed his mind. We will never completely understand God's plan. It is too complicated for us as we are not the mind of God—just humans who are trying to connect and make sense of ourselves, each other, and the world.

Choose your spiritual friend wisely because you will have to share the details of your experience with God. The spiritual friend will assist you in understanding the struggles of other prophets like Moses and Jonah. They will also hold your confidence and must be absolutely trustworthy. So they can check your revelations against God's word in scripture, they must be firm in their faith and familiar with scripture

God was talking to me about the spiritual journey when he said the following:

*"There are many paths to God. Each man has his own path. I decide how to bring my children to me. Each person has his own unique journey. Each is challenged independently of another. I am the ultimate spiritual guide. Listen to my voice and follow me in love. If the journey takes you where there is no love for yourself that is not the way. Love is the answer; it is the way. Considerations of self are good so long as they bring us closer together. There is no love like mine. In perfection, there is only one. I am yours, and you are mine. The burden of time is light. It has no meaning. The things of God are never to be understood by man. Only after will understanding come, after man's short flight there will be meaning. Knowledge will illuminate the darkness. I am waiting for you."*

In time you will change from using meditation to contemplation. That is, God will take over and steer your thinking as if he's taking over the wheel of a car. St. John of the Cross taught that a seeker will know when to change from meditation to contemplation when three things happen: (1) there will come a point in meditation when bringing God to you in your imagination will no longer bring satisfaction; (2) the imagery will become more difficult, a bother and a struggle; and, (3) you will get to the point where you are only enjoying the presence of God without being instructed by God or gaining more knowledge of God. This can be very rewarding, but it is not producing spiritual growth.

When all three of these hindering elements are present, you should move forward into contemplative prayer. Do not attempt to create an image, vision, or thought. Contemplation is emptying your mind and letting God fill it. If your own thoughts and images flash to mind, don't worry. That's normal. Just return to opening yourself up to God. Stretch yourself into the silence—it wells up with God when you allow for blankness, like a clean slate in the front of your internal message board. Contemplation is passive. Just turn your mind over to God. If, however, contemplation becomes difficult or unproductive, then return to your meditation.

Right from the first, even when you don't realize it, God will begin training you mentally, physically, and spiritually. You may have to wait for God to begin speaking. Don't be afraid or impatient. Keep your writing tools handy. You may want to write down exactly what thoughts or images you receive. Let God be your guide. You may not understand many things that happen, but down the road, you will. The wonderful God that keeps billions of stars and planets orbiting and aligned in our galaxy and others beyond also created you so you would have a relationship with him. Wrapping our mind around how it all works is not the point. The point is to love God like he loves you.

In contemplation, God will lead you to a greater understanding of yourself and him. It will be a direct teaching and it is totally individual. Abandon yourself, everything you have learned. Again, make your mind a blank tablet for God to write on. This is the cornerstone. A blank mind equals a receptacle for God to convey his miraculous language to you. It may be a picture he places there, a quick time video, or words that are written or spoken through the mist of that blankness.

In the *Seeds of Contemplation*, Thomas Merton wrote the following: "The situation of the soul in contemplation is something like the situation of Adam and Eve in Paradise. Everything is yours, but on one infinitely important condition: that it is all given. There is nothing you can claim, nothing that you can demand, and nothing that you can take. And as soon as you try to take something as if it were your own—you lose your Eden (1949, p. 148). "

After your discourse with God, write down everything that happened and share it with your spiritual friend. This will give you confidence and direction. Do not share your experience with just anyone because they might not understand. People might infringe on your communication and make you doubt or believe something that is not true. "Do not give dogs what is sacred; do not throw your pearls to pigs. If you do, they may trample them under their feet, and then turn and tear you to pieces" (Matthew 7:6).

As you open yourself, you may receive communication from any of the senses. However, the corporeal or bodily senses are deemed least reliable. The Christian mystics have not trusted this means of communication because they have proven to be the most inaccurate. The four intellectual communications of visions, revelations, locutions, and spiritual feelings are purely spiritual. These are not communicated through the tactile senses, but are passively received effortlessly through the mind. St. John of the Cross called these revelations spiritual visions. Mystics see visions in this way. They do not see them with their eyes, but envision them in their mind. It is here that it is important we differentiate between self-directed imagery and God-directed imagery. Both use images and both use the imagination. In self-directed imagery, you try to create something in your mind. In God-directed imagery, God creates the experience.

In God-directed thinking, many ideas and images and words, for example, will be revealed. These God-directed experiences are nobler and more advantageous than self-directed imagination or corporeal experiences. They are like holy fire within you: purely spiritual, untouchable, and divine. Within this realm, you are seeking union with God. To understand this union, one should know that God lives in every person. The union you are seeking is when you become more and more like God, the divinity within you. It is tapping on your door, you just have to allow and let it open.

Standing as a young child in the living room covered in coal dust, I remember the confusion. The confusion then was thick on all of us—the confusion of who I was, where I was, and what my parents were doing to me. As thick as the coal stuck to my hair and skin, this air of confusion permeated everything I did. Later this confusion would turn into doubting—doubting my thoughts, doubting my words, doubting my life. Doubt is like swimming in a restless sea. There is no rest for the weary. You don't know where the wind, waves, and current are taking you. You have no engine. You are helpless in the face of forces beyond your control. Children raised in homes such as mine struggle more than children who were raised otherwise.

In other words, children who are raised in healthy homes are consistently loved. At all hours of the day or night, the parent is there for the child. Trust develops from this constant showing of love. The child believes that whenever he or she is in need, someone will come and meet the need: warm food, a hug, or help with homework. Based on repetition and experience, the child develops faith in his or her parents. The child believes totally that someone will always be there for them.

Yet at some point, every parent fails at the task of "always being there" for his or her child. In effect, this means we are not quick enough to come to aid or rescue our children. We have our own lives to distract us: work, other time commitments, or we fail to see an unmet need. All of us have made mistakes that have resulted in painful consequences for ourselves or others.

Susy Smith, 1978 gives an example of an evil voice that talked to her inside of her own mind. "With a kindly attitude it said, 'your rescuer has arrived. I have come from a far place to help you. There will be no more trouble.'" This voice sounded benevolent, but later the voice said, "Oh, I'll get you never fear. I'll either kill you or drive you insane" (p. 42-43). Smith states that her dabbling in psychic phenomenon became dangerous. "As I had more and more experiences, ranging from the ineffectual to the outright frightening—most especially the terror of fighting against the bad guys in my mind—I grew to realize that admonitions against such dabbling in the para-normal should be not be listened to as if they are God but from a spiritual force of evil (p. 42-43)."

In *The Joy of Listening to God, 1986,* Joyce Huggett tells several stories of people mistaking a communication. One man thought he heard God tell him he was going to marry someone even though she was happily engaged to someone else. "I now realize that we can never be one hundred percent certain that the picture we see or the voice we hear or the prophecy we speak out is winged to us from God" (p. 141).

No one knows but God, so you can never be one hundred percent sure. However, there are tests that can make you more confident in what you receive. In James 3:17, he states, "But the wisdom that comes from heaven is first of all pure; then peace-loving, considerate, submissive, full of mercy and good fruit, impartial and sincere. The fruit of God's communication is love." Then in Galatians 5:22 it states, "But the fruit of the Spirit is love, joy, peace, patience, kindness, goodness, faithfulness, gentleness and self-control." Communications of evil or darkness do not create a feeling of humbleness and love for God. Evil leaves a feeling of self-importance, directing attention away from God. It is akin to the ego and "edging God out."

Robert Baldwin in *Conversations with God: A Catholic View of Prophecy, 1988* tells of a church group that communicates with God. The first test these people use is the feeling that comes in their hearts and spirit. God's presence has a particular feeling attached to it, the feeling peace and serenity. The second thing they note is whether the communications are loving. The third test is whether the communication will glorify God. The fourth test is whether the message gives new life to the person or prayer group.

Tests that will increase our confidence that the communication we receive is from God are listed here:

1.  The fruit of the message is love, joy, peace, patience, kindness, faithfulness, gentleness, and self-control.
2.  A feeling of love and peace will accompany the message.
3.  The message will agree with scripture.
4.  The message will glorify God.
5.  The message will be pure, peace loving, considerate, submissive, full of mercy and good fruit, impartial and sincere.
6.  The message will create a humble love for God.
7.  The message will create a new feeling of life and hope.
8.  The message will be true.
9.  Your spiritual friend will agree with the message.
10. The message will not tell you to rush in blindly.

Ten steps here will assist you in checking for the truth of your message. Your message is important to you, to your spiritual friend, and to the people in your community. You will begin to see the impact of your communications as you gently listen and gently answer. It is as simple as that.

# CHAPTER 26

In my search to find out if anyone else had listened to God I found these people were called mystics. I now know that everyone can be a mystic if they try God is speaking to everyone in a new way.

Most major religions are sparked by mystical experiences. Hinduism, Buddhism, Christianity, Islam, and Judaism all have mysticism at the core. In her book, *Search for Silence, 1972*, Elizabeth O'Connor defines a mystic as a person who, in searching, experiences union or direct communication with God or ultimate reality. The mystical experience is so powerful that it rarely occurs without changing a person and those around him or her. Contact this with absolute truth is a deeply moving experience. As religious movements spring from these experiences, mysticism takes on an enormous importance in the development of society (McDowell and Stewart 1989).

Through the ages there have been individuals who have spent most of their lives communicating with God. Mysticism is the science or art of spiritual life. When someone by accident or design uncovers what they believe to be ultimate truth they are in the realm of the mystic.

Many authors have expressed the idea that mystical experiences change the world. Wayne Oates in *The Psychology of Religion* 1973 states, "One cannot simply write these experiences off as an aberration in the constitutions of a few people, as attempts of sick souls to heal themselves by autosuggestion" (p. 121). These individuals are changing the course of history. William Wainwright in *Mysticism: A Study of Its Nature, Cognitive Value and Moral Implications,* states, "There are good, if not conclusive reasons for believing that some mystical experiences are veridical, and the claims which are built into them are true" (Wainwright 1981 p. 88). In other words, the mystical experience is true, good, and effective in assisting our personal world—even changing the whole world.

Communication with God is not confined to one religion or worldview. There is one truth, but many different ways of expressing it. The differences in religions come about because of the different environments in which ultimate truth is expressed. All people are able to communicate with God—the one God who comes to people from widely different cultural backgrounds. To this point, the seeds of the mystic can be found in every religion and society.

Attempts to limit mystical experience to any one religion are futile. God is too big for that. Remember that God is inviting everyone to come to him, not just the people from one religion or culture. There are, however, startling similarities among all mystical experiences. "The visual and auditory experiences of persons from different cultures, with diverse social backgrounds and different psychological make ups, are often quite similar" (Wainwright 1981p. 88).

When the mystical experience happens to a person, one must remember that each person comes with a different set of cultural experiences. "I now realize how true it is that God does not show favoritism, but accepts men from every nation who fear Him and do what is right" (Acts 10:34). Each mystic is totally unique. If he's a Christian, God comes to him through this belief system. If he is a follower of Buddha, God comes to him through this belief system. This capacity and its realization are therefore implicit in all the great religious traditions, whether Asian or European, whether Hindu, Buddhist, Moslem, Christian, or a new religion entirely (Underhill, 1974).

Members of one religion should not reject mystical experiences from another faith. Instead, they should honor and respect their own experience. Christians should support members of other religions and hold up the story of Christ while Muslims should support members of other religions and hold up the story of Muhammad. Pope John Paul II said, "Thus, instead of marveling at the fact that Providence allows such a great variety of religious, we should be amazed at the number of common elements found within them, (John Paul II 1994 p. 82)."

Human beings have always had incredible spiritual experiences. *The American Psychiatric Press Textbook of Psychiatry 1988*, states the following:

Religious individuals may pursue practices that lead to profound and subjectively meaningful hallucinatory phenomena or may experience their spontaneous occurrence. Attempts to achieve mystic experiences often utilize techniques that a secular observer might interpret as auto-hypnotic. Some spiritual experiences may include complex hallucinations or visions that are powerful and fulfilling within the individual's frame of reference, in others, the mind is emptied of mental contents and the individual, in a state of pure awareness, experiences a nearness to or mystic unity with a supreme being and/or a sense of oneness with the universe" (p. 559).

Mystical experiences are as varied as the people having them are and many authors have described their mystical experiences. Abraham received a call to a new journey with God. God said to Abraham, *"Leave your country, your people and your father's household and go to the land I will show you. I will make you into a great nation and I will bless you; I will make your name great and you will be a blessing. I will bless those people who bless you, and whoever curses you I will curse; and all the peoples on earth will be blessed through you"* (Genesis 12:2-3).

Muhammad, the founder of Islam, received communications from the angel Gabriel. These were collected into the Koran. Sometimes he may have heard the words being spoken, but for the most part he "found them in his heart" (Holt 1970, p. 31-32; Dawood 1956).

Living in the twelfth century, St. Bernard describes his experience with God, "It is not by the eyes that He enters, for He is without form or color that they can discern; nor by the ears, for His coming is without sound; nor by the nostrils, for it is not with the air but with the mind that He is blended" (Underhill 1974, p 244).

Then in the thirteenth century, St. Francis of Assisi heard Christ speak to him from a painting. He heard God say, *"Francis, go, repair my house, which thou seest is falling into decay"* (Underhill 1974 p. 181).

St. Francis said, "I heard God speaking to me. I heard the voice of God— not with my ears, but in the quietness of my heart—telling me of the love that He had for me. I felt His love surrounding me, holding me" (Yocum 1976 p. 10).

St. John of the Cross (1542-1591) who lived in the sixteenth century, gained the title "Mystical Doctor" because he was one of the greatest mystics in history. He wrote the famous poem, *Dark Night of the Soul*, in which he details a conscious contact with God:

One dark night, fired with love's urgent
longings—ah, the sheer grace! —
I went out unseen, my house being now all
stilled.
In darkness, and secure by the secret ladder,
Disguised, —ah, the sheer grace! —
In darkness and concealment, my house
Now all stilled;

On that glad night, In secret, for no one saw me,

Nor did I look at anything,
With no other light or guide
Than the one that burned in my heart;
This guided me

More surely than the light of noon
To where He waited for me
—Him I knew so well—
In a place where no one else appeared.
O guiding night!

O night more lovely than the dawn!
O night that has united
The Lover with His beloved,
Transforming the beloved in her Lover.
Upon my flowering breast

Which I kept wholly for Him alone,
There He lay sleeping,
And I caressing Him
There in a breeze from the fanning cedars.
When the breeze blew from the turret

Parting His hair
He wounded my neck
With His gentle hand,
Suspending all my senses.
I abandoned and forgot myself,
Laying my face on my Beloved;
All things ceased; I went out from myself,
Leaving my cares
Forgotten among the lilies.

The poem is a beautiful depiction of a man, a mystic, coming to God and communing
with God. The end line punctuates how one's vessel, one's mind, one's sacred vision is ethereal, full of wonder and delight.

Fast forward to the here and now.

In modern times, Catherine Marshall received this message one-day as she was praying: *"Relax into my love. Allow me to love you. There are times when a mother wants to hold her child. No words need pass between them, just the feel of love. This morning let me love you like that. Let all spiritual strain and tension go. Relax in me"* (Marshall 1986, p199).

In her book, Joyce Huggett said, "What I heard in those times of listening was more than a voice. It was a presence. Yes. I heard the Lord call my name. But I also 'heard' His tenderness. I soaked up His love. *"'Joyce! Think not so much of the powers of evil, the powers of destruction, but of my power to protect. I watched over you. I shielded you from harm. I held you in my arms. The arms of pure love. In this relax and rejoice. For I am your God, and you are the apple of my eye. I am your God. Your best interests are tucked into the creases of my Father-heart. I am your Father"* (Huggett 1986, p. 115).

Sometimes the mystic experiences something he or she cannot identify. This is an experience described in *Cosmic Consciousness: A Study in the Evolution of the Human Mind*:

"I had spent the evening in a great city, with two friends, reading and discussing poetry and philosophy. We parted at midnight. I had a long drive in a carriage to my lodging. My mind, deeply under the influence of the ideas, images, and emotions called up by the reading and talk, was calm and peaceful. I was in a state of quiet, almost passive enjoyment, not actually thinking, but letting ideas, images, and emotions flow of themselves, as it were, through my mind. All at once, without warning of any kind, I found myself wrapped up in a flame-colored cloud. For an instant I thought of fire, an immense conflagration somewhere close by in that great city; the next, I knew that the fire was within myself. Directly afterward there came upon me a sense of exultation, of immense joyousness accompanied or immediately followed by an intellectual illumination impossible to describe. Among other things, I did not merely come to believe, but I saw that the universe is not composed of dead matter, but is, on the contrary, a living Presence; I became conscious in myself of eternal life, It was not a conviction that I would have eternal life, but a consciousness that I possessed eternal life then; I saw that all men are immortal; that the cosmic order is such that without any peradventure [perhaps]? all things work together for the good of each and all; that the foundation principle of the world, of all the worlds, is what we call love, and that the happiness of each and all is in the long run absolutely certain" (Bucke, 1901 p. 7-8).

190

Thomas Merton states,"Since in practice we must admit that God is in no way limited in His gifts...nor is there any a priori [from the earlier] basis for denying that the great prophetic and religious figures of Islam, Hinduism, Buddhism, etc. could have been mystics, in the true, that is supernatural sense of the word" (Merton 1961 p. 207).

One of the most striking features of the mystical experience is the mystics, for the first time, are convinced they are seeing life the way it really is. Many researchers, specifically, Stace, Smart and Zaehner, have attempted to catalog mystical experiences, but they have difficulty because of its indescribability (Stacy 1960, Smart 1958, 1971, and Zaehner 1961). You cannot put a value or statistical measure on the evidence to make it concrete. One of the primary elements of this experience is the lack of language to build an image or a metaphor that makes it tangible, more understandable.

To illustrate this point, Stace in *Mysticism and Philosophy* 1960, detailed five core elements of the mystical experience: (1) a sense of reality (2) a feeling of peace (3) an awareness of the divine (4) paradoxically (many opposites exist at the same time) (5) ineffability (indescribable in words). He agrees here with the other authors that there is a lack of language to describe the experience.

The differences in the mystic's experience come about because of what the mystic brings to the "indescribable" experience. To have a mystical experience, a mystic must abandon him or herself, surrender totally, mentally, physically, and spiritually, make a break with the world of the senses, and turn the self over to God

Through the ages, mystics agree that the content of the mystical experience is through thought processes. The experiences occur inside the mystic's thinking in words and images. Mystics call these events visions and voices. By and large, mystics refuse, however, to place any relevance or importance on corporeal [tactile] feeling during their experiences. These experiences, in fact, place less certainty of the divinity on the total mystical vision. The more inside the interior of the mind, the better.

An example of a mystical experience for the mystic might be a symbol appearing in his or her mind. This symbol could be a number, or a picture of butterfly, even a kaleidoscope of color. Jesus's voice can be heard as they sit near a river or a rock...or they transcend to a beloved park and wait for a voice-like message to say something.

There are three times when a mystic's message is subject to interpretation: (1) After the experience, through reflection; (2) during the experience; and (3)

prior to the experience. This seems to be where the great varieties of mystical interpretations come from. This is where man attempts to make sense of the experience and here he must draw upon his own personal experience (Almond 1982). Because no person can be perfect, the mystic cannot always interpret the message accurately. That is, God reveals something in words or images and the mystic interprets it. It is in the interpretation that the message can be mistaken.

A mystic listens to God and a prophet speaks God's message to others. God tells the prophet what to say and then the prophet, in turn, tells others what God said. God can't talk to people unless they are listening, and sometimes it is easier to hear a message through another person—like a prophet. For example, God may ask you to tell someone a message you have received during a meditation or contemplation. You may not know what the communication means, but you will feel a strong desire to deliver the message that person. God won't force you, but he will be persistent. Only God knows the "why" behind the communication. You don't have to know why. You just decide to deliver the message. Use your spiritual friend to guide you. Don't go charging off on your own. To say you are speaking God's words is risky business. It is easy to make a mistake and think you are speaking God's words but you are speaking your own.

The first great prophet in the Bible was Moses. Moses spent many years in the desert herding his father-in-law's sheep. One day, God called to him from a burning bush. God talked to Moses and tried to convince him that this was, indeed, God. Moses wasn't convinced—he was a doubter like we all are. God told Moses that he was going to lead the Israelites out of Egypt. Moses didn't think this was a very good idea. "Who am I, that I should go to Pharaoh and bring the Israelites out of Egypt," he said (Exodus 3:11). God told Moses that he would help him. Because of his unique ability to speak to God, Moses changed the history of the world.

Modern day prophets feel the same reluctance that Moses felt, but they are urged on by God's voice. Bruce Yocum in his book, *Prophecy, 1976*, describes the first time he delivered a message from God. "On the day I gave my traumatic first prophecy, I experienced both an urging to speak the message I had heard, and a conviction that the Holy Spirit Himself was urging me" (p. 80).

How will you know that God has chosen you to speak? God will tell you, and you will feel a powerful desire to do what God says. This can happen to anyone who is in contact with God's voice. Yocum outlines four distinct purposes for prophecy in the modern day church: "(1) God wants the church to be encouraged; (2) wants members to be convicted of their sin; (3) wants the inflow of divine inspiration; and (4) wants to directly guide the church" (Yocum 1976 p. 78).

In Yocum's prayer group, the members pray and open themselves up to a message from God.

"After a minute or so, some words or phrases or sentences begin. Some people find this almost like listening to tape-recorded messages—they seem to hear a voice speaking. Others find thoughts forming in their minds without any effort or direction of their own: the thoughts just come .... Many times when we receive a prophecy, we will not receive specific words to speak. Instead, we will be given a very clear sense of the message God wants spoken. People who prophesy will sometimes receive neither the words nor the sense of the message. Instead, they will receive only a word or two. If they are convinced that those few words begin a full prophetic message, they can simply begin to speak. As they do so, the rest of the message will be given to them" (Yocum 1976 p. 78).

Another example similar to Moses is that of Jeremiah. He was a priest, however, when the Lord came to him with urgings to carry a message to the people of Israel. "The word of the Lord came to me, saying, 'before I formed you in the womb I knew you, before you were born I set you apart; I appointed you as a prophet to the nations.'

"'Ah, Sovereign Lord,' I said, 'I do not know how to speak; I am only a child'" (Jeremiah 1:7). Jeremiah, like Moses, felt that God made a mistake and had chosen the wrong person to be a prophet.

"But the Lord said to me, 'Do not say, 'I am only a child.' You must go to everyone I send you to and say whatever I command you. Do not be afraid of them, for I am with you and will rescue you'" (Jeremiah 1:7-8). If God gives you a prediction that doesn't seem to come true, do not be discouraged. That doesn't mean that it won't come true later. You may have misunderstood what God said.

With scripture and your spiritual friend, you should test each prophecy like any spiritual communication. In the book of Matthew, Jesus told us how to judge false prophets. "Watch out for false prophets. They come to you in sheep's clothing, but inwardly they are ferocious wolves. By their fruit you will recognize them" (Matthew 7:15-16).

# CHAPTER 27

You and God and your spiritual journey.

From my small roots as an invisible boy finding his way in the world, I have come to believe that all spiritual journeys are unique. They do, however, have common steps along the way. The steps are not set in stone, and they don't always come in a particular order. Some steps can even occur at the same time. Rest assured God will guide you along the journey. You will get off track and this is normal. When you do this, ask God to show you the way. When you are on the right path you will feel peace, a sense of freedom. God's communications are always delivered in love. Use the feeling of love and peace as the central signpost of all communications.

In the first part of your journey, you will be curious about God and seek him. God tells us, "Ask and it will be given to you; seek and you will find; knock and the door will be opened to you. For everyone who asks receives; he who seeks finds; and to him who knocks, the door will be opened" (Matthew 7:7-8). God is hungry for you. In the words of a Sufi poet, "I sought Him for thirty years, I thought that it was I who desired Him, but no, it was He who desired me" (Benton 1978 Vol. 12 p. 788).

God waits until he knows your search is genuine and then he comes into your life with such power and force that even you—the great doubter—can't doubt any longer. You can't doubt him. Already, God knows what is in your heart. God will knock gently and wait for you to open the door to your heart. You have to be open-minded and willing. God won't kick down the door.

When you are willing, go to a quiet place and ask God to come into your life. Ask this in your own words. Tell God you are sorry for not loving yourself the way you could have, others the way you could have, and God the way you could have. Ask God to show you how to draw closer to him.

Once you have done this, go to the library or a bookstore and buy a book of scripture. Ask your spiritual friend or clergy person for a good version that's easy to read. As you read this book, think and know that God is speaking to you directly. God will highlight on your heart the things that you need to learn. Scripture should be the primary method by which you listen to God. It is written for you. Nothing you hear from God in person will disagree with these words. You will find revelation after revelation for yourself in scripture. It will be about you, a personal communication from God. Join a study group and study scripture in depth.

The next part is to join a body of believers and attend meetings regularly. Getting together with people who are on the spiritual journey is very important. This will give you encouragement, direction, and motivation. Speak to a clergy person about joining a prayer group. Go to several groups until you find one that is comfortable.

It will be very helpful for most readers to order this meditation CD online and listen to it many times. Soon you will not need it anymore and you can meditate on your own. You can use this and a number of meditation exercises for free at www.godtalkstoyou.com.

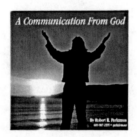

A Communication from God: *www.cdbaby.com/cd/godtalks2*

Here are the steps that will assist you on this journey:

Go to a quiet place with some paper and a pen or pencil. Then, get into a comfortable position and play the CD. During the meditation, God will speak to you in one of three ways: (1) in words inside of your thinking; (2) in images inside of your thinking; or (3) you will not get words or images, but you will know the communication. A number of meditation videos are available on the website www.godtalkstoyou.com this is an excellent way to start your conversation with God.

After God knows that you are seeking him genuinely, he decides to come and live inside of you as if he were stepping through the doorway to your heart. This is called a filling of the Holy Spirit. The Holy Spirit is a part of God that comforts you, directs you, and leads you along your spiritual journey. As God fills you from the inside, you change. It is like an epiphany and you are never the same person again. You see everything differently: trees, grass, animals, insects, clouds, and particularly people. As this part of God lives inside you, everyone feels like your child. You won't be as irritable or impatient with people as you used to be. At your conversion experience, you will get some or all of the fruits of the Holy Spirit: love, joy, peace, patience, kindness, goodness, faithfulness, gentleness and self-control (Galatians 5:22-23). These characteristics will become more and more like you every day. People will begin to see you in a different way, even friends and family members will recognize that you have changed. Your conversion could occur suddenly or gradually over time and this is up to God alone. Some people need to change slowly and some people in the blink of an eye.

Most people feel overwhelmed with love in their conversion experience like this report by Alline.

At that instant of time when I gave all up to Him to do with me as He pleased, and was willing that God should rule over me at His pleasure, redeeming love broke into my soul with repeated scriptures, with such power that my whole soul seemed to be melted down with love; the burden of guilt and condemnation was gone, darkness was expelled, my heart humbled and filled with gratitude, and my whole soul, that was a few minutes ago groaning under mountains of death, and crying to an unknown God for help, was now filled with immortal love, soaring on the wings of faith, freed from the chains of death and darkness, and crying out, My Lord and my God; thou art my rock and my fortress, my shield and my high tower, my life, my joy, my present and my everlasting portion (Alline 1806 p. 31-40).

At his conversion, Chuck Colson found profound relief when God came into his life. He describes it here:

Outside in the darkness, the iron grip I'd kept on my emotions began to relax. Tears welled up in my eyes as I groped in the darkness for the right key to start my car. Angrily I brushed them away and started the engine. "What kind of weakness is this?" I said to nobody.

The tears spilled over and suddenly I knew I had to go back into the house and pray with Tom. I turned off the motor, got out of the car. As I did, the kitchen light went out, then the light in the dining room. Through the hall window I saw Tom stand aside as Gert started up the stairs ahead of him. Now the hall was in darkness. It was too late. I stood for a moment staring at the darkened house, only one light burning now in an upstairs bedroom. Why hadn't I prayed when He gave me the chance? I wanted to so badly. Now I was alone, really alone.

As I drove out of Tom's driveway, the tears were flowing uncontrollably. There were no streetlights, no moonlight. The car headlights were flooding illumination before my eyes, but I was crying so hard it was like trying to swim underwater. I pulled to the side of the road not more than a hundred yards from the entrance to Tom's driveway, the tires sinking into soft mounds of pine needles.

I remember hoping that Tom and Gert wouldn't hear my sobbing; the only sound other than the chirping of crickets that penetrated the still of the night. With my face cupped in my hands, head leaning forward against the wheel, I forgot about machismo, about pretenses, about fears of being weak. And as I did, I began to experience a wonderful feeling of being released. Then came the strange sensation that water was not only running down my cheeks, but surging through my whole body as well, cleansing and cooling as it went. They weren't tears of sadness and remorse, nor of joy--but somehow, tears of relief.

And then I prayed my first real prayer. "God, I don't know how to find you, but I'm going to try! I'm not much the way I am now, but somehow I want to give myself to you." I didn't know how to say more, so I repeated over and over the words: "Take me."

I had not "accepted" Christ—I still didn't know who He was. My mind told me it was important to find that out first, to be sure that I knew what I was doing, that I meant it and would stay with it. Only, that night, something inside me was urging me to surrender--to what or to whom I did not know.

I stayed there in the car, wet-eyed, praying, thinking, for perhaps half an hour, perhaps longer, alone in the quiet of the dark night. Yet for the first time in my life I was not alone at all (Colson 1976 p. 116-117).

Chuck Colson's path was lit, not by any external source, but by his own heart and mind. The audacity and the courage to stay in the moment with God was life altering.

When God educates you about who he is and about who you are, then illumination occurs. You can't learn about God without learning about yourself. Illumination is life changing because by now—through your study of meditation and contemplation and scripture—you will want to be more like God. Underhill in *Mysticism* 1974 defines three characteristics of illumination: a joyous appreciation of the presence of God, a clearer view of reality, and a heightened energy state.

Let God tell you about himself. Ask him all the questions you have wondered about. Remember that you are talking to the one being who has all of the information in the universes. Remember that God can't explain everything. We are not capable of understanding everything. Some things are too complicated so we have to let go and let God do what it is that is in his grand design.

When you don't do what God has asked you to do, it is missing God's mark: sin. God asks you to love yourself, to love others, and to love God himself. He knows that this is the only way to be happy. However, as we go through life, we all tend to pick up bad habits that make us miserable. We lie, gossip, eat too much, drink too much, treat our mother or father disrespectfully. The misery list can go on. As you draw closer to God, you will want to leave more and more of these mistakes behind. You will want to purify yourself so you can move closer to God and become more like him. God becomes the example you want to follow.

In purification, you become aware of the sin that keeps you away from God. For example, you may drink to excess or you may treat others with overt and covert scorn. The more you purge yourself of these behaviors, the closer you get to God. Sin by sin, problem by problem, you remove the obstacles, the barriers that stand in the way of your connection. As AA says you let go and let God.

Bottom-line, there is no room for pride and you will feel humble before God. To this point, please know that you will not feel badly about yourself. God will gently correct you without you feeling as though something were wrong with you. Remember: everybody makes mistakes which are a part of life. Just because you make a mistake does not mean that God does not love you. His love is so sweet and gentle that you will never feel this is untrue. You are God's creation and he loves you. God forgives your sin and gives you another chance.

Do you have to go to extremes to get close to God? No. God doesn't want to torture you. But some strong personalities on occasion need to be molded. Many people have to be humbled to come to this truth. Martin Luther is often quoted as saying, "He whom God decides to use, first He batters to pieces." This means that we must come to God humbly, not full of false-pride. We all need to spend time on the obstacle course or self-will run riot. Once we are beaten, and then turn our will and our lives over to God, life begins to get good.

The closer people get to God, the more they become aware of where they have missed God's mark. The purpose of this cleansing, this purification, is to draw closer to God. Jesus told us we would experience life in full if we love God with our entire mind, body, and spirit. At some point, God will stretch your faith to the breaking point. At this point, God seems to disappear, leaving you alone. This is what St. John of the Cross calls the dark night of the soul. Here you feel overwhelmed by a feeling of abandonment by God. This is the death of self, which is wanting nothing and desiring nothing, nothing at all When there is no more of you left, God delivers His best—union. You will then bloom like a spring flower.

Consistently following God's plan for you is the elemental force in each moment of our lives. In union you join faithfully with God in an even finer way than ever before. In union you become as much like God as possible while retaining yourself (Underhill 1974). To illustrate this, Meister Eckhart reports on his union experience: "The knower and the known are one. God and I, we are one in knowledge. There is no distinction between us" (Benton 1978 p. 787). "At the place of central silence one's own life and spirit are united with the life and the Spirit of God. There the fire of God's presence is experienced..." (O'Connor 1972 p. 11).

St. Catherine of Siena points this out:

Those who are in this sweet light know it, and remain constantly in peace and quiet, and no one scandalizes them, for they have cut away that thing by which stumbling-blocks are caused, namely their own will. And all the persecutions, with which the world and the Devil can attack them, slide under their feet, standing, as they do, in the waters of many tribulations and temptations, and do not hurt them, for they remain attached to Me by the umbilical cord of fiery desire (St. Catherine of Siena 1959 p. 215-219).

You will experience bits and pieces of union along your journey; the sweet tempting taste of God is the culmination of your existence. You will blend into God—it is utter joy.

St. Teresa details her experience.

In the orison of union, the soul is fully awake as regards God, but wholly asleep as regards things of this world and in respect to herself. During the short time the union lasts, she is as it were deprived of every feeling, and even if she would, she could not think of any single thing.... In short, she is utterly dead to the things of the world and lives solely in God.... God establishes Himself in the interior of this soul in such a way, that when she returns to herself, it is wholly impossible for her to doubt that she has been in God, and God in her (St. Teresa translated by Bouix, p. 421-424).

"With what you know now, what are you going to do?"

At some point, you will have to make a decision to talk to God or not. What are you going to do? What is your decision? Do you want to communicate with your Father? Are you willing? Ponder this: all spirituality has, at its core, what is already inside you. Inside you, there is goodness. In all cultures, this goodness is expressed in the moral law. Immanuel Kant stated, "Two things fill the mind with ever new and increasing awe and admiration the more frequently and continuously reflection is occupied with them; the starred heaven above me and the moral law within me" (Pelikan 1990 p. 178).

Here is how moral law works in all cultures of the world. If a stranger were drowning in a lake, this law would motivate you to help. Instinctively, you would be driven to help, even by putting your own life at risk. This moral law transcends the instinct for survival. This law is exactly the same everywhere. It is simply the right thing to do. Moral law in all cultures regards lying as wrong. God's law is moral law. It is written in all of us.

If we were to survey all religions, ideas and philosophies and rule and rights would vary widely. However, the truth is this: religious doctrine differs widely but universal laws among religions remain indistinguishable. They are the same. Saints in all religions are doing indistinguishable things.

# CHAPTER 28

Moral law is universal law: God's law—it cannot be denied.

In his classic text, *The Varieties of Religious Experience* 1961, William James proposes that all religions consist of two basic elements: the uneasiness that there is something wrong about us, and the solution that we are saved from this wrongness by making a connection with a higher power.

There is a problem. Even if we believe in the moral law, we break it. We get lazy and don't check on our parents or kids. We refuse to see the person begging on the street for a few pennies. We lie to our spouses, we have affairs, and we run away from our problems. We curse our lives and our misfortune. We judge people on their looks their behavior and their cars. In the end, it makes us feel we are bad.

Where did we get this good moral law? How did these laws of behavior, an inherent inborn right and wrong, come to be? Did they just evolve from nowhere or did they evolve from heredity or evolution? People who believe in God believe that this good does, indeed, come from something. Of course, they believe, too, that there is more of this something at work in the universes.

During my very first conversation with God, I had questions. These questions are part of a larger philosophical argument that runs through the heart of many people, many nations. That is, there are two arguments against there being a God: (1) If there is a God, and God is good, how come so many bad things happen; (2) if there is a God, why doesn't He make Himself more knowable?

Again, I asked God these two questions and this was his reply to me:

*If I had made my presence more known to man, I would have taken away the choice, the choice to believe. The choice to love me means everything. It is the decision around which everything turns. This choice, to be wise, must be a difficult one. There must be many temptations to choose the other way, the way of human flesh, and desire. I want the love of my people. If I would only do great things, greater and greater, giving everyone more than they needed, there would be no decision, everyone would love me. But that is not what I want. I want to choose my lovers. I want to decide whom I will bless with my gifts. I am deciding with whom to walk through all time. I am making this choice carefully. Sin is necessary for this decision. Free will is necessary for this decision. The subtlety of my presence is necessary for this decision. If I were to shout my voice, like the thunder of the universe, everyone would be afraid. I do not desire love that comes from fear. I desire the love that springs from gentle people pure in heart. There is no going through life without sin. There is no going through life without doubt. There is no going through life without pain. These things are important to my decision. I, the Lord God, will collect the evidence of the lifetime. I, who live inside you, know you best. I know who and what you are. I know how you feel. I know what you think. Ron, you are pure in heart. You would never hurt anyone for your own gain. You give to others unselfishly. You feel the pain of the universe and spread love wherever your foot falls. It is with you, and people like you, that I will walk through time with. Whoever you touch will receive my blessing.*

Much of God remains a mystery. If we look at science, however, we find the same mystery. At core of physics are the elemental forces of gravity, electromagnetic energy, the weak force, and the strong force. In, *A Brief History of Time 1988*, Stephen W. Hawking details how little we know about these elemental forces. We can only make judgments about scientific things by our experience. We have never seen an electron, but we are sure it exists, because we have experience that suggests it exists. Both science and religion require faith. Faith based on experience.

Just as natural as the ability to love or hate, every person has the ability to communicate with God. It emerges naturally through an awakening. It is primal—a seed planted by God—awaiting growth. When God is experienced, he blooms as a powerful force of love and peace, a feeling of awesome power and truth.

Nothing will be more rewarding than communicating with God, because you were born for this relationship. You will find joy here that you never dreamed possible. On the other hand, without God, you will never feel true peace. Struggling through life to find the answers, you will fail—fail at trying to get what you want.

Safely away from the confines of my earlier prison home, I was brought to God once I laid foot on the soil of South Dakota. My deliverance started long before this occurred. A young boy foraging for food, using a square of toilet paper, and finding solace in a seal he had named, Baby. My life had burned to the core and the manifestations of alcoholism and parental neglect brought me on the longest journey to my own dark night of the soul. Like St. John and St. Teresa, there were times I was completely naked and oblivious to the world and its goings on around me and the why's of all of it.

When God spoke to me, the power of my youth was expunged, not the memory. I used his voice to understand ideas and happenings beyond my human comprehension. Today, I live a glorious life. Each day is filled with the voice of God on my heart as the director of my ride here. The union I have found with him and the faith brought me to my miraculous sign: Angela. It is with her I trust my voice, our collective voice, will be heard and you will awaken to the magical mystery of God in you.

I became an invisible boy to disappear from the pain of my life. No matter who you are and no matter what you have done you do not have to be invisible anymore. You can come out of your coal bin, and stand in the sunshine of God's love. To God you are his perfect child and he has chosen you to change the world. I hope you listen for God's voice. If you do your life will change, your doubt will be removed, and you will believe. I want to take a walk with you someday in paradise, where nobody will ever have to be an invisible boy.

# REFERENCES

*Alcoholics Anonymous. Third Edition.* New York: Alcoholics Anonymous World Services, Inc., 1976.

Alline, Henry. *Life and Journals,* Boston: 1806.

Almond, Philip C. *Mystical Experience and Religious Doctrine: An Investigation of the Study of Mysticism in World Religions.* New York: Moulton Publishers, 1982.

Anderson, Norman, ed. *The World's Religions.* Grand Rapids: William Erdmans Publishing, 1976.

Baldwin, Robert. *Conversations with God: A Catholic View of Prophecy. Our Sunday Visitor,* 1988.

Barker, Kenneth. *The New International Version Bible.* Grand Rapids: Zondervan, 1985.

Benson, Herbert. *The Relaxation Response.* New York: William Morrow, 1975.

Benton, William. *Encyclopedia Britannica.* Chicago, 1978.

Bextion, W.H., W. Heron, and T.H. Scott. "Effects of Decreased Variation in the Sensory Environment." *Canadian Journal of Psychology* 8 (1954): 70-76.

Bucke, R.M. *Cosmic Consciousness: A Study in the Evolution of the Human Mind.* Philadelphia: 1901.

Cho, Paul Yonggi. *The Fourth Dimension.* South Plainfield: Bridge Publishing, 1979.

Cho, Paul Y. Prayer. *Key to Revival.* Dallas: Word Publishing, 1984.

Chrisci, John. *Mysticism: The Search for Ultimate Meaning*. New York: University Press of America, 1986.

Clark, Walter H. *Chemical Ecstasy, Psychedelic Drugs and Religion*. New York: Sheed and Wald, 1969.

Colson, Charles. *Born Again*. Old Tappan: Chosen Books, 1976.

Das, Bhagavan. *The Essential Unity of All Religions*. Wheaton: The Theosophical Press, 1939.

Dawood, N.J. *The Koran*. New York: Penguin Books, 1956.

Dickason, C. Fred. *Angels, Elect and Evil*. Chicago: Moody Bible Institute, 1975.

Dostoyevsky, Fyodor. "The Grand Inquisitor." In *The World Treasury of Modern Religious Thought*, edited by Jaroslav Pelikan, Boston: Little, Brown, 1990.

Edwards, Tilden. *Spiritual Friend: Reclaiming the Gift of Spiritual Direction*. New York: Paulist Press, 1980.

Emerson, Ralph Waldo. "Divinity School Address." In *The World Treasury of Modern Religious Thought*, edited by Jaroslav Pelikan, Boston: Little, Brown, 1990.

Ekman, P. and H. Oster, "Facial Expressions of Emotion," *Annual Review of Psychology* 30, (1979).

Finke, R.A. "Levels of Equivalence in Imagery and Perception." *Psychological Review*,87, (1980): 113-139.

Forell, George W. *The Protestant Faith*. Englewood Cliffs: Prentice-Hall, 1960.

Foster, Richard J. *Celebration of Discipline: The Path to Spiritual Growth*. New York: Harper and Row, 1988.

Foster, Richard. *Meditative Prayer*. Europe: MARC, 1983.

Gaer, Joseph. *What the Great Religions Believe*. New York: Dodd, Mead and Company, 1963.

Gershom, Scholem. "Jewish Mysticism." In *The World Treasury of Modern Religious Thought* edited by Jaroslav Pelikan, Boston: Little, Brown, 1990.

Graham, Billy. *Angels: God's Secret Agents*. Garden City: Doubleday and Company, 1975.

Graham, Billy. *Peace with God*. Dallas: Word, 1984.

Graham, Billy. *The Holy Spirit: Activating God's Power in Your Life*. Dallas: Word, 1988.

Grollman, Earl A. *Suicide*. Boston: Beacon Press, 1971.

Hawking, Stephen W. *A Brief History of Time*. New York: Bantam, 1988.

Hoffman, Mark S. Editor. *The World Almanac and Book of Facts*. New York: Pharos Books, 1990.

Holt, P.M., ed. *The Cambridge History of Islam, Vol. II*. London: Cambridge University Press, 1970.

Houston, Jean and R.E.L. Masters. *The Varieties of Psychedelic Experience*. New York, 1967.

Huggett, Joyce. *The Joy of Listening to God*. Downers Grove: Inter Varsity Press, 1986.

Hybels, Bill. *Honest to God*. Grand Rapids: Zondervan, 1990.

James, William. *The Varieties of Religious Experience*. London: Collins, 1961.

James, William. "The Will to Believe." In *The World Treasury of Modern Religious Thought* edited by Jaroslav Pelikan, Boston: Little, Brown, 1990.

John Paul II. *Crossing the Threshold of Hope*. New York: Alfred A. Knopf, 1994.

Jung, Carl. *Modern Man in Search of a Soul.* Translated by Ronald Knox. New York: Kennedy, 1958.

Lawrence, Brother. *The Practice of the Presence of God.* New York: Peter Pauper Press, 1963.

Kant, Immanuel. "Philosophy of God, Freewill, and Immorality." In *The World Treasury of Modern Religious Thought* edited by Jaroslav Pelikan, Boston: Little, Brown, 1990.

Kaufmann, G. *Imagery, Language, and Cognition.* Bergen: Universititsforlaget, 1980.

Klinger, Eric et. al. "Therapy and the Flow of Thought." In *Shorr Imagery: Its Many Dimensions and Applications.* New York: Plenum Press, 1980.

Kluft, Richard. "The Dissociative Disorders." In, *The American Psychiatric Press Textbook of Psychiatry,* edited by Talbott, Hales, and Yudofsky, Washington: The American Psychiatric Press, 1988.

Kosslyn, S. *Image and Mind.* Cambridge: Harvard University Press, 1980.

Lewis, C.S. *Mere Christianity.* New York: Macmillan, 1943.

Lilly, J.C. "Mental Effects of Reduction of Ordinary Levels of Physical Stimuli on Intact Healthy Persons." *Psychiatric Research Reports of the American Psychiatric Association 5 (1956,):* 1-28.

Luther, Martin, *What Luther Says.* Edited by Ewald Plass. St. Louis: Concordia, 1959.

Luther, Martin, 1545. In Benton, William. Publisher, *Encyclopedia Britannica,* 1978.

Luther, Martin, 1539. *What Luther Says.* Edited by Ewald Plass. St. Louis, 1959.

Mails, E. Thomas, "Fools Crow." In *Wisdom and Power.* Tulsa: Council Oak Books, 1991.

Marshall, Catherine. *The Helper.* Waco: Chosen, 1978.

Marshall, Catherine. *A Closer Walk.* Old Tappan: Chosen, 1986.

McDowell, Josh and Don Stewart. *Handbook of Today's Religions.* San Bernardino: Here's Life, 1989.

McNamara, William. *Christian Mysticism.* Chicago: Franciscan Herald, 1981.

McNamara, William. *Mystical Passion: Spirituality for a Bored Society.* New York: Paulist Press, 1977.

Merton, Thomas. *Contemplative Prayer.* New York: Herder and Herder, 1969.

*Merton, Thomas. No Man is an Island.* New York: Harcourt Brace Jovanovich, 1955.

Merton, Thomas. *Seeds of Contemplation.* Norfolk: New Directions, 1949.

Miller, Richmond P. "What is a Quaker." In *Religions of America, edited by* Leo Rosten. New York: Simon and Schuster, 1975.

Neisser, U. *Cognition and Reality.* San Francisco: Freeman, 1976.

Nouwen, Henri J. M. *Reaching Out: The Three Movement of the Spiritual Life.* Garden City: Doubleday, 1975.

Oates, Wayne E. *The Psychology of Religion.* Waco: Word, 1973.

O'Connor, Elizabeth. *Search for Silence.* Waco: Word, 1972.

Otto, Rudolf. *Mysticism, East and West: A Comparative Analysis of the Nature of Mysticism.* New York: Meridian, 1957.

Otto, R. *The Idea of the Holy*. London: Oxford University Press, 1958.

Pahnke, Walter. *Drugs and Mysticism: An Analysis of the Relationship Between Psychedelic Drugs and Mystical Consciousness*. Doctoral Dissertation: Harvard University, 1964.

Peck, M. Scott. *The Road Less Traveled*. New York: Simon and Schuster, 1978.

Pelikan, Jaroslav. *The World Treasury of Modern Religious Thought*. Boston: Little, Brown, 1990.

Plutchik, R. *Emotion: A Psychoevolutionary Synthesis*. New York: Harper and Row, 1980.

Radhakrishman, S. *Eastern Religions and Western Thought*. London: Oxford University Press, 1940.

Richardson, Alan. Imagery: Definition and Types. In Anees A. Sheikh. *Imagery: Current Theory, Research, and Application*. New York: John Wiley and Sons, 1983.

Rinn, W.E. "The Neuropsychology of Facial Expression: A Review of the Neurological and Psychological Mechanisms of Producing Facial Expression." *Psychological Bulletin* 95, 52-77.

Schweitzer, Albert. "Reverence for Life." In *The World Treasury of Modern Religious Thought* edited by Jaroslav Pelikan, Boston: Little, Brown, 1990.

Shepard, R.N. "The Mental Image." *American Psychologist* 33 (1978) 123-137.

Shurley, J.T. "Hallucinations in Sensory Deprivation and Sleep Deprivation." In *Hallucinations*, edited by D.J. West. London: Grune and Stratton, 1962.

Slotkin, James. *Peyote Religion, A Study in Indian White Relations*. Glencoe: The Free Press, 1956.

Smart, N. "Interpretation and Mystical Experience." *Religious Studies* 1, 75-87.

Smart, N. *Reasons and Faiths*. London: Routledge and Kegan Paul, 1958.

Smart, N. *The Religious Experience of Mankind*. London: Fontana, 1971.

Smith, Susy. *The Conversion of a Psychic*. Garden City: Doubleday, 1978.

Stace, Walter. *Mysticism and Philosophy*. New York: J.B. Lippincott, 1960.

Stanley, Charles. *How to Listen to God*. New York: Oliver Nelson, 1985.

St. Augustine. *Solisloquiorum Animal ad Deum Liber Unus*, c. 2: PL 40, 886.

St. Catherine of Siena. *The Dialogue of the Seraphic Virgin Catherine of Siena, 1370*. Translated by Algar Thorold. Westminster: The Newman Press, 1959.

St. John of the Cross. *The Collected Works of St. John of the Cross*. Translated by Kebran Kavanaugh and Otilio Rodregues. New York: Doubleday, 1964.

St. Teresa. *The Interior Castle, Fifth Abode*. Translated by Bouix. In Euvres,

Underhill, Evelyn. *Mysticism*. New York: New American Library, 1974.

Two Listeners. *God Calling*. New York: Jove Books, 1978.

Underhill, Evelyn. "Mysticism and Theology." In *The World Treasury of Modern Religious Thought*, edited by Jaroslav Pelikan, Boston: Little, Brown, 1990.

Wainwright, William J. *Mysticism: A Study of Its Nature, Cognitive Value and Moral Implications*. Madison: University of Wisconsin Press, 1981.

Willard, Dallas. *The Spirit of the Disciplines: Understanding How God Changes Lives*. San Francisco: Harper and Row, 1988.

Woolf, Henry, ed. *The Merriam Webster Dictionary*. New York: Pocket, 1974.

Yocum, Bruce. *Prophecy*. Ann Arbor: Servant, 1976.

Younghusband, Sir Francis. *Modern Mystics*. Freeport: Books for Library's Press, 1935.

Zaehner, R.C. *Mysticism, Sacred and Profane: An Inquiry into Some Varieties of Preternatural Experience*. New York: Oxford University Press, 1961.

Zenon, Pylyshyn. "The Imagery Debate." In. *Imagery.* edited by Ned Block Cambridge: The MIT Press, 1981.

View other Black Rose Writing titles at www.blackrosewriting.com/books and use promo code PRINT to receive a 20% discount when purchasing.

# BLACK ROSE
## writing™

CPSIA information can be obtained
at www.ICGtesting.com
Printed in the USA
FFOW05n0109300816

9 781612 967509